T0152030

Wonderful Ethiopians of the Ancient Cushite Empire

By Drusilla Dunjee Houston

BOOK I

Black Classic Press
P.O. Box 13414
Baltimore, MD 21203

Wonderful Ethiopians of the Ancient Cushite Empire

Library of Congress Control Number: 89-090991
Print book ISBN: 978-1-57478-213-4
E-book ISBN: 978-1-57478-082-6

Printed by BCP Digital Printing (www.bcpdigital.com)
an affiliate company of Black Classic Press Inc.
For a virtual tour of our publishing and printing facility visit:
https://www.c-span.org/video/?441322-2/tour-black-classic-press

Purchase Black Classic Press books from your favorite book seller
or online at: www.blackclassicbooks.com.

For inquiries or to request a list of titles, write:
Black Classic Press
P.O. Box 13414
Baltimore, MD 21203

DRUSILLA DUNJEE HOUSTON: AN INTRODUCTORY NOTE ABOUT THE AUTHOR AND HER WORK

Drusilla Dunjee Houston (1876-1941), daughter of John William and Lydia Taylor Dunjee, was a teacher, journalist, self-trained historian and by any standard a remarkable woman. Born at Winchester, Virginia in 1876,* she lived most of her adult life in the Southwest—first in Oklahoma and later Phoenix, Arizona. She had moved with her family to Oklahoma from Minnesota, where her father worked for the American Baptist Home Mission Society as an educator, fundraiser, and church building missionary. John Dunjee has been credited with instilling in the young Drusilla "a sense of race pride." Visits to the family home by her father's close associates, Frederick Douglass, Blanch K. Bruce and other prominent Blacks, further enhanced this sense of race pride and left lasting impressions on the young writer-to-be. Significantly, it was in her father's expansive library that she first pored over what she would later refer to as "the dry bones of history."

At twenty-two years of age Drusilla eloped and married Price Houston, a storekeeper eleven years her senior. One child, a daughter, was born to this union. Drusilla settled with her husband in McAlester, Oklahoma. There she opened the McAlester Seminary, a school she operated for twelve years.

In 1915, Mrs. Houston's younger brother Roscoe purchased a small printing plant from which he published "one of the best edited weekly's in the Southwest," **The Black Dispatch**, of Oklahoma City.

Keeping **The Black Dispatch** alive during its early days was a difficult task. It exacted a tremendous price of devotion and commitment from the young editor, who had sold vegetables to earn the money to buy the printing plant. Seldom was there enough money to pay writers, assistant editors or staff. Drusilla supported her brother's efforts during those early days and served as a contributing editor for the publication. Her columns were regularly featured in **The Black Dispatch**. Those dealing with "Negro" history and Black social concerns were frequently syndicated to Black newspapers throughout the United States by the Associated Negro Press; consequently gaining for Drusilla recognition and a wide Black readership.

A conscientious student of African history, she was further inspired in her studies after reading W.E.B. Du Bois' **The Negro**, first published in 1915. **The Negro** was a landmark book, representing one of Du Bois' earliest attempts to refute the racist notion of Africans having no history before the coming of the European. Although limited by the size of the volume, Du Bois nevertheless attempted to outline African history from an African perspective. In addition, he set forth an early framework for viewing the unity of African people throughout the diaspora.

Thoroughly aroused by Dr. Du Bois' theme and his writing, Mrs. Houston, committed

---

*Mrs. Houston's place of birth and exact birth date are issues that merit further research. James Spady believes she was born at Harpers Ferry, West Virginia. (See his commentary, this volume.) However, a signed statement from her brother, Roscoe Dunjee, indicates she was born at Winchester, Virginia.

herself to the task of writing a multi-volume history of the Black race.

Her labourious efforts were culminated in 1926 with the publication of **Wonderful Ethiopians of the Ancient Cushite Empire, Volume I**; most often referred to as **The Wonderful Ethiopians**. Massive in its scope, the volume takes the reader on a journey beginning with the origin of civilization. It moves rapidly into ancient Egypt and Ethiopia. It then moves on to establish connecting linkages among the ancient Black populations of Arabia, Persia, Babylonia and India. In each case, she concluded that the ancient Blacks who inhabited these regions were culturally linked and had been the progenitors of civilization in these areas.

Significantly **The Wonderful Ethiopians** was favorably reviewed by most of the major Black newspapers and journals of the day. This did not mean Mrs. Houston's self-trained approach to history was not criticized. Mary White Ovington, writing for **The Chicago Defender**, criticized the book for having "no footnotes, no bibliography and no index" but went on to compliment Mrs. Houston for presenting,

> Such a mass of facts that one cannot but be impressed by the majesty of the Cushite dynasties and the former greatness of Black men.

When J.A. Rogers, the noted journalist and self-trained historian, reviewed **The Wonderful Ethiopians** for a New York paper, **The Amsterdam News**, he criticized Mrs. Houston's work for having at least one flaw "...too many laudatory adjectives." Perhaps because his own work had received similar criticism, Rogers believed that while Mrs. Houston's style of writing made the volume more interesting to the average reader, it detracted from the volume's scholarship.

In spite of his criticism, Rogers too was impressed by the abundance of sources used by Mrs. Houston to support her conclusions.

> . . . All of which shows a trememdous amount of research on the part of Mrs. Houston and some of which this reviewer (Rogers) must admit is new to him.

Rogers went on to recommend that **The Wonderful Ethiopians** be placed in every "Negro" home and school in the land.

Perhaps the most favorable review of the work was written by Arthur A. Schomburg, a dedicated "race man", bibliophile and historian. Schomburg welcomed the appearance of Mrs. Houston's work, and in a column syndicated to several Black newspapers, Schomburg showered the book with praise:

> I can assure everyone that the author must have used considerable oil in her lamp represented by her exhaustive research, the indefatigable labor that resulted in the astonishing compilation before me. . . We are indebted to Drusilla D. Houston for this illuminating and comprehensive book. . .

The Wonderful Ethiopians also received favorable endorsment from other influencial Blacks and whites. Robert L. Vann of the **Pittsburgh Courier** wrote, "we know of no book published in the last 25 years which offers such reputable inspiration to the black people of the earth." Cornelius Edwin Walker, a white author wrote, "you prove your contention from the first that civilization came from the black race." Dr. I. W. Young, president of Langston University, predicted a bright future for Mrs. Houston's writings:

> By far she is the most interesting writer among us. Equipped with splendid education and home training her writings will permanently affect race conditions in this country.

From all evidence collected, it appears that volume two and three of Mrs. Houston's epic saga were completed, but never published. The evidence also seems to suggest these volumes may have been subjected to revisions, updating and title changes as they awaited publication. In a letter written to Schomburg in 1927, she discussed **The Wonderful Ethiopians** and its companion volumes.

> The book you read was only one of three that are <u>completed</u>.* I do not know when the other two can be. (sic)** Number two is Ancient Cushites in Western Europe... Then there is book three that I think is the more beautiful of the three.

Mrs. Houston also referred to the two volumes at varying times in her syndicated column. In her column of September 15, 1934, which was published by the **Louisiana Weekly** and other papers under the heading "Wondrous History of the Negro", she described the two volumes.

> One is the origin of Aryans... the book will be valuable because it reveals the root of the strange and undying race hatreds of Western Europe. The other, **Wonderful Ethiopians of The Americas**, is a book on which I have been at work for 25 years.

The NAACP's William Pickens, a close friend of Drusilla's brother Roscoe, provides further proof of the existence of the two volumes. In a profile of Mrs. Houston and her work, he described the two volumes as portraying the Black race's remarkable evolution from "the origin of civilization" to the "dawn of a New World." He went on to indicate that economic barriers had prevented Mrs. Houston from publishing the remaining volumes.

While it certainly appears that lack of finances was an important factor preventing publication of the second and third volumes, Mrs. Houston's failing health was also a major deterrent. The last days of her life were spent in relative seclusion in Phoenix, Arizona. There she waged a losing battle against tuberculosis and passed out of this existence, February 2, 1941. At the time she was working on yet another volume of "Negro" history.

The uniqueness of Drusilla D. Houston's achievements are striking. To appreciate them fully we must keep in mind that she was at a terrible disadvantage when she conducted her research and wrote **The Wonderful Ethiopians** and its companion volumes. Lacking adequate financial resources, she was forced to work without the benefit of a staff of assisting researchers. Most of her research was conducted in Oklahoma, far away from major libraries and universities. As she became more involved with her research, her circle of associates narrowed. Her preoccupation with a task few

---

*My Italics
**Mrs. Houston did not complete this sentence although she ended it with a period. Apparently she was indicating that she did not know when the volumes would be published.

members of her community understood or fully appreciated earned her the label of being "unsociable" and "uppity".

In spite of these handicaps, she became a self taught encyclopedia of facts and data about people of African descent. Her mastery of facts enabled her to become a member of an elite, loosely affiliated grouping of Black self-trained historians who used history as a positive weapon of propaganda. These historians practiced an art that was effectively used to correct the distorted and negative manner in which Blacks were portrayed by most white historians. At the same time, they used their art to soothe the psyche of the Black masses by repeatedly insisting "that not only are you somebodies, you are great somebodies." Using newspapers, books and pamphlets, often self-published, these historians prevailed against the odds, keeping a sense of "true" Black history alive among the Black masses. They nursed and cuddled Black history until, strong enough, it became one of the driving forces of the Black liberation movement during the 1960's and 1970's.

It is just as important to note that Mrs. Houston broke new ground when she published **The Wonderful Ethiopians** and "established" herself as an expert on the history of ancient Africa, its people and the world. She boldly entered a domain that was ruled largely by white male His-storians. To accomplish this feat she was forced to overcome societal biases of race and sex which characterized the late nineteenth and early twentieth centuries. Women and Blacks of this era were increasingly victimized by pseudo-scientific studies in eugenics and craniology. These studies often provided a "scientific" rationale for the continued oppression of Blacks and women. Both groups were said to possess distinctly smaller brains than their white male counter-parts. Unfortunately this deficiency limited the abilities of Blacks and women to become "intense abstract thinkers."

A pioneer in what today is known as "the Black Studies Movement, she documented history from a Pan-African perspective. As did Du Bois, she recognized the cultural and blood-ties which connect African people the world over. In this sense, she precedes, anticipates and shares in the views articulated by contemporary Pan-African minded scholars: Chancellor Williams, Cheikh Anta Diop, Yosef Ben-Jochannon, John Henrick Clarke and others. Invigorated by her research and her findings, she proclaimed an African origin of civilization; this in 1926, a year when one Black American was lynched in the United States every twenty-three days; brutal evidence of the nation's attempt to reinforce the concept of Black inferiority. It was this false concept that Drusilla Houston's **Wonderful Ethiopians** attacked.

Mrs. Houston was not the first African-American woman to establish herself as a chronicler of Black history. But she is the earliest known to use her knowledge and "abstract thinking" to author a multi-volume study of ancient Africa and its descendants. In doing this, she not only made a significant contribution to Black women's history, she also expanded the foundation of Black historiography in general. In a resolute manner she refused to see her accomplishments as individual victories; preferring to see them as contributions in the struggle for race pride and dignity. In every sense of the word, she was a "race woman," who believed her work was God inspired and that it would ultimately help eradicate ignorance, which she held to be one of the principle causes of race prejudice.

Regrettably, the work, as well as its author, have been relegated to obscurity. The **Wonderful Ethiopians** is seldom if ever discussed when scholars examine the foundation of Black historiography. Moreover, Drusilla Houston's name is rarely included among those Black women writers of the 1920's and 1930's, leading one to conclude that Black women writers of this period limited themselves to fiction, poetry and other forms of writing—but not history and certainly not ancient African history. Drusilla Dunjee Houston and her efforts have all but been forgotten.

We owe a great debt to this Black woman. A debt William Pickens recognized when he wrote:

> If her race were culturally ready and economically able to buy her books, what an historic foundation she could lay for them. . . The patience with which she has dug into the past history of races and especially her own is genius. If there was no race prejudice in America she would have wealth and much greater fame than she has. . . Perhaps some day we will build her a statue, or name a university after her, when we have finished starving to death and buried her.

Black Classic Press is pleased to reintroduce Mrs. Houston and **Wonderful Ethiopians of the Ancient Cushite Empire** to the public. An index prepared by Mrs. Julia W. Bond of Atlanta, GA creatively includes a bibliographic listing of sources cited by Mrs. Houston. Commentary by James G. Spady and the Afterword by Asa G. Hilliard do much to place Mrs. Houston and her work within a more comprehensive perspective.

Our efforts to reintroduce Mrs. Houston and her work to the public have been aided by numerous persons. Relatives, friends and former students of Mrs. Houston proved to be most helpful. A special note of appreciation must be extended to Mrs. Mary Lou Harvey of Phoenix, Arizona, a niece of Mrs. Houston, who provided introductions to family members in Phoenix and Oklahoma City.

Appreciation is also extended to Mr. Kinya Kiongozi of Baltimore, a consummate reader and student of the Black world experience. It was he who first brought Mrs. Houston to our attention, more than a dozen years ago.

Valuable assistance was provided by the reference librarians of the Schomburg Center for Research in Black Culture. Just as important has been the support and interest expressed in this project by members of the Moorland-Spingarn Research Center at Howard University, most notably, Dr. Elinor Sinnette, who read, made helpful suggestions and criticized my introductory notes.

W. Paul Coates
January 24, 1985

Wonderful Ethiopians
OF THE
Ancient Cushite Empire

BY DRUSILLA DUNJEE HOUSTON.

BOOK I.

NATIONS OF THE CUSHITE EMPIRE.
MARVELOUS FACTS FROM AUTHENTIC
RECORDS.

THE UNIVERSAL PUBLISHING COMPANY
OKLAHOMA CITY, OKLA., U. S. A.

1926.

TABLE OF CONTENTS.

Preface—The Origin of Civilization.

IVORY STATUETTE OF A KING OF THE FIRST
DYNASTY.
(From Petrie's "Abydos," Part II.)

SYNOPSIS OF CONTENTS.

PREFACE.

THE ORIGIN OF CIVILIZATION.

The minds of men today are stirred with eager
questionings about the origin of civilization and
about the part the different races of mankind
played in its development from primitive ages.
The remains that archaeologists are uncovering
in Egypt, old Babylonia, and South America, reveal that there were significant factors in the first
development of the arts and sciences that history
has failed to make clear. Scientists are busy today studying the types of those old civilizations
and comparing them with those of the present.
Our modern systems do not function for the
masses to give them development and happiness as did some of the ancient cultures. Books
upon the early life of man are very hard to secure.
Few have been written that are authentic, because
it requires technical skill to assemble and con-
dense such matter. Exhaustive research work
is necessary to secure this kind of information,
with only a line here and there in modern books
to help the reader to reach definite conclusions.
Only the trained mind holds the multitude of details and possesses the ability to impartially weigh
and classify the facts, that prove the influence of
the races upon the civilization of today.
The quest for the innumerable and startling
facts of the succeding volumes arose, much as

teachers of the Romans; then we follow the life
and tragedy of the fleeting Pelasgians, who were
the fountain out of which later Greek culture
welled. They were the people of the legends of
Greek mythology. It is almost impossible to find
anything but scanty fragments in the world's
literature about any of these people of pre-historic days, but our text has compiled these fragments, so many of them, as to form fascinating
chapters. Today all of these subjects remain unexplained mysteries in the average book. We
dwell for a while on the marvels of the lost civilization of the Ægean and stop to study the Greece
of Homer and the meaning of the Greek legends.
All having direct relation to the ancient Cushites.

Historic Greece in all her glory, but viewed
from new angles, passes before us with the older
and superior civilization of Asia Minor, which
has been almost entirely overlooked in modern
literature. \ Next we come to the fact that the
Phoenicians called themselves Ethiopians and
that the Hebrew writers gave them the same
name;\then we reflect upon the strange relationship of the family of Cushite tongues to the so-
called Indo-European group of languages. The
trail leads us high up to where we get a breath-
less view of the astounding Ethiopian religion,
which gives us the answer to many strange and
incomprehensible traits in the Ethiopian of today. Next follows the chapter on the ''Wonderful Ethiopians,'' who produced fadeless colors
that have held their hues for thousands of years,
who drilled through solid rock and were masters

of many other lost arts, and who many scientists believe must have understood electricity, who made metal figures that could move and speak and may have invented flying machines, for the "flying horse Pegasus" and the "ram of the golden fleece" may not have been mere fairy tales. Next out of the forgotten wastes of the dark continent rise before us ancient African empires, representing other lost civilizations of the time of the Cretan age. Then across the screen comes flashing the "Ancient Cushite Trade Routes," which contrary to our notion were the medium by which rich and varied products were interchanged.

In the chapter on "Ancient Cushite Commerce," we follow the ships of these early, daring and skillful seamen, who before the dawn of history had blazed out the ocean trails that the Phoenicians later followed. We find irrefutable evidence of the presence of these daring conquerors in the primitive legends, religion, customs and institutions of America. Next out of the dim haze of far antiquity, rise the indistinct lines of "Atlantis of Old," the race that gave civilization to the world, the race that tamed the animals and gave us the domestication of plants. The gods of the ancient world were the kings and queens of mystic "Atlantis." The chapter the "Gods of Old" makes plain that the deity of Greece and Rome were also the kings and queens of the ancient Cushite empire of Ethiopians, which was either the successor or the most famous branch of the Atlantic race. It was about these princes

and heroes that all the wonderful mythology of
the ancients was woven. They were the deity that
were worshipped in India, Chaldea, Egypt, and
in Greece and Rome, which nations themselves
must have been related to the race of Atlantis,
that tradition said had been overwhelmed by the
sea. Atlantis could not have been mythical, for
her rulers were the subjects of the art and literature of all the primitive nations until the fall of
Paganism long after the birth of Christ.

Another division of Atlantis was trans-At-
lantic America. There the mysterious Mound
Builders represent the ancient Cushite race. We
study the peculiar culture and genius of the fierce
Aztec, who acknowledged that he received the
germs of civilization from the earlier Cushite
inhabitants. We pass southward and examine
the higher development of the wonderful Mayas
of North America, whose ruins are attracting
special study today, and we find there transplanted the Cushite arts of the ancient world.
Next flash the pictures of the marvelous culture
and arts of the Incas, superior to those of Western Europe in 1492. From America the story
turns to the "Bronze and Iron Ages," we seek
the origin of the mysterious bronze implements
of Western Europe found in the hands of seemingly barbarous people. We seek for the place
and the race that could have given the world the
art of welding iron. The trail reveals that the
land of the "Golden Fleece" and the garden of
the "Golden Apples of Hesperides" were but
centers of the ancient race, that as Cushite Ethio-

pians had extended themselves over the world.
These are subjects that have attracted the study
of world scholarship. They represent not mere
myths but are all that vast ages have left to us
of events of primitive race history. "Cushite
Art" and "The Heart of the African" answer
many questionings of our hearts about Ethiopians. The series closes with a comparison of
ancient culture with modern forms. The intelligence of the Cushite, his original genius is held
up beside the decadence of true ideals in the art
and literature of the present. The "Revolt of
Civilization" and "Dawn of a new World" voice
the concern of the thoughtful over the present
decay of culture.

We are sending forth this information because so few men today understand the primitive
forces that are the root of modern culture. So
superficial and prejudiced has been most modern
research, that many important and accepted theories of universal history have no actual basis in
fact. The average modern historical book con-
tradicts what the ancients said about the nations
that preceeded them. We cannot solve the stupendous problems that the world faces until we
can read aright the riddle of the evolution of the
races. Uninformed men make unsafe leaders.
that is the primal cause for so many errors of
judgment in state and national councils. We look
upon them not as statesmen but as promoters of
petty politics, for out of their deliberations spring
no alleviation of the woes of the world. It is
from this lack of understanding in leadership

that the world suffers most today. We could dis-
criminate between the true and false in our civilization, if we knew more about primitive culture.
The way by which the first man climbed must ever
be the human way. Racial prejudices are the
greatest menace to world progress. Classes clash
because the wealth of the world concentrates more
and more in the hands of a few. The tragedy of
human misery increases, the increase of defec-
tives, the growing artificiality of modern living,
compels us to seek and blazen forth the knowledge of the true origin of culture and the fundamental principles that through the ages have been
the basis of true progress. Only by this wisdom
shall we know how to lift human life today.

In most modern books there seems to be pre-
concerted understanding to calumniate and dis-
gust the world with abominable pictures of the
ruined Ethiopian, ruined by the African slave
trade of four hundred years. There seems to be
a world wide conspiracy in literature to conceal
the facts that this book unfolds. Because of this
suppression of truth, world crimes have been easily made possible against the Ethiopian. These
people are held in low estimation because truth
is hidden which proves that today though more
favored races are at the apex of human accom-
plishment; yet in the earlier ages the wheel of
destiny carried upward those, who now seem
hopelessly under. To wipe away the black stain
of the slave trade, modern literature has represented the slave trader as having trafficked in de-
praved human beings. Today the lower types of

the Aryan race look upon them as creatures only
fit for political and economic spoilation, to fill the
coffers of the colonial renegade, who could not
succeed at home. This type of the world finds it
easy to stifle the life of ruined and defenceless
races. This spoilation of the weak, returned in
a counter stroke from which it was impossible to
escape in the world war. Belgium reaped in identical measure and kind, what this type had meted
out to the defenceless people of the Congo. Nations must reap what they sow.

This is not the nature or intention of the better men of the civilized nations but we are uninformed about alien peoples. We are narrow and
provincial in our views. The hatred of the races
springs out of misunderstanding. The men of the
world who have traveled, and read, and thought,
upon ethnological problems are the men who have
the cultivated instincts of human brotherhood.
Shall England, France, Germany, America, suffer
further because we have not taught the uninformed of the nations that we must pay a still
heavier toll for a continued measure of injustice
to weaker peoples? Innocent must suffer with
the guilty, for it is in our power to inform and
curb the power of the selfish. The question looms
large in the minds of thinking men today, whether
Ethiopians are worthy of equal opportunity. Let
us settle forever out of time's irrefutable evidence, whether if we gave him the chance, the
Ethiopian would treat us as we have treated him.
There need be no conjecturing; for the archives
of the past hold the facts. The history of the

Cushite Ethiopians down through the ages is one of the most thrilling as well as tragic of all time's age old stories. It is almost incredible that its rich treasure for developing our understanding has so long remained veiled.

The Ethiopian is a great race, probably the oldest. It is a race that does not die out under adversity. When other races are sullen, or despairing and turn to self destruction, these people cheerfully press on. When they think the way is blocked they turn aside to pick flowers along the pathway of pleasure. We hear their happy voices in the cotton field, they can be the life of the carnival, their zealous fervor in camp meeting and the swing song of the marching black regiments of the world war and the stevedore regiments in peace, show these people as they employ themselves, patiently waiting for bars to progress to rot down, if nothing else will remove them. Then again they take up the steady march onward, that has been the wonderful element of their history on down through the ages. We need our eyes opened, this type that we in ignorance despise, built the eternal pyramids of Egypt and laid the foundation of the civilization of the historic ages. Because the slave trade broke the threads of remembrance, they walk among us with bowed heads, themselves ignorant of the facts that this story unfolds.

Lift up your heads, discouraged and downtrodden Ethiopians. Listen to this marvelous story told of your ancestors, who wrought mightily for mankind and built the foundations of civilization true and square in the days of old. Awake ye sleeping Aryans, become aware of the acute need of the world today of this enchained energy and ability. The absence of this power is the cause of many a breakdown in modern civilization. Out of our own accepted sciences, the chapters of this book, prove the Cushite race to have been the fountainhead of civilization. If you desire truth, if you desire to be fair minded, to be educated in vital knowledge not possessed by the average college student, if you desire to be an authority upon the life of the ancients, go down with me as archaeology, ethnology, geology and philology disclose; not in a dry and tedious way, but through the unfolding of this the most intensely interesting and startling drama of the ages. The Cushite race, its institutions, customs, laws and ideals were the foundation upon which our modern culture was laid. Let this not stir the pride of the modern Cushite, but rather inspire him to a greater consecration to the high idealism that made the masteries of olden days.

Knowledge of the primal strength and weaknesses of each world group must be possessed by world leadership or we shall still further go astray. Without this knowledge international councils cannot intelligently assign each race to its rightful place in the consummation of God's plan of the Ages. Without this truth the nations cannot put over their programs. The world war proved that we have no international stability. The world's securities and diplomatic relations are propped. Because the real history of mankind is not a part of our general knowledge, we are discounting factors most needed to secure world balance. There can be no more needed contribution to civilization, than to gather from the archives of the past and present day science all the truth about the origin of culture. Only thus will we know how to develop better men today. If we knew just what contribution each race has made to art, science and religion, we would know what would be its fitness to take part in world government and control. Has the influence of a race been creative or destructive throughout the ages? That should point plainly to the part they would be likely to play today.

Because we are without this knowledge, we cannot read aright the past or present history of civilization. Modern crimes of injustice toward weaker peoples have been made easy by this suppression of truth. It has been popular and remunerative to write and speak on the side of prejudice. A better spirit is rising in the world. Men are eager for information, for the truth. Through the teaching of sociology, the most popular and crowded classes of our great universities, in a scientific way, man is beginning to see the need of a realization of our common brotherhood and to reach out to solve unmastered problems and unfulfilled duties. Many problems are an international consternation because they are too gigantic for the handling of any one world group. Civilization was appalled at its helplessness in the world war. The leading nations faced annihilation, yet were unable to walk out of the trap until the flower of European manhood had perished. The noblest offered themselves for sacrifice, the more selfish remained at home. The world may never be capable of calculating its artistic and moral loss. We see the difference in the crime and debauchery breaking down the culture of today. Unless we can rouse men to truth and united effort, there is no hope for our civilization which is tottering and must fall.

In justice to that Divine Leading that piloted this search of a decade over trails, that otherwise might not have been found in a lifetime, in tribute to the pluck and consecration to a purpose— to add to the light of truth, that has gathered such an avalanche of testimony from authoritative sources, we speak of this work which has taken all those spare moments, that are our right to spend in leisure, that a frail unflagging spirit might make possible this marvelous story, as strange as any olden fairy tale; yet by the light of our accepted sciences true, We lift the veil lightly lest the careless skim over these pages carelessly, little recking what they have cost. Often when limbs and weary brain cried out in protest, the searcher pressed on, seeing fully the power in this truth if patiently, carefully gathered, to lift the men of all races to a clearer comprehension of the contribution of each race to all that we prize in civilization, and to stir within us the determination to lift and bear aloft the "torch" lit in primitive ages by a race today despised and misunderstood. The average book has its dozen helpers and advisors, this work has been done in hermitage. The hermitage of a life submerged in service. Humbly, reverently, this truth is offered in love to all races. Ten years more may be devoted to its final setting but the facts imbedded in these pages are too important to be longer withheld.

THE AUTHOR.

CHAPTER I.

THE EMPIRE'S AGE AND SCOPE.

The excavations of Petrie revealed in Egypt the remains of a distinct race that preceeded the historic Egyptians. The earliest civilization was higher than that of the later dynasties. Its purer art represents an "Old Race" that fills all the background of the pre-historic ages. It colonized the first civilized centers of the primitive world. The ancients called this pioneer race, which lit the torch of art and science, Cushite Ethiopians, the founders of primeval cities and civilized life. The wonders of India, to which Europe sought a passage in the age of Columbus, the costly products and coveted merchandise of Babylon, and the amazing prehistoric civilization of Asia Minor, sprang from this little recognized source. The achievements of this race in early ages were the result of co-operation. Cushites reached the true zenith of democracy. Their skillful hands raised Cyclopean walls, dug out mighty lakes and laid imperishable roads that have endured throughout the ages. This was the uniform testimony of ancient records. Modern writers seem of superficial research, either being unaware of these facts, or knowing, purposely ignore them. Archaeologists dig up the proofs, ethnologists announce their origin, but history refuses to change its antiquated and exploded theories.

General history informs us that when the curtain of history was lifted, the civilization of Egypt was hoary with age. It was a culture that must have developed from thousands of years of growth. Why is the scholarship of the world so silent as to what lay behind historic Egypt? No nation throughout the ages has "as Athene sprung full fledged into knowledge of all the arts and sciences." The story of what lay behind Egypt fascinated the whole ancient world. The culture of Egypt did not originate upon the Lower Nile. Who then was her teacher? It was the ancient Cushite empire of Ethiopians, which weighty authorities tell us ruled over three continents for thousands of years. Should the world wait longer to test the truth of these ancient witnesses? Beside these gigantic achievements, the petty conquests of Alexander the Great, Julius Caesar, and of Napoleon Bonaparte, fade into insignificance. There seems to be fear to tell about these ancients, who built mighty cities, the ruins of which extend in uninterrupted succession around the shores of the Mediterranean Sea. Traces of this hoary empire, works appearing to have been wrought by giants, bearing marks of Cushite genius, have been found by scientists all over the primitive world.

We marvel at the wonders recently unearthed in Egypt. Let us look behind her through the glasses of science at the "Old Race" of which she was in her beginning, only a colony. Ethiopia was the source of all that Egypt knew and transmitted to Greece and Rome. We are accustomed to think of Ethiopia as a restricted country in Africa but this was not true. The study of ancient maps and the descriptions of the geographers of old, reveals that the ancient Land of Cush was a very widespread and powerful empire. Rosenmuller shows us that the Hebrew scholars called Cush, all the countries of the torrid zone. It was the race that Huxley saw akin to the Dravidians of India, stretching in an empire from India to Spain. The Greeks described Ethiopia as the country around the Indus and Ganges. (*Rosenmuller's Biblical Geography*, Bk. III, p. 154.)

H. G. Wells says that the Hamitic tongue was a much wider and more varied language than the Semitic or Aryan in ancient days.* It was the language of the Neolithic peoples who occupied most of western and southern Asia, who may have been related to the Dravidians of India and the people of George Elliot's Heliolithic culture. Sir H. H. Johnson says that this lost Hamitic language was represented by the scattered branches of Crete, Lydia, the Basques, the Caucasian-Dravidian group, the ancient Sumerian and the Elamite. The people of this race were the first to give the world ideas of government. Stephanus of Byzantium, voicing the universal testimony of antiquity wrote, ''Ethiopia was the

*Outline of History, Vol. 1, p. 158.   Wells.

first' established country on earth and the Ethiopians were the first to set up the worship of the gods and to establish laws.'' The later ages gained from this ancient empire, the fundamental principles upon which republican governments are founded. The basic stones of that wonderful dominion were equality, temperence, industry, intelligence and justice.

The average historical book ignores this testimony and disputes in its theories the records and monuments of Egypt and Chaldea. They group the races in utter contradiction to the records of the Greeks and Hebrews. In the light of reason, who would know about the ethnic relations of the ancients, the scholars and historians of Egypt, Chaldea and Greece, who are more and more corroborated by the findings of science, or the theories of the men of today?' The modern writer whose research has been superficial does not know that before the days of Grecian and Roman ascendency, the entire circle of the Mediterranean and her islands was dotted with the magic cities and the world-wide trade of Ethiopians. The gods and goddesses of the Greeks and Romans were but the borrowed kings and queens of this Cushite empire of Ethiopians. So marvelous had been their achievements in primitive ages, that in later days, they were worshipped as immortals by the people of India, Egypt, old Ethiopia, Asia Minor and the Mediterranean world.

Rawlinson, after his exhaustive research into the life of ancient nations, says, ''For the last

three thousand years the world has been mainly
indebted to the Semitic and Indo-European races
for its advancement, but it was otherwise in the
first ages. Egypt and Babylon, Mizraim and
Nimrod, both descendants of Ham, led the way
and acted as the pioneers of mankind in the various untrodden fields of art, science and literature. Alphabetical writings, astronomy, history,
chronology, architecture, plastic art, sculpture,
navigation, agriculture and textile industries
seem to have had their origin in one or the other
of these countries." (*Rawlinson's Ancient Monarchies*, Vol. 1.) The taming of the animals was
the gift to us of these prehistoric men. By skill
and perseverence they developed from wild plants
the wheat, oats and rye that are the foundation
of our agriculture. This work was done so many
ages ago, that their wild origin has disappeared.
The average man little realizes the gifts of the
prehistoric ages, or how helpless we would be
without them today. ›

'Rawlinson continues, "The first inventors of
any art are among the greatest benefactors of
mankind and the bold steps they take from the
known to the unknown, from blank ignorance to
discovery, are equal to many subsequent steps
of progress." Bunsen says in his *Philosophy of
Ancient History*, "The Hamitic family as Rawlinson proves must be given the credit for being
the fountainhead of civilization. This family
comprised the ancient Ethiopians, the Egyptians,
the original Canaanites and the old Chaldeans.
The inscriptions of the Chaldean monuments

prove their race affinity. The Bible proves their relationship. It names the sons of Ham as Cush, Mizraim, Phut and the race of Canaan. Mizraim peopled Egypt and Canaan the land later possessed by the Hebrews. Phut located in Africa and Cush extended his colonies over a wide domain." (*Philosophy of Ancient History*, Bunsen, p. 52.)

Bunsen concludes by saying, "Cushite colonies were all along the southern shores of Asia and Africa and by the archaeological remains, along the southern and eastern coasts of Arabia. The name Cush was given to four great areas, Media, Persia, Susiana and Aria, or the whole territory between the Indus and Tigris in prehistoric times. In Africa the Ethiopians, the Egyptians, the Libyans, the Canaanites and Phoenicians were all descendants of Ham. They were a black or dark colored race and the pioneers of our civilization. They were emphatically the monument builders on the plains of Shinar and the valley of the Nile from Meroe to Memphis. In southern Arabia they erected wonderful edifices. They were responsible for the monuments that dot southern Siberia and in America along the valley of the Mississippi down to Mexico and in Peru their images and monuments stand as voiceless witnesses." This was the ancient Cushite Empire of Ethiopians that covered three worlds. Some of our later books recognizing their indisputable influence in primitive culture, speak of them as a brunet brown race representing a mysterious Heliolithic culture.

Wells testifying from researches of Eliot Smith admits that this culture may have been oozing round the world from 1500 B. C. to 1000 B. C. He calls it the highest early culture of the world. It sustained the largest and most highly developed communities, but as in other modern books there is failure to give us clearer light upon this ancient culture and its origin. Baldwin speaking more frankly affirms that Hebrew writers describe these first inhabitants of cities and civilized life as Cushites. "The foundations of ancient religions, mythology, institutions and customs all had the same source. He considered the Egyptian and Chaldean civilizations as very old but the culture and political organization of Ethiopia was much older. They belonged to what Egyptians and Chaldeans regarded as real antiquity, ages shrouded in doubt because they were so remote. The oldest nations mentioned in history did not originate civilization, the traditions of Asia bring civilization from the south, connecting it with the Erythraean Sea. These traditions are confirmed by the inscriptions found upon the old ruins of Chaldea." (*Prehistoric Nations,* Baldwin.)

Wilford, that eminent student of the literature of India, found that Ethiopia was often mentioned in the Sanskrit writings of the people of India. The world according to the Puranas, ancient historical books, was divided into seven dwipas or divisions. Ethiopia was Cusha-Dwipa which included Arabia, Asia Minor, Syria, Nubia, Armenia, Mesopotamia, and an extended region

in Africa. These Sanskrit writings prove that in
remote ages these regions were the most powerful richest and most enlightened part of the world.
From these authoritative records and the conclusions drawn by historians of deeper research we
would decide that many ancient peoples, who have
been assigned to other races in the average historical book of modern times, were in reality
Ethiopians. There were nations that called themselves Cushites who never knew themselves under
the titles and classifications that superficial students have given them. The Phoenicians in the
days of Christ called themselves Ethiopians. The
Scriptures and ancient records called the Samaritans Cushites. To create a true story of the ages
the entire fabric of the ethnological relationship
of the races will have to be torn down to be more
honestly laid.

This Ethiopia, which existed for long ages
before its wonderful power was broken, cannot
be limited to the short chronological period of
history, that, the facts of geology prove to be in
error. The Bible gives no figures for the epochs
of time. It speaks of Creation and its after periods in God cycles that we cannot resolve into figures. We read in *Prehistoric Nations*, "In the
oldest recorded traditions, Cushite colonies were
established in the valley of the Nile. Barabra
and Chaldea. This beginning must have been
not later than 7000 or 8000 B. C. or perhaps earlier. They brought to development astronomy
and the other sciences, which have come down to
us. The vast commercial system by which they

joined together the "ends of the earth" was created and manufacturing skill established. The great period of Cushite control had closed many ages prior to Homer, although separate communities remained not only in Egypt but in southern Arabia, Phoenicia and elsewhere." (*Prehistoric Nations*, pp. 95, 96.) Baldwin continues, "5000 B. C. Egypt and Chaldea became separate. The Cushites were still unrivalled. 3500 to 3000 B. C. the kingdom divided again. We do not know what caused the breaking up of the old empire, which for thousands of years had held imperial sway." It may have been that the first cities and civilization extended beyond the "Deluge." The Sabaeans, Himyarites, and Ethiopians maintained supremacy almost to modern times; but the ancient glory had departed previous to the rise of Assyria 1300 B. C. Not long before the Arabian peninsula had been overrun by Semites, chiefly nomads, who became the permanent inhabitants. The previous conquests of the ancient world denominated by modern books as Semitic were Cushite Arabian and not of the later Semitic Arabian race. Through this error many ancient branches of the Hamitic race are lined up as Semitic. After the rise of Assyria, the Ethiopians above Egypt became the central representatives of that power that had exercised world empire for thousands of years. What kind of race could this have been that could throw such giant shadows upon time's dawn?

The stories of the "*Arabian Nights*," which

so enthralled us in childhood and to which the
childhood of the world clings as though they were
true has this historic basis. They picture the
activities and world wide scope of Cushite civilization in the declining days of Ethiopian glory.
Its scenes represent India, Persia, Arabia and
Chaldea, which were primitively Cushite, in the
decline of the Gold and Silver Ages of ancient
tradition. Archaeological research and findings
are proving that there were such ages. The tales
of the Arabian Nights, so marvelous and gripping
in interest, did not spring from mere fancy alone,
and because of this have for mankind an alluring
and undying fascination. These tales minus their
genii and fairies form an imperishable book pic-
turing a far distant but powerful civilization. In
the land of the ancient Chaldean, in Egypt, in
happy "Araby the Blest," and along the shores
of the Mediterranean, the evidences of this prehistoric civilization are being dug up in wonder
by the archaeologists of the civilized nations today. Relics in their way as wonderful as the
gems called up by Alladin's Lamp, hidden just as
were his finds in chambers of the earth.

Heeren, whose researches furnish invaluable
information to the later historians says, "From
the remotest times to the present, the Ethiopians
have been the most celebrated and yet the most
mysterious of nations. In the earliest traditions
of the more civilized nations of antiquity, the
name of this most distant people is found. The
annals of the Egyptian priests were full of them;
and the nations of inner Asia on the Euphrates

and the Tigris have woven the fictions of the
Ethiopians with their own traditions of the wars
and conquests of their heroes; and at a period
equally remote they glimmer in Greek mythology." Dionysus, Hercules, Saturn, Osiris, Zeus
and Apollo were Cushite kings of the prehistoric
ages. Around these and other Ethiopian deities
the people of the Mediterranean and the Orient
wove their mythologies. Prejudice and ignorance
may have marked their deeds as fabulous but the
imperishable monuments that they left are not
imaginary. They are the realistic reminders of
a people who deeply impressed and colored the
life, art and literature of the ancient world.

The prehistoric achievements of Cushite heroes
were the theme of ancient sculpture, painting and
drama. They were the object of worship of all
the nations that appear civilized at the dawn of
history. The literature and music of Greece and
Rome was permeated by this deep Ethiopian
strain. These classic forms and ideals
maintain supremacy in the art of modern
times. Heeren continues, "When the Greeks
scarcely knew Italy and Sicily by name, the Ethiopians were celebrated in the poems of their bards.
They were the remotest nation, the most just of
men, the favorites of the gods. The lofty inhabitants of Olympus journey to them and take part
in their feasts. Their sacrifices are the most
agreeable that mortals can offer and when the
faint beams of tradition give way to the clear
light of history, the lusture of the Ethiopians is
not diminished. They still continue to be objects

of curiosity and admiration; and the pens of cautious and clear sighted historians often place them in the highest rank of knowledge and civilization.''

CHAPTER II.

OLD ETHIOPIA—ITS PEOPLE.

Because of the great lapse of time, it seems almost impossible to locate the original seat of the old Ethiopian empire. Bochart thought it was "Happy Araby," that from this central point the Cushite race spread eastward and westward. Some authorities like Gesenius thought it was Africa. The Greeks looked to old Ethiopia and called the Upper Nile the common cradle of mankind. Toward the rich luxurience of this region they looked for the "Garden of Eden." From these people of the Upper Nile arose the oldest traditions and rites and from them sprang the first colonies and arts of antiquity. The Greeks also said that Egyptians derived their civilization and religion from Ethiopia. "Egyptian religion was not an original conception, for three thousand years ago she had lost all true sense of its real meaning among even the priesthood." (Budge, *Osiris and the Egyptian Resurrection*—Preface.) Yet Egyptian forms of worship are understood and practiced among the Ethiopians of Nubia today. The common people of Egypt never truly understood their religion, this was why it so easily became debased.

Ptolemaic writers said that Egypt was formed of the mud carried down from Ethiopia, that

Ethiopians were the first men that ever lived, the only truly autochthonous race and the first to institute the worship of the gods and the rites of sacrifice. Egypt itself was a colony of Ethiopia and the laws and script of both lands were naturally the same; but the hieroglyphic script was more widely known to the vulgar in Ethiopia than in Egypt. (Diodorus Siculus, bk. iii, ch. 3.) This knowledge of writing was universal in Ethiopia but was confined to the priestly classes alone in Egypt. This was because the Egyptian priesthood was Ethiopian. The highly developed Merodic inscriptions are not found in Egypt north of the first cataract or in Nubia south of Soba. These are differences we would expect to find between a colony and a parent body. Herodotus (bk. ii, p. 29) says that Meroe was a great city and metropolis, most of its buildings were of red brick. 800 B. C. at Napata, the buildings were of hard stone. (*Meroe*—Crowfoot, pp. 6, 30.)

The *Cyclopedia of Biblical Literature* says, ''There is every reason to conclude that the separate colonies of priestcraft spread from Meroe into Egypt; and the primeval monuments in Ethiopia strongly confirm the native traditions reported by Diodorus Siculus, that the worship of Zeus-Ammon originated in Meroe, also the worship of Osiris. This would render highly probable the opinion that commerce, science and art descended into Egypt from the Upper Nile. Herodotus called the Ethiopians ''Wisemen occupying the Upper Nile, men of long life, whose manners and customs pertain to the Golden Age, those virtuous mortals whose feasts and banquets are honored by Jupiter himself.'' In Greek times, the Egyptians depicted Ethiopia as an ideal state. The Puranas, the ancient historical books of India, speak of the civilization of Ethiopia as being older than that of Egypt. These Sanskrit books mention the names of old Cushite kings that were worshipped in India and who were adopted and changed to suit the fancy of the later people of Greece and Rome.

The Hindu Puranas speak of the Cushites going to India before they went to Egypt, proving Hindu civilization coeval with that of Chaldea and the country of the Nile. These ancients record that the Egyptians were a colony drawn out from Cusha-Dwipa and that the Palli, another colony that made the Phoenicians followed them from the land of Cush. In those primitive days, the central seat of Ethiopia was not the Meroe of our day, which is very ancient, but a kingdom that preceeded it by many ages; that was called Meru. Lenormant spoke of the first men of the ancient world as ''Men of Meru.'' Sanskrit writers called Indra, chief god of the Hindu, king of Meru. He was deified and became the chief representative of the supreme being. Thus was primitive India settled by colonists from Ethiopia. Early writers said there was very little difference in the color or features of the people of the two countries.

Ancient traditions told of the deeds of Deva Nahusha, another sovereign of Meru, who extended his empire over three worlds. The lost

literature of Asia Minor dealt with this extension
of the Ethiopian domain. An old poem "Phry-
gia," was a history of Dionysus, one of the most
celebrated of the old Ethiopians. It was written
in a very old language and character. He preceeded Menes by many ages. Baldwin says that
the authentic books that would have given us the
true history concerning him, perished long before
the Hellenes. The Greeks of historical times distorted the story of Dionysus and converted him
into their drunken god of wine. "They miscon-
strued and misused the old Cushite mythology,
wherever they failed to understand it, and sought
to appropriate it entirely to themselves." One
of the poetical versions of the taking of Troy, on
the coast of Asia Minor, was entitled "The
Æthiops," because the inhabitants of Troy, as
we shall prove later, who fought so valiantly in
the Trojan war, were Cushite Ethiopians. This
version presented the conflict as an Egyptian
war.

In those early ages Egypt was under Ethiopian domination. In proof of this fact, the *Cyclopedia of Biblical Literature* says, "Isaiah often
mentions Ethiopia and Egypt in close political
relations. In fine the name of Ethiopia chiefly
stood as the name of the national and royal family
of Egypt. In the beginning Egypt was ruled from
Ethiopia. Ethiopia was ruined by her wars with
Egypt, which she sometimes subdued and sometimes served." Modern books contain but little
information about the country of the Upper Nile,
but archaic books were full of the story of the

wonderful Ethiopians. The ancients said that
they settled Egypt. Is it possible that we could
know more about the origin of this nation than
they? Reclus says, "The people occupying the
plateau of the Blue Nile, are conscious of a glorious past and proudly call themselves Ethiopians." He calls the whole triangular space between the Nile and the Red Sea, Ethiopia proper.
This vast highland constituted a world apart.
From it went forth the inspiration and light now
bearing its fruit in the life of younger nations.

Hereen thought, that excepting the Egyptians,
no aboriginal people of Africa so claim our attention as the Ethiopians. He asks, "To what
shall we attribute the renown of this one of the
most distant nations of the earth? How did the
fame of her name permeate the terrible deserts
that surrounded her; and even yet form an in-
superable bar to all who approach. A great many
nations distant and different from one another
are called Ethiopians. Africa contains the greater
number of them and a considerable tract in Asia
was occupied by this race. The Ethiopians were
distinguished from the other races by a very dark
or completely black skin." (Heeren's Historical
Researches—*Ethiopian Nations*. Ch. 1, p. 46)
Existing monuments confirm the high antiquity of
Meroe. In the Persian period Ethiopia was an
important and independent state, which Cambyses vainly attempted to subdue. Rosellini thinks
that the right of Sabaco and Tirhakah, Ethiopian
kings, who sat upon the throne of Egypt in the
latter days, must have been more by right of de-

scent than by usurpation or force of arms. "This may be judged," he says, "by the respect paid to their monuments by their successors." The pictures on the Egyptian monuments reveal that Ethiopians were the builders. They, not the Egyptians, were the master-craftsmen of the earlier ages. The first courses of the pyramids were built of Ethiopian stone. The Cushites were a sacerdotal or priestly race. There was a reli-gious and astronomical significance in the position and shape of the pyramids. Dubois points to the fact that in Upper Egypt there were pictured black priests who were conferring upon red Egyptians, the instruments and symbols of priesthood. Ethiopians in very early ages had an original and astounding religion, which included the rite of human sacrifice. It lingered on in the early life of Greece and Rome. Dowd explains this rite in this way: "The African offered his nearest and dearest, not from depravity but from a greater love for the supreme being." The priestly caste was more influencial upon the Upper Nile than in Egypt. With the withdrawal of the Ethiopian priesthood from Egypt to Napata, the people of the Lower Nile lost the sense of the real meaning of their religion, which steadily deteriorated with their language after their separation from Ethiopia.

If we visit Nubia, modern Ethiopia today, we can plainly see in the inhabitants their superiority to the common Egyptian type. The Barabra or Nile Nubians are on a footing of perfect equality in Egypt because that was their plane in ancient

RACE TYPE OF THE EARLY DYNASTIES.
(From Ridpath's History.)

days. Baedecker describes them as strong, muscular, agricultural and more warlike and energetic than Egyptians. Keane says the Nubians excel in moral qualities. They are by his description obviously Negroid, very dark with full lips and dreamy eyes. They have the narrow heads which are the cranial formation of Ethiopia. Race may be told by shape of the skull far better than by color or feature, which are modified by climate. The members of the Tartar race have perfectly rounded skulls. The head of the Ethiopian races is very elongated. Europeans have an intermediate skull. The cranial formation of unmixed races never changes. Keane concludes by saying, ''All Barbara have wooly hair with scant beards like the figures of Negroes on the walls of the Egyptian temples.'' The race of the Old Empire approached closely to this type.

Strabo mentions the Nubians as a great race west of the Nile. They came originally from Kordofan, whence they emigrated two thousand years ago. They have rejected the name Nubas as it has become synonymous with slave. They call themselves Barabra, their ancient race name. Sanskrit historians call the Old Race of the Upper Nile Barabra. These Nubians have become slightly modified but are still plainly Negroid. They look like the Wawa on the Egyptian monuments. The Retu type number one was the ancient Egyptian, the Retu type number two was in feature an intermingling of the Ethiopian and Egyptian types. The Wawa were Cushites and the name occurs in the mural inscriptions five thousands years ago. Both people were much intermingled six thousand years ago. The faces of the Egyptians of the Old Monarchy are Ethiopian but as the ages went on they altered from the constant intermingling with Asiatic types. Also the intense furnace-like heat of Upper Egypt tended to change the features and darken the skin.

In the inscriptions relative to the campaigns of Pepi I, Negroes are represented as immediately adjoining the Egyptian frontier. This seems to perplex some authors. They had always been there. This was the Old Race of predynastic Egypt—the primitive Cushite type. This was the aboriginal race of Abyssinia. It was symbolized by the Great Sphinx and the marvelous face of Cheops. Take any book of Egyptian history containing authentic cuts and examine the faces of the first pharaohs, they are distinctively Ethiopian. The "Agu" of the monuments represented this aboriginal race. They were the ancestors of the Nubians, and were the ruling race of Egypt. Petrie in 1892 exhibited before the British Association, some skulls of the Third and Fourth Dynasties, showing distinct Negroid characteristics. They were dolichocephalic or long skulled. The findings of archaeology more and more reveal that Egypt was Cushite in her beginning and that Ethiopians were not a branch of the Japheth race in the sense that they are so represented in the average ethnological classifications of today.

Egyptians said that they and their religion had come from the land of Punt. Punt is generally accepted today to have been Somaliland south of

Nubia. On the pictured plates at Deir-el-Baheri, the huts of the people of Punt were like the Toquls of the modern Sudanese, being built on piles approached by ladders. The birds were like a species common among the Somali. The fishes were not like those of Egypt. The wife of the king of Punt appears with a form like the Bongo women with exaggerated organs of maternity. This was a distinctive Ethiopian form. The king had the Cushite profile. The products carried by the wooly haired porters were ebony, piles of elephant tusks, all African products and trays of massive gold rings. Punt is mentioned in the inscriptions as a land of wonders. We find marvelous ruins in southeastern Africa that substantiate these reports. The inscription in the rocky valley of Hammat tells how 2000 B. C. a force gathered in the Thebaid to go on an expedition to Punt to bring back the products that made the costly incense of the ancients. The Stage Temple at Thebes showed in gorgeous pictures another expedition in 1600 B. C. We now know that Somaliland yielded the frankincense of ancient commerce, which was used in the ceremonials of all ancient kingdoms. Punt was called the "Holy Land" by the Egyptians.

In Egypt today, the most effective battalions are those commanded by black Nubians. In ancient ages the Egyptians followed the lead of the Ethiopian to battle and it is instinctive in them to do so today. Cushites were the backbone of the Egyptian armies in the earliest ages. The Egyptian has no warlike qualities. It was the Cushite

who was the head and brains of the foreign conquests. It was the Cushite element of the Old
Empire that extended itself in foreign colonization eastward and westward around the world.
Across Arabia and southwestern Asia, even to
the central highlands, inscriptions and massive
images in stone stand as voiceless witnesses that
they were the commanders of the Egyptian armies
and that the Ethiopian masses accompanied the
soldiers as trusted allies and not as driven slaves.
We must remember that in the early ages they
were not a subject race but that their power as
a great empire was at its zenith.

The Egyptian of today much changed from the
ancient whom Herodotus called black, is content
to live in a mud hut beside his beloved Nile. He
is despised by the prouder Nubian, who saves his
earnings to buy a home and piece of ground in
his native Ethiopia. Reclus tells us that the dis-
like between Egyptians and Nubians is carried to
such a great extent that the Nubians even in
Egypt will not marry an Egyptian woman and
that he refuses his daughter in marriage to the
Egyptian and Arab. This could have come down
alone from an age-old consciousness of superiority. He knows the proud traditions of his race.
In books careless of ethnography, we find the Nubian classed with Semitic stock. They have no
affinities at all with this race. Nubians are never
able to speak the Arabic tongues gramatically.
Nubian women are seldom seen in Egypt. They
are the most faithful to the manners and customs
of the Old Race. The Egyptian of today makes

little showings of ambition or the spirit for great
deeds. He squanders his earnings upon trinkets
and seems content in the same mud hovel in which
the masses of Egyptians primitively lived.
Prichard recognizes two branches of the Nubians, the Nubians of the Nile and those of the
Red Sea. In the age of Herodotus, the countries
known as Nubia and Senaar were occupied by two
different races, one of which he includes under
the name Ethiopian; the other was a pastorial
race of Semitic decent which led a migratory life.
This distinction continues to the present day.
The Red Sea nomadic tribes are extremely savage and inhospitable. The Nile Nubas or Barabra
are the original Ethiopians. They are agricul-
aural and have the old Hamitic traits. They plant
date trees and set up wheels for irrigation. These
are the Ethiopians mentioned in chronicles as
possessing war chariots. Their allies were the
Libyans. Semites at that age of the world had
no possession of iron vehicles. Heeren says,
"that the ancestors of these Ethiopians had long
lived in cities and had erected magnificent temples and edifices, that they possessed law and government, and that the fame of their progress in
knowledge and the social arts had spread in the
earliest ages to a considerable part of the world."
Maurice, that reliable authority on ancient remains, declares, "The ancient Ethiopians were
the architectural giants of the past. When the
daring Cushite genius was in the full career of
its glory, it was the peculiar delight of this enterprising race to erect stupendous edifices, exca-

vate long subterranean passages in the living rock, form vast lakes and extend over the hollows of adjoining mountains magnificent arches for aqueducts and bridges. It was they who built the tower of Babel or Belus and raised the pyramids of Egypt; it was they who formed the grottoes near the Nile and scooped the caverns of Salsette and Elephante. (These latter are wonders of Hindu architecture.) Their skill in mechanical powers astonishes posterity, who are unable to conceive by what means stones thirty, forty and even sixty feet in length from twelve to twenty in depth could ever be raised to the point of elevation at which they are seen in the ruined temples of Belbec and Thebais. Those comprising the pagodas of India are scarcely less wonderful in point of elevation and magnitude." (*Maurice's Ancient History of Hindustan.*)

CHAPTER III.

ANCIENT ETHIOPIA, THE LAND.

The Nubo-Egyptian desert was once abundantly watered and a well timbered region. With the exclusion of the narrow Nile valley, all of this is generally a barren waste today. Geology reveals that in the primitive ages, this country had a moist climate like the Congo basin; but these conditions prevailed in remote geographical times, probably before the creation of the delta. The changes that turned the Sahara into a burning waste in time made Upper Egypt dry and torrid. Keane describes its climate as often fatal to all but full blooded natives. Under those brazen skies the children of even Euro-African half castes seldom survive after the tenth or twelfth year. Passing southward, we find that ancient edifices occur throughout the whole extent of Ethiopia. In the olden days, the climate there was favorable to the nurturing and development of a high type of civilization and produced an Ethiopian so superior to the later types, that they were called by the ancients, "the handsomest men of the primeval world."

The whole of the space between the Nile and Abyssinia, and northward to Lower Egypt once constituted Ethiopia. It was called Beled-es-Soudan (land of the blacks). Once Egypt ex-

tended to Lower Nubia. The ancient kingdom of
Meroe was Upper Nubia and was divided into
agricultural and grazing lands. Crowfoot tells
us in his *Ancient Meroe*, p. 29, that Meroe at the
height of its prosperity was established upon as
broad an economic basis as Egypt or Mesopotamia. Ancient authorities tell us that they grew
grains upon lands richer and wider than the
whole of Egypt, with pastures of limitless plains.
Theirs were lands of heavy rains. Precious
stones were there in abundance. They produced
beautiful painted pottery and their princes were
robed in magnificence. The yearning of the Ethiopian for all things beautiful, his love for ceremony and costly attire may not be mere imitation
but springs from inheritance, from the possession of these things by his ancestors thousands
of years ago.

Herodotus II, 29, says, "Meroe was a great city
and metropolis." Here Zeus Ammon was worshipped in temples of the utmost splendor. The
Cyclopedia of Biblical Literature explains, "The
early prosperity and grandeur of Ethiopia sprang
from the carrying trade of which it was the center,
between India and Arabia on the one hand and
the interior of Africa and especially Egypt on
the other. There was intimate connection between Egypt and Ethiopia commercially. Thebes
and Meroe founded a common colony in Libya."
This would prove the close relationship of Thebes,
which was Nubian and Meroe. Meroe was the
seat of a great caravan route from the north of
Africa. Another route went westward across the

Soudan. Strabo spoke of this open way in the day of Tartesus, long before the ancient Gades was built. From Meroe eastward extended the great caravan route by which the wares of southern Arabia and Africa were interchanged. The great wealth of the Cushites arose from this net work of commerce which covered the prehistoric world.

Biblical Literature asks these pertinent questions, ''Whence did Egypt obtain spices and drugs with which she embalmed her dead? Whence the incense that burned on her altars? Whence came into the empire the immense amount of cotton in which her inhabitants were clad, and which her own soil so sparingly produced? And whence came into Egypt the rumors of the Ethiopian gold countries which Cambyses set out to seek? Whence that profusion of ivory and ebony that Greek and Phoenician artists embellished? Whence the early spread of the name of Ethiopia celebrated by Jewish poets as well as by the earliest Grecian bards? Whence but from the international commerce of which Ethiopia was the center and seat?'' These principal trade routes may still be pointed out by a chain of ruins, extending from the shores of the Indian Ocean to the Mediterranean. The cities Adule, Axum, Meroe, Thebes and Carthage were the links in the chain The ''merchandise of Ethiopia'' of which the Bible so often speaks passed along this line of cities to less civilized portions of the earth.

Heeren in his Ancient Nations of Africa, tells us that commercial intercourse existed between the countries of southern Asia, between India and Arabia, Ethiopia, Libya and Egypt, which was founded upon their mutual necessities; and became the parent of the civilzations of these peoples. The fame of the Ethiopians, as a civilized people had forced its way into Greece in the time of Homer. Meroe, the hundred gated Thebes, Jupiter-Ammon, and the oracles in Lybia and Greece were woven with the most ancient Greek myths. The Argonautic Expedition, the Triton Sea, and the Garden of the Hesperides, were flashes from this ancient Ethiopian commerce. Its introduction into Hellas must have been made at a very early period as shown by the oracle and sanctuary of Dodona. Ethiopian commerce was carried on under the protection of sanctuaries. The priests of Ammon said, that the oracles were founded in Greece from Thebes and Meroe. The Pelasgians adopted the Egyptian names of these deities and passed them on to the later Greeks.

Heeren continues, "Meroe from time immemorial had been an oracle of Jupiter. Its soil was extremely fertile. As late as 1000 B. C. it was one of the most powerful states of the ancient world. Accounts left us by the ancients have been considered fabulous but not so to those who have viewed the ruins now covering the site of this once powerful and highly civilized state. Remnants of mighty buildings covered with sculptures, representations of priestly ceremonies and battles, rows of sphinxes and colossi, give rise to the question, as to which nation Ethiopia or Egypt imparted its knowledge to the other."

Until historical times Ethiopia furnished Egypt
with gold. Her ravines were worked until the
middle of the 12th century. Gold was extracted
by crushing, a very costly method, proving that
these mines had been very rich and must have
been a source of the great profusion of golden
articles found in many African ruins and graves.
Keane describes the Fayum district, which
grew in great profusion, roses, vine olives, sugar
cane and cotton. Here the orange and lemon trees
attained the size of our apple trees. The district was in more primeval times an arid depres-
sion. An early pharaoh cut a deep channel
through the rocky barrier toward the Nile and let
in the western river. Since the Twelfth Dynasty
this lake had been one of blessing and abundance.
This tract thus reclaimed from the desert was
justly a wonder of Egypt. Here the marvelous
Lake Moeris received the discharge of the Bahr
Yusef, which was one half the volume of the Nile.
It was one of the astounding engineering feats
of the old world and still ranks as one of the most
marvelous achievements of mankind. Notwith-
standing the drying up of Lake Moeris the Fayum
is still an important and fertile province.

Gold appears in the Elba Hills. Topaz mines
are worked, while perhaps its emerald mines were
then the oldest and most extensive in the world,
and the only ones known until the conquest of
Peru. Ethiopia seems to have had an inexhaustible supply of building material of the first quality, sandstone, limestone and granite were worked
there for ages. In ancient days the buildings

seem to have been of red brick, now the people live in mud huts. Barth speaks of the numerous ruins of Upper Nubia, which attest the splendor of the ancient cities. The average student does not know that in Nubia are infinitely more monuments and temples than in Egypt; besides this Arabs say that Europeans are acquainted with few of the monuments concealed by the encroaching sands in the desert. Twelve miles north of Naga is a labyrinth of ruined buildings. The Arabs call it Massaurrat. The central building is one of the largest known edifices, being 2700 feet in circumference. Its columns are fluted but without hieroglyphics. (*The Earth and Its Inhabitants*—Reclus. Vol. I, p. 246.)

The two temples of Jebel Arden' are covered with sculpture, representing the victories of a king who bears the titles of one of the Egyptian pharaohs. One of the buildings is approached by an avenue of sphinxs. The pyramids, temples, colonades, avenues of animals and statutes are still standing at Meroe. Their sandstone was not so durable as that of Egypt. Eighty pyramids have been damaged by sightseers. Lepius with difficulty prevented the systematic destruction of the monuments of Meroe. Cairo was built by removing the marble facing of the Great Pyramid. Thus have many ancient ruins disappeared. The pyramids of Meroe do not compare with those of Egypt in magnitude, though they are more artistic. Reclus describes the two temples at Abu Simbel, that take their place as marvels of ancient art. They are the monuments of Ib-

sambul. The southern temple is hewn out of the
living rock. Before the gate sit four colossi over
sixty feet high, of noble and placid countenance.
All these colossi are covered with inscriptions.
In the interior of the rock, follow three large
halls in succession and twelve smaller ones whose
walls contain brilliant paintings. If you will examine the faces of these colossi in any book of
authentic cuts you will find that they are the
faces of full featured Ethiopians.

"Many temples succeed these as far as the
first cataract, containing burial grottoes, gateways and towers. Almost buried in the sand,
travelers find the ancient town of Mahendi, whose
tunnel shaped gallaries like those of Crete are
still to be seen passing under the houses. We
see Dakka with its gigantic gateways only possible of erection by the hand of the ancient Cushite. In the sepulchral cave Beit-el-Walli are
sculptures representing triumphal processions,
assaults, court and battle scenes. These have
been rendered more populuar by engravings than
any other. The colors of these paintings are still
remarkably brilliant." (*The Earth and Its Inhabitants*, Vol. I, p. 306.) The temples of Dabod and
Dakka were built by the Ethiopian king Ergam-
enes. Many of these ruins and this art appear
to us as Egyptian but as Sayce points out the
little temple of Amada in Nubia built by Thotmes III in honor of his young wife, in delicately
finished and brilliantly painted sculpture on stone,
is worth far more than the colossal monuments
of Ramses II. Ramses cared more for size and

An Ancient Cushite.
RAMESES II, SURNAMED "THE GREAT."
From a group in red granite. Tanis. Photographed by
Mr. W. M. F. Petrie.

number of buildings than for their careful construction and artistic finish. Sayce describes the building of his era as mostly scamped, the walls ill built and the sculpture coarse and tasteless. Even here in Nubia the monument of Abu Simbel forms a striking contrast. Wrought by the hands of Nubians it forms one of the world's wonders carved in rock. It is as Sayce says the noblest monument left us by the barren wars and vain glorious monuments of Ramses-Sesostris. (*Ancient Empires of the East*—A. H. Sayce.)

Meroe had an army of 250,000 trained men and 400,000 artisans when her rule reached Syria. One note-worthy feature was the enormous size of the city of Meroe. It covered an almost unbelievable area. The ruins that Pliny described had disappeared in Roman times, so ancient was their origin. That is why so little can be learned about Ethiopia by the study of the country today. The period of her ancient glory was too far beyond the ages of our times. Hoskins thought the pyramids of Gizeh magnificent and wonderful in effect and artistic design. There were pyramids used for burial places at the site of Meroe. On the reliefs on the walls of the burial chambers the rulers appear purely Cushite. Calliund thought Massaurrat, a unique place having no parallel in Egypt, to have been a great college. Heeren thought it the site of the oracle of Jupiter, at whose command colonies issued forth which carried civilization, arts and religion from Ethiopia into the Delta, to Greece and to far Nordic lands.

The *Encyclopedia Britannica* says, "The Nubians are supposed by some authorities to agree with the ancient Egyptians more closely than the Copts, usually deemed their representatives." According to Dr. Pritchard, it is probable that the Barabra may be an offshoot from the original stock that first peopled Egypt and Nubia. It was the Old Race of the higher civilization that ruled Egypt in the pre-dynastic ages. It was from this nation went forth the colonies that spread civilization. This old race of the Upper Nile, th ˙ ʒu or Anu of the ancient traditions, spread their arts from Egypt to the Ægean, from Sicily to Italy and Spain. Mosso Angelo says that the characteristic decorations on the pottery of the Mediterranean race of prehistoric times is identical with that of pre-dynastic Egypt. Reisner in 1899 examined 1200 tombs in the Nile valley. He found the remains of a distinct race who buried their dead with legs doubled up against abdomen and thorax. This was an old Ethiopian form of burial, which preceeded embalming and may be traced through ancient Cushite lands.

Earnest and consciencious students, seeking the facts about ancient Ethiopia, find but scanty and unsatisfactory references in modern books. Going back to ancient records we find voluminous testimony. Out of this material the modern author selects what he sees fit and rejects much authentic history about Ethiopia. One book will tell us that the Ethiopians belonged to the Japhetic stock, in fact this is the favored theory; yet the encyclopedia says that Nubians are a Negroid

stock. Others say that they are Semitic. There
is a world of contradiction in modern books from
an ethnological standpoint. Without the untan-
gling of these threads one must have a narrow
and twisted conception of true history. In ancient days the African nations were proud and
mighty. Cambyses marched against the Egyptians because their king had refused him a daughter in marriage. A stele in the British museum
shows how the fleet of Cambyses was destroyed
by Ethiopians on the Nile and the land forces
succumbed to famine. At this time the temples
of Napata were already in ruins.

Pyramids were erected for a long line of queens
called Candace. The high treasurer of one of
these queens was converted to Christianity under the preaching of Philip. To prove how lasting is the religious impression upon the heart of
the Ethiopian, Abyssinia is the only great Christian nation of any importance in the east today.
The Candace queens ruled over an Ethiopia that
included Abyssinia, but their center was near
Meroe, where they were buried. The Scriptures
spoke of the treasure of queen Candace, accumulated from the merchandise and wealth of Ethiopia. Strabo spoke of a queen warrior of Ethiopia. This line of queens was of a race type never
seen among Egyptians. They had the pronounced
Bushman figure. The renowned queen of Sheba,
queen of the south, who visited Solomon belonged
to this line of queens.

Ethiopia furnished the perfumes of the ancient
world. ''From Meroe to Memphis the most com-

mon object carved or painted in the interior of the temples was the censor in the hands of the priest. They worshipped the presiding deity with gold and silver vessels, rich vestments, gems and many other offerings. Various substances were used for incense but the most esteemed came from Ethiopia. It was from these costly products that this nation derived much of its wealth that has seemed fabulous to the thoughtless. For the embalming of the dead, spicery in vast quantities was used. The Hindu and Egyptians use incense to this day. The Hebrews burned incense. Nineveh, Persepolis, the earthenware of China, all show innumerable forms of censors; Greece, Rome and on down to our day in Catholic ceremonies we find that the incense, first necessary to allay the odors of animal sacrifice, and finally taking its place, still persists. In ancient days when the dead were buried in churches, the burning of incense was thought necessary to preserve men's health. For these reasons we must recognize how enormous must have been the traffic to supply such demands. Early writers said that Ethiopians had fountains with the odor of violets, and that her prisoners were fettered with gold chains.

Considering the natural products of Ethiopia, her commerce, the strength of her armies, spoken of by the Scriptures as a thousand thousand, we find them a substantial foundation for ancient traditions about that nation. Another remarkable people of these regions were the Microbians, Herodotus describes the visit of the ambassadors of Cambyses to them. He directed his expedition against them because of their reputed wealth. His spies brought presents to this king of the Ethiopians. They were a very tall race and the king was chosen for his great stature. They were a civilized people with their own laws and institutions. The spies brought a purple robe, gold and perfumes, and a cask of palm wine. This king looked at their presents and despised them. He inquired how long they lived and what they ate. When told that they lived eighty years, he said, "I do not wonder that you who feed upon such rubbish should live no longer. The Microbians," he said, "lived one hundred and twenty years and sometimes longer," their chief food being flesh and milk. This diet was evidence of civilization. He sent a message to the Persian king that filled him with rage, "When you can bend the bow which I send you then you may undertake an expedition to the Microbians."

The ambassadors were shown the "Table of the Sun," a meadow at the outskirts of the city in which much boiled flesh was laid, placed there every night by the magistrates. This seems a strange custom to the unthinking, but was a part of the commercial policy of the Ethiopians, a way by which the vast trains of caravans that swept through the country were fed. At the table of the Sun, all who wished might eat. The ambassadors were next led to the prisons, where the captives were bound with gold fetters. This was before the iron age. Ethiopia had a skill in embalming superior to Egypt. The Ethiopian mummy could be seen all around and they were preserved in columns of transparent glass. The Egyptian mummy could only be seen from the front. In the sepulchers the corpses were covered with plaster on which were painted lifelike portraits of the deceased. They were then placed in the cases of crystal which was dug up in abundance. This report of Herodotus proves the Ethiopians in possession of laws, prisons, commerce, knowledge of working metals and the fine arts.

CHAPTER IV.

THE AMAZING CIVILIZATION OF ETHIOPIA.

At the beginning of the historical period of Egypt most inhabitants of the earth were rude savages. In western Europe and northern Asia the half-human Neanderthal lived in caves under overhanging ledges and fed upon the untamed products of the wild. ! Outside of Africa, we find over the earth the rude stone tools of the first barbaric inhabitants, that mark the evolution of these races, from savagery, through long stages of development to the civilized state. In Africa we find no evidences of this slow progress of man up from the barbaric state. The Soudan shows no evidence of a stone age. The African seems to have passed directly to the use of metals without intermediate steps. The Semitic and Japhetic races upon the more sterile lands of the east, and north, as nomadic shepherds, were slow to change to the more settled life, that developed naturally in the rich regions of Egypt and the Upper Nile. Without agriculture they could not advance to the handicraft stage. Going back only three thousand years we find these nations still very ignorant. Semites made no showings of culture until the rise of half barbarous Assyria, which copied its arts and sciences from Cushite

Chaldea. The Hebrews learned agriculture and building from the Hamitic race of Canaan.

Some one civilized race of prehistoric times had tamed the domestic animals; for when the curtain of history was raised we find them in attendance upon man. With the same infinite patience, this race developed wild plants into tamed fruits and cereals. The Cushite was the only race that could have performed this service, for the other races in historic times despised agriculture. Nomadic races are fierce and impatient, they have a nature the opposite to habits that make for patient and perseverence, which are the steps to art and literature. Before the dawn of history Cushites were working in metals and they had perfected the tools with which we conquer the forces of nature today. Our masons tools are identical with those unearthed in Egypt. Joly calls the three significant factors of progress in the life of man: the hearth, the altar and the forge. All three of these were given to the world by the African. The ancients said that Ethiopians first taught them the worship of the gods and sacrifice. The agricultural Ethiopian developed the idea of a settled hearth and home. He developed very early the art of smelting iron, which is found in the pyramids and gave knowledge of its manufacture to the world.

Donnelly points out that in the thousands of years since the domestication of animals, the historic nations of our times have tamed one bird. In the light of these facts, is it helpful to our development, that we blazen forth the boast that from later races has come the sum total of civilization? Ancient Africans yoked the wild ox, tamed the cow, the horse and sheep. This is why animals play such an important part in the old Cushite mythology. Africans subdued the elephant as early as the Cushites of Asia. Ancient sculptures show the African lion tamed. These indefatigable men domesticated wheat, barley, oats, rye and rice, in fact all the staple plants of our civilization were fully developed so far back in the distant ages, that their wild species have disappeared. Think how helpless we would be today without them. Reclus declares, "We are indebted to the African for sorghum, dates, kaffir, coffee and the banana, also for the dog, cat, pig, ferret, ass and perhaps for the goat, sheep and ox. The first African explorers, found the country covered with cattle parks, in which the natives kept thousands and tens of thousands of cattle of remarkable breeds, rare skill being shown in their handling.

A botonist of the Smithsonian Institute recently traveled nine thousand miles through Africa, finding species from which valuable grasses, grains, forage, and fruit may be obtained. We are still reaping the fruits of the earlier zeal and genius that tamed the first plants. Ancient Ethiopians were wonderful agriculturalists. The melon and sweet potato produced there are far more delicious than ours. The races to which agriculture was not native present the spectacle today of crowding their populations into cities.

Ethiopians developed long staple cotton, millet, kaffir and Soudan grass. The unusual size and flavor of African fruits were not the result of accident but of labored perseverance and skill. Primeval man gave us the gift of language. Myers says, "Rich and copious languages were upon the lips of the great peoples of antiquity, when they first appear in the morning light of history." This was of incalculable value to succeeding ages. They also gave us the alphabet. Baldwin affirms that the writings used by the peoples of the first ages of history were all derived from a common source. The Phoenicians said the art was invented by Taut. The primitive worship of the Ethiopians was pure. They worshipped one supreme being. Their rulers were priest-kings and at death were deified. As the ages ensued this extended itself in ancestor worship, which was original with the Cushite race. It flourishes on the African continent today. Ancestor worship spread over all the countries which the Cushites conquered. Frobenius, the great anthropologist, says, "Ethiopia is an ancient classical land. In olden days its inhabitants were considered the most pious and oldest of mankind. In many quarters Meroe is thought to be indebted to primitive Egypt. From a standpoint of ethnology, we must unhesitatingly reject this supposition. The Nubians possessed an independent and individual religion in the earliest known times, the cult of which impressed the Egyptians, who gave an account of it to the authors of old." (*Voice of Africa.* Vol. II p. 621.)

Champollion, the father of Egyptology, in his
valuable memoirs declared, that the Lower Valley
of the Nile was originally peopled from Abyssinia
and Meroe. The most ancient cities that they
founded were Thebes and Edfou. In the beginning Egypt was ruled by priest-kings, who
reigned in the name of some deity. This sacerdotal class were overthrown by the warrior caste,
whose chiefs raised themselves to the rank of
kings. This new establishment of power took
place about 2000 B. C. Thebes under them
reached the height of her glory. The Old Race
of the first dynasties, the race of Thot, Amen-Ra
and Osiris had turned its greatest strength in
wider and wider circles across North Africa and
up the coast of western Europe. To the eastward
they had civilized the Mesopotamian plains and
had swept on to India. Their relation toward
Egypt became more and more hostile, though full
blooded Ethiopians still sat upon the throne. The
idols of Egypt to the last detail were gods of
Meroe.

Heeren says, ''The best informed travelers
and the most accurate observers recognize the
same color, features and mostly the same fash-
ions and weapons in the inhabitants of the Upper
Nile as they find portrayed on the Egyptian monuments. The race which we now discover in the
Nubian, though by loss of liberty and religion
much degenerated; yet, which was once the ruling
race in Egypt. This Nubian race did not come
from Arabia. Their color, language and manner
of life were different. According to their own

traditions the Egyptians were originally savages without tillage or government. They lived in huts made of reeds. A race of different descent and color settled among them and lifted them to civilization. The men of this race were the ancestors of the Nubians, who planted other colonies in opposite regions of the world, in Greece, Colchis, Babylonia, and even India." All of these regions had priest-kings.

There had been a rich literature in ancient Ethiopia, which endured until the time of Christ. There are now in existence more than two thousand Ethiopian manuscripts. The early Christian missionaries who entered Ethiopia considered it a duty to destroy all the ancient pagan literature. The two thousand extant are but a remnant of olden writings, which if in the possession of the world today would unfold many a baffling mystery. The literature of Ethiopia that remains is almost wholly Christian. Nubia long resisted the inroads of foreigners. The Barabra knew what the entrance of aliens would mean to their land, but its confiscation and violence to their rights. Nubians mothers would drown or mutilate their daughters, that they could not carry away, to save them from dishonor. Virtue is highly prized among them today. Frobenius tells us that Nubians adopted Christianity as early as 500 A. D. Determinedly for a thousand years they refused to accept Mohammedism. When Islam began to persecute the Christians in Egypt, Nubia sent her cry, "Stay your hand," ringing down the

Nile with both energy and effect. The Arab spared Egypt for fear of the Nubian.

The Barabra or Nubian hated the Turk and the Arab and were right in their determination not to let them enter their land, which was blooming and prosperous but which later came to utter ruin. Sir Samuel Baker describing the Nile between Berber and Karthum said, that as late as 1862 the banks were crowded with populous villages. The land everywhere was cultivated and produced heavy crops. Under the Turks in thirty years it had become a howling wilderness. Gaps in the bank show where wheels once stood, which have entirely disappeared. Their channels have been choked for years. Budge paints a pathetic picture of the few inhabitants who remain, who are nearly naked and slowly starve for months. They lack sufficient covering at night, the cold being intense. These Nubians get up long before dawn and sit shivering, waiting for the needed warmth of the sun. They love their independence and are content to endure hardship.

700 A. D. Moslem Arabs overran the Delta and transformed the old Retu type of Egyptian into an Arab speaking fellahin. The old Egyptian intermixed with Greeks, Romans and Arabs, produced a physical type quite unlike the people of earlier days. Along the Nubian Nile ancient prestige prevented their onrush. The old Ethiopian empire with its northern and southern capitals, blocked Moslem progress for almost a thousand years. In 1316, this Christian kingdom was overthrown but the race loving Nubian peasantry

clung to and still retain their Hamitic speech, which is the key to their origin. After 1300 A. D. massacre was introduced to compel the Nubian to change his faith. Slave raiding brought inconceivable ruin. ''Four-fifth of the population was destroyed and the greater part of this once best cultivated region of the world went back to wilderness. The cattle were killed, the young men slain, and the daughters of Ethiopia ravished.''

A look at Ethiopia today in her ruined condition, makes it difficult for the average observer to receive the deductions of explorers, geologists and ethnologists. The great lapse of time has erased traces of a civilization that was decaying in the days of Cambyses. Many of the massive ruins and relics of those declining days as described in books are conceived by the readers to be products of the lower Nile, when they existed far up in Nubia. The museums of the world contain much of Ethiopian art that is labeled as Egyptian. Ferlini in 1820 found in the tomb of the Great Queen of Meroe, a bronze vessel, the handles of which were ornamented with Dionysus masks, also necklaces, bracelets, rings and other articles of jewelry. Dionysus was the Bacchus of the Greeks, the Osiris of Egypt and a very famous ruler of the ancient Cushite empire of Ethiopians. These jewels and the bronze jar are in the museum at Munich. Ferlini was greatly surprised at the workmanship, which he considered finer than any to which the Greeks had attained. (*Egyptian Soudan*—Budge.)

In 1863, Marriette discovered at Jebel Barkal

among the monuments, five columns of the highest importance, proving Ethiopia to have had a very important position among the Egyptian dynasties, in later historical times. These Ethiopian kings residing in Nubia ruled Egypt. One of these conquerers, Takarka carried his expeditions into Asia. He was doing no more than Ethiopians of earlier ages had done. European museums contain some of the monuments of Jebel Barkal. Groups of pyramids are near the temple. In twenty-five structures at Nuri in interior vaults is a method of support, until recently thought to be an Etruscan invention. At the time of the Old Empire the population of Upper Egypt was Nubian. In the Sixth Dynasty Nubia was a part of the Egyptian Kingdom. In the inscriptions of Ethiopia the ruler is called ''King of the Two Lands'' and the symbol of the Uraei proves their authority over Egypt and Ethiopia. The pyramids of the Queens of Meroe show the authority of this line over the Two Lands. This was why Egyptian monarchs so often married princesses of Ethiopia. It seemed to strengthen their claim to the throne.

Late excavations of Harvard University in old Ethiopia have unearthed at Napata a royal cemetary more than two thousand years old. At Nuri they examined the tombs of twenty kings and twenty-five queens of Ethiopia from 660 B. C. to 250 B. C. The line of Candace was highly honored in Ethiopia. Their jewelry was very elaborate and purely Merotic in style and workmanship. At the feet of the Great Queen were the gods of the north and south tying the two lands together. The two lands that in their beginning had been one. The symbolic representation of the union of the north and south is found at a very early period in Egypt. Her Pharaohs bearing the title, King of the Two Lands. Hoskins infinitely preferred the pyramids of Meroe for their elegance of architectural effect to those of Gezeh. He viewed the ruins of Meroe as the last architectural efforts of a people whose greatness had passed away. These rulers were fully Ethiopian in feature and hair. In their titles was the name Amen-Ra.

Some of the largest temples of Nubia were built by this line of kings and queens. The power of Tarkaka and Pankhi who subjugated Egypt is attested by the sculptured reliefs of the scenes of their battles. In XXII Dynasty of Egypt, the country having become so intermingled with foreign blood, the main body of the priests of Amen, who had ruled so long at Thebes, emigrated into Ethiopia. Favors shown foreigners so displeased the military class that they deserted in a body to Ethiopia, 240,000 soldiers. Pharaoh made overtures to them but they would not return. These were the former ruling class of Egypt returning to the land and culture from which they had originated.

The term Nubia was unknown to the ancients. Everything south of Egypt was called Ethiopia, the land of the dark races. Though the local traffic is small, a very large caravan trade still passes through Nubia between Central Af-

rica and Egypt. The Nuba tribes of Kordofan
seem to constitute the original stock. The Nile
Nubas are closely allied to the Nubas of Kordofan who are admittedly, says Britannica (Vol.
XVII. Nubia.), of Negro stock and speech, so the
Nile Nubas must be regarded as essentially a
Negro people. The Nile above Egypt has always
been occupied by this people. Many Nubians are
artizans, small dealers, porters and soldiers in
Egypt where they are noted for their honesty and
cheerful and frank temperaments. The native
tongue is very sonorous and expressive. It is of
distinctly Negro character. These Barbarians in
Nubia are labored agriculturists, faithful, obedi-
ent, cleanly and Keane insists that nearly all of
them understand arithmetic and know how to
read and write.

Many Nubians recall the Retu type upon the
Egyptian monuments. These people of old Ethiopia wear today the plaited turned up beard of
the Egyptian gods and a style seen in Etruscan
sculptures. Amen-Ra, from whom a long line of
Egyptian monarchs descended, was an Ethiopian
god. He was the most terrible of the Egyptian
gods to look upon, with his blue-black complexion.
Ancient Egyptians were so determined to represent him as black that they produced a singular
black effect by laying on a dead black color and
treating it with blue through which the black remained visible. The Soudan in those ancient days
was considered as but a continuation of Egypt.
The greatest of the Soudanese gods ranked with
the Egyptian gods. Thotmes III of Egypt called

himself royal son of the land of the south. His son, Amenhotep, appears on the reliefs of the temple of Thelmes making offerings to the Nubian gods. Reclus tells us that at Dongola, the capital of Nubia, is the ruin of one of the largest and finest specimens of ancient architecture. The columns are as elegant as those of Greek temples. The crests of the neighboring rocks are crowned with towers and strongholds and walls of ancient entrenched camps. Nubian castles differ but little from those of the Rhine. They were both built by the descendants of the Cushite dolmen builders. These Nubian castles are the remnants of a feudal system similar to that of Europe. This system is still alive in Abyssinia today. In the Nubian castles the battlements, keeps and roofs are all broader at the base than at the summit and all the towers are conical. Remses II built wonderful temples in Nubia, the rock hewn temple of Abu Simbel for simple grandeur and majesty is second to none in all Egypt. He built another temple to Amen-Ra at Napata. The Harvard expedition found the ancient Ethiopian kingdom had been called Seba or Sheba. It was that part of the empire from which the Queen of Sheba had come with rich gifts to Solomon. Josephus, the Jewish historian called her a queen of Egypt and Ethiopia. This was in the ages when Egypt probably was the Two Lands.

CHAPTER V.

PREHISTORIC EGYPT, THE LAND OF WONDERS.

The native name of Egypt was Khem, the black land. The name came not so much from the color of the soil as the hue of the inhabitants. Egypt was called the "Gift of the Nile," because Lower Egypt was formed out of soil brought down by the mighty river. Without the Nile, Egypt would be but a desert. The ancient peoples seemed to know more about the sources of the Nile than later nations. In our age Livingston explored the branches of the White and Blue Nile far into the highlands of the equator. The land through the ages has been raised by the deposits left by each annual overflow. Failure of the river to rise means drouth and famine. At the time of overflow Egypt is a vast sea with her cities on the tops of continuous natural mounds. Numerous canals traverse the country connecting the natural channels. Egypt was inhabited in ancient days by two races or two distinct divisions of one race. Ancient records all testify that the ruling class in those times was the Ethiopian. They founded the powerful priest caste. "This priesthood included the judges, physicians, astrologers, architects—in a word they united within themselves all the highest culture and the most distinguished offices of the land." (*Biblical Literature.*)

Calumet testifies, that from ancient accounts and from all recent research, culture and civilization spread into Egypt from the south and especially from Meroe. Egypt, ruled at first by several contemporary kings, was finally united into one great kingdom. A priesthood seemed to have governed the land. The head of the state was a priest. The sacred books of the Hindu speak of an "Old Race," that came down from Upper Egypt and peopled the delta. They mentioned the Mountains of the Moon and the Nile flowing through Barabra. Herodotus says in his Second Book, "They say that in the time of Menes all Egypt except the district of Thebes was a morass, and that no part of the land now existing below Lake Myris was then above water. To this place from the sea is seven days passage up the river." Diodorus Siculus says in Book Three, "The Ethiopians say that the Egyptians are a colony drawn out of them by Osiris; and that Egypt was formerly no part of the continent; but a sea at the beginning of the world, and that it was afterwards made land by the river Nile."

This testimony is corroborated by geology. Rennel after scientific investigation says, "The configuration and composition of the low lands of Egypt leave no room to doubt that the sea once washed the base of the rocks on which the pyramids of Memphis stand; the present base of which is reached by the inundations of the Nile at an elevation of seventy or eighty feet above the Mediterranean." How remote must be the period when Egypt was not the gift of the Nile. Renan

declares that Egypt had no infancy because its
first colonists had been civilized in Ethiopia.
Egypt did not begin with Menes. Sayce thinks
that when Abraham went down in Egypt 4000
years ago, the origin and meaning of the Sphinx
was lost in mystery.

The Syhinx and the pyramids were symbols of
some form of religion of the Old Race. Baldwin
quotes from Diodorus Siculus, "The laws, customs, religious observances and letters of the
ancient Egyptians closely resembled the Ethiopians, the colony still observing the customs of
their ancestors." Egyptians in later days affirmed, that they and their civilization came from
the black tribes of Punt. Some scholars seek to
derive Egyptian civilization from some Oriental
source. There is evidence that the culture of
Egypt was not developed in Egypt from their
traditions and their earliest remains. It did not
come from the north or east but must have been
imported from the south for as Budge affirms,
Egyptians had all the characteristics of an African race. Sergi shows that the discoveries of
Flinders Petrie and De Morgan prove that prehistoric Egypt was not influenced by any Oriental
civilization.

The primitive people of Egypt, as revealed by
archaeology, dressed in skins and used rude stone
implements of the stone age men. They lived in
mud and reed huts and hunted wild animals. We
do not find any such rude beginnings for the race
of the Soudan. From these people of Punt, came
Cushite colonists bearing to the children of Miz-

raim knowledge of copper, bronze, cereals, oxen, sheep, goats, and brickmaking. The historic Egyptian rose probably from the union of the aborigines and the invaders. Sayce says that the ancient Egyptians had the elongated type of skull. With the intermixture of later times the heads of the Egyptians have widened. The race of today has returned to the aboriginal mud hut on the bank of the Nile. In the days of Egyptian supremacy the cranial formation was Ethiopian. James Henry Breasted, world famous archaeologist, discovered in Egypt the studio of an Egyptian sculptor of 1400 B. C. It was called the house of the chief sculptor Thutmos. All the portraits were remarkable in that they were unmistakably African.

The early population of Thebes was Nubian. The reign of Menes was no nearer our time than 4000 B. C. One of the temple records calls him a Theban. Thebes was settled from Meroe. Menes had been a priest of Upper Egypt, the older of the two countries. He made a change in the channel of the Nile. Many ages of civilization had preceded him. Bunsen believed that the time preceeding Menes was greater than since. Lepius says, "Under the Fourth Dynasty, six thousand years ago, the nation had approached the highest development at which we find her, of which the ruins still bear witness. The admirable system of monumental writings showed its highest perfection in the oldest ruins. This certainly indicated a long previous development." This was the age when Egypt was under domina-

tion of the Ethiopians. The farther back we go
the more perfect the art and the purer the ideals.
The ancient temples were almost covered with
inscriptions. So universal was education that
even workmen wrote upon the stones.

Chronology as we have computed it, makes no
allowance for the many ages through which
Egypt must have passed to have reached the high
stage of culture which she had obtained at the
dawn of recorded history. The chronology of
Berosos, Mantheo, and the Hindu sages, include
ages of which other races possess no history and
seem incomprehensible to us. These were Cushite
races, the first men, and bring over a record of
ages preceeding the Deluge. Their chronology
is backed by the findings of science, which has
shown that the earth is older than the puny period allowed by *Usher's Chronology*. The Bible
says that a thousand years with our God is as
a day. Examination of prehistoric culture, reveals that the rich languages, complex systems
of religion, and astounding architectural achievements, which appear when the curtain of history
was lifted, are proof that the earth is older than
we perceive.

The priests of Sais said to Solon, "You Greeks
are novices in all the knowledge of antiquity. You
are ignorant of what passed here or among your-
selves in the days of old. The history of eight
thousand years is deposited in our sacred books,
but we can ascend to much higher antiquity and
tell you what our fathers have done for nine
thousand years. I mean their institutions, their

laws, and their brilliant accomplishments."
Baldwin points out that neither Solon nor Plato
thought this improbable. The Greeks could tell
nothing of their progenitors and but little of the
Pelasgian race that preceded them in Hellenic
lands. "There can be no doubt," says Baldwin,
"that the Egyptians preserved old records of the
early period of their history extending beyond
Menes." This knowledge was lost to our times by
the destruction of the Alexandrian library and
the fanatical zeal which destroyed all pagan manuscripts.

Again the significant questions arise, why were
the Greeks so ignorant as to their ancestors, and
why did Egypt hold the knowledge of earlier
Hellenic life? It must have been that the historic
Greeks were but emigrants into Hellenic lands;
that in prehistoric ages had been filled with the
rich culture of another race akin to the Egyptians.
That the deluge did not reach this portion of the
human race, may be the reason why Ethiopia
was able to introduce civilization to the other
races. All of the races of the earth have their
traditions of a universal deluge but the African.
They may have brought over to us the knowledge
of the arts and wisdom of the ante-diluvian world..
Reclus also declares, "All the marvels of Egypt
were not the work of the Retu. Neither Usher's
chronology nor the little country Phoenicia can
suffice to explain that mighty and widespread influence of the Cushite race in human affairs,
whose traces are visible from Farther India to
Norway."

Egypt falls into natural divisions, Lower and Upper. Lower Egypt stretches from the Mediterranean to the limit of the Delta. Upper Egypt extends six hundred miles south of the Delta to the first cataract. The broad plains of the Delta and the comparatively narrow valley higher up, make up the divisions of Egypt. In the primitive days Upper Egypt was wholly Ethiopian. Bunsen says that the early monuments reveal the primitive Egyptian, with head low and elongated, the forehead not amply developed, the nose short, thick, the lips full and large, the chin short and receding. In those days the rulers of Egypt were wholly Ethiopian. Look at authentic plates of early Egyptian Pharaohs, they are undeniably Cushite. The Great Sphinx, emblematic of an earlier king, is the full featured Ethiopian type. Look at the astounding countenance of Cheops. The counterpart of such a face can only be found among Ethiopians today. He is a perfect representation of the Cushite Ethiopian race, that cast such giant shadows on time's dawn.

The Delta is a rich cultivated plain, which travelers describe as dotted with lofty mounds, under which lie buried cities. Here and there on the mounds are villages in groves of palm, where they may be above the flood waters of the Nile. Dews as well as rains are more copious toward the sea. At Alexandria, after sunset, clothes exposed to the dew become soaked as if it had rained. When rain falls in Lower Egypt there is general rejoicing. The people assemble in the streets and sing. From the middle of spring one sees nothing but grey dusty soil full of cracks and chasms. At the time of the autumnal equinox, the whole country presents an immeasurable surface of reddish yellow water out of which rises date trees and villages. After the water retreats, we may see only black and slimy mud. In winter nature puts on all her splendor. Egypt is then a beautiful garden, a verdant meadow, sown with fields of waving grain.

Upper Egypt is a rich narrow valley hemmed in by mountains. It has a clear dry climate and is much healthier than Lower Egypt. The atmosphere has a brilliance, which is almost intolerable, and the torrid sun is unrelieved by any shade. This is all right for the races that can bear great heat. Rain rarely ever falls up the Nile valley. Because of this scarcity of moisture, agriculture depends upon canals much below the level of the land. Their greatest need lies in proper machines by which the water may be lifted. This extreme difference in Upper and Lower Egypt accounts for the physical difference in the the two race types of the land. The bronzed hues are in the Delta but the black hues are under the brazen skies of Upper Egypt. In the Delta many diseases are prevalent, due to the weakness and poverty of the people and the insufficient food because of the exploitation of a rapacious government. The plague and dissentry cause many deaths. In Upper Egypt all is different. Disease is not prevalent and the natives are comely, kindly and thrifty.

The Egyptian in general is simple, cheerful and

hospitable. These are genuine African traits. The fellahs are a quiet, contented, submissive race. Amrou says, that they have always been toiling for others never for themselves. The love of the fellah for his native Egypt is deep and absorbing. Remove him and he perishes. He would rather die than revolt. The whole family fortune is lavished upon diadems and necklaces of true or false gems. They have no other wealth. The Egyptian was made for peace, not for war, though his patriotism is intense, he has no spirit for conquest. The miseries of soldiers is a favorite subject for satire with Egyptian literary men. At the first rumor of war, half the tribe takes refuge in the mountains, until the recruiting agents are gone. The armies of ancient Egypt were led and very largely manned in the days of her supremecy by the Ethiopian element, which today is much more warlike than the fellah. Egyptians make themselves cripples to escape military service. This would also lead us to decide that it was the Old Race, not these, who extended themselves over so great an area of the ancient world.

Because of mistreatment the Egyptian of today resorts to fraud, trickery, and subterfuge, that is easily detected. Nubians are frank and honest. We have every reason to see why the nature of the Egyptian can be no better. Niebhur says, "When we reflect that Egypt has been successively subdued by Persians, Greeks, Romans, Arabians, and Turks, and has enjoyed no interval of tranquility or freedom but has been

constantly oppressed and pillaged, we need not
be surprised that agriculture has been ruined or
that her cities have declined. The population is
decreasing and the inhabitants of this fertile
country are miserably poor. The exactions of the
government leave him nothing remaining to lay
out in the improvement or culture of his land,
and many unhappy restraints render it impossible
for him to engage in any lucrative occupation.
They are reduced to a small number compared
to the Arabs who have poured like a flood over
the country." The mass of Egyptians live in a
mere hut or heap of clods dug out of a neighboring ditch. A few cakes of durrah suffice to nour-
ish him.*

Reclus says, "The Retu still greatly resemble
their fathers, in spite of interminglings, the Copts
are still known as the people of Pharaoh. Under the Ptolemies they must have been greatly
mixed. The Copts concentrate chiefly in Upper
Egypt. They possess whole villages to themselves. In the towns they are artizans, money
changers, and employers. They marry later than
other Egyptians and regard more the family ties
and their children. The old Coptic language, key
to the hieroglyphics, is no longer spoken anywhere. Since the seventeenth century, Arabic is
the general language throughout Egypt, simply
the language imposed upon them by conquerors.
Scribes and notaries are found among the Copts.
They constitute the lower official class, and are

*Niebhur's Travels, Vol. 1, p. 104.

decidedly voracious and more corrupt than the
Turnish officials themselves. Copts are somewhat
darker than Arabs. Their hair is of a soft wooly
texture, their noses short and their lips wide.
They are supposed to be the direct descendants
of the Pharaohs and are about one sixteenth of
the population of Egypt. Reclus thinks they do
but little credit to those ancient sovereigns.
(*Africa*, Vol. I, Reclus.)

Modern research is leading us to the belief that
culture was spread in Egypt from the south, especially from Meroe. The country was first ruled
over by contemporary kings, who were at war
with each other. At last the common difficulties
in harnessing the Nile united them under Menes
5500 years B. C. For a thousand years the capital remained at Memphis. This was the Old
Kingdom, the period of the Pyramid builders.
Sayce found the shape of the skulls subsequent
to the Sixth Dynasty different from those that
preceded it. This was a period of absolute decadence and must represent the domination of
some other race in which time the monuments are
silent as to any true achievement. It must have
been during this silent period that Ethiopia
turned from continued colonization in Egypt to
send her swarms westward into the European
continent and spread out into that broad band of
nations that extended from India to Spain and
in whom Huxley said there was a common origin.
Sayce tells us in *Ancient Empires* that with the
passing of the Old Empire the religion of Egypt

became gloomy and that in art the light-hearted freedom of the Ethiopian was gone.

2400 to 2000 B. C. was the beginning of the Middle Kingdom. This period is represented by the rise of Thebes, with its magnificent temples and its introduction of mysteries. A new deity Amen-Ra, god of Thebes presides. It had been thought that Amen was not one of the gods of Egypt until this 11th Dynasty, but when the pyramids of the 5th and 6th Dynasties were opened Amen was there. The Pharaohs claimed to be literal and lineally descended from Amen-Ra. This was implicitly believed by their subjects. Let us seek to trace who Amen-Ra was. He was originally the god of Ethiopia. Amen-Ra was Cush, the son of Ham from whom the Cushites sprang. He was not one of the oldest deities of Egypt because he was preceeded by the gods of the ages of Noah (Saturn) and Ham. About the time of the rise of Thebes his name from his worldwide conquests must have been entered into the cycle of gods; for Africans deified their dead kings. Undoubtedly descendants of the great Cush sat upon the throne of Egypt. This is why his name and form appear in the 11th Dynasty and its line of kings assumed his name.

His became the predominent shrine of Egypt and its enrichment became the chief object of the Pharaohs. Amen or Cush was recognized by Egypt as its chief god. All the mummery of the world which tries to resolve the gods of old into anything else presents the hight of folly. The ancients looked upon Zeus, Apollo and

Osiris as persons. Amen-Ra was the Zeus of
Greece, that was why they said the gods ban-
queted with the Ethiopians. He was the Jupiter of Rome. Zeus was king of kings because he
was chief ruler in Ethiopia and over the lesser
kings in his wide domains stretching from India
to farther Norway. Horus, Apollo, Belus and Nimrod his son, were recognized and worshipped by
all Cushite colonies. In the sculptures the Negro
types of Africa are the assistants at the festivals
in Amen's honor. He, himself, was of the same
ancestry. In the later chapters of the Egyptian
ritual his name is in the language of the Negroes
of Punt.

CHAPTER VI.

EGYPT AND HER "GOLDEN AGE."

There are few voices to be heard underrating the greatness of Egypt. Reclus declares, that when the whole of Europe was still overrun by savage tribes, that have left no records behind them, Egypt existed a civilized power of greatness. Astronomical observations, arithmetic, geometry, architecture, all the arts, and nearly all the sciences, and industries of the present day, were known when the Greeks were still cave men. The origin of the sciences and many moral precepts, still taught from the wisdom of the ancients were recorded upon the Egyptian papyri or on the monuments. The very groove of our present thought had its origin upon the banks of the Nile. (*The Earth and Its Inhabitants. Africa.*— Vol. I. p. 207.) Earlier works of art show the Egyptians to have been a kindly people who did not believe in charms. As the ages succeeded and Egypt became mingled with other races, her arts declined, she seemed to forget the meaning of her religion, and finally only animal worship remained.

Reclus continues, "So ancient is the civilization of Egypt, that it is known by virtue of its decadence. The most powerful epoch is the most ancient known to us. After Ramses II there

was a rapid decline in art.'' Unlike the eastern
rulers who had the power of life and death over-
their subjects, the life of the Pharaoh was pre-
scribed by religious rule. The rights and
property of his subjects were protected by law.
In the earlier creative days Egypt attained some
arts not yet equaled and some that today are lost.
They, perhaps, developed embalming, because of
the dampness of the soil from the rising Nile.
Embalming enabled them to better preserve the
body. Sayce described the statue of Khaf-Re in
the museum of Gizeh as a living portraiture.
There is a sublime charm about it. The work is
of exquisite finish; yet it is carved out of diorite
rock, the hardest of hard stone. The stone mason of today possesses no tools with which to
work it.

Donnelly affirms that Egypt, Chaldea, India,
Greece and Rome passed the torch of civilization
from one to another. They added nothing to the
arts that existed at the earliest period of Egyptian history. These arts continued without material change until two or three hundred years
ago. For all these years men did not improve,
but perpetuated. The age of Columbus possessed only printing that was unknown to the
Egyptians. Egyptian civilization was highest at
its first appearance showing that they drew
from a fountain higher than themselves. In that
day Egypt worshipped only one supreme being.
At the time of Menes, this race had long been
architects, sculptors, painters, mythologists and
theologians. What king of modern times ever

devoted himself to medicine and the writing of
medical books to benefit mankind, as did the son
of Menes? For six thousand years men did not
advance beyond the arts of Egypt.
The primitive religious beliefs of the Egyptians lie back in obscurity. The later monuments reveal the worship of many gods. De
Rouge thinks that this polytheism developed from
the worship of one God. Ptah was the greatest
of the Egyptian gods. He was Lord of Truth,
Ruler of the Sky, and King of both Worlds. After
Ptah came Ra, the god of the Sun. His worship
was more general than that of any deity save
Osiris. The Ethiopians said that Egypt was a
colony drawn out of them by Osiris. The greatest of all the Egyptian myths centered about
Osiris and Isis. Their primitave seats of worship were at Philae and Abydos high up the Nile.
Here Petrie found many relics of the Old Race.
At Abydos was the tomb of Osiris. Every Egyptian of sufficient wealth and dignity desired to be
buried there. Horus was the son of Osiris and
Isis. Isis wears the horned cresent, the moon
disk between. She was a black goddess of the
Soudan. Thot was a magician priest. One text
calls him the brother of Osiris. He was the
chief Moon-god and deity of knowledge, wisdom
and art. The seat of Moon worship was the
Soudan. Thot originally was of those regions.
After Thot, from whom the ancients said
came writing, were many lesser gods. Certain
animals were sacred to each. No intelligent
Egyptian worshipped the bull. It was only the

symbol that represented Osiris. Any offense
to it was an insult to him. Therefore the sacred
animals were respected as deities. To injure
one meant death from the fury of the populace.
The sacred animals were chosen by certain mark-
ings, they were fed the finest of foods, clad in
costly raiment and at their death, the wealth of
the king and the noblemen was squandered in a
gorgeous funeral. Osiris had the power of awak-
ening life out of death. He examined the soul
and judged its deeds. Each spirit must pass before the judgment seat of Osiris. Thot recorded
the sentence of eternal doom. All the art and
literature of Egypt was woven about her religion
and in honor of her gods. 3500 B. C. Egypt believed that God became incarnate in man.

Circumcision was a rite universally practiced
as a part of the religion of the old Egyptians, as
long as the native institutions flourished. It was
a rite of the ruling Ethiopian element. Under
Greek and Roman rule it fell into disuse but was
always retained by the priesthood and those who
desired to cultivate ancient wisdom. Herodotus
said that all Ethiopians circumcised. Lenormant calls it original with them. The Coptic
church practices it to this day. Abyssinians do
the same. They did not adopt it from the Jews
for they circumcise both sexes. Oldendorpe finds
the rite in western Africa. It must be a relic of
ancient African customs. It is older than Mohammed, who did not regard it as a religious
rite. Southern Arabia had the rite from Ethiopia.
Himyartic Arabs (Cushites), circumcise their

children on the eighth day. Pocock found that
other Semitic Arabs circumcise between the tenth
and fifteenth years.

Budge in *Osiris and the Egyptian Resurrection*, preface, tells us, "that the knowledge of the
Egyptian priests of the real meaning of their
religion after 1200 B. C. seemed extremely vague
and uncertain. The early beliefs became buried
in magic spells and amulets." Only a few clung
to the old faith. 3400 B. C., Egypt had possessed
a conception of truth, justice and righteousness.
He continues page XIV, "that all characteristics
indicate that the Egyptian religion was of African rather than Asiatic origin. Its true form
died about 3000 years ago. The best explanation
of the Egyptian religion could only be obtained
from the religion of the Soudan." The priest
caste of Egypt had been Ethiopian and the first
rulers priest-kings. As they were overthrown
the priesthood was not able so perfectly to do-
minate the thought of the empire. When the
priests of Amen, the Ethiopian priesthood emigrated to Napata it is clear why Egypt lost the
inner meaning of the religious cults.

In commercial life the Egyptians were con-
ciencious and honest. In the towns there was
little quarrelling or disorder. Justice was ad-
ministered speedily and impartially. Among the
many crafts were blacksmiths, gold and coppersmiths, cabinet makers, weavers, upholsterers,
potters, glass blowers, shoe makers, tanners, tail-
ors and armorers. West describes them as workmen of marvelous dexterity, masters of processes

that are now unknown. Weavers in particular produced delicate and exquisite linen, almost as fine as silk, workers in glass and gold were famous for their skill. Jewels were imitated in colored glass so artfully that only an expert today can detect the fraud by appearance. The belief that a good life would win reward after death appeared upon the monuments hundreds of years before the Hebrew Ten Commandments. Some of their writings were medical treatises. One a recipe for an application whereby Osiris cured his father Amen-Ra of the headache. (*World Progress*—West.) It seems unreasonable that Osiris could have done this if Amen-Ra was the sun.

Unlike the Cretan and Ethiopian inscriptions, the Egyptians never took the final steps to a true alphabet. "Their writing remained to the end a queer mixture of hundreds of signs of things." Sayce speaks of Egyptian manuscripts that contain versions of stories very similar to those we have read in the Arabian Nights. There are tales with plots like Cinderella. The Taking of Joppa, is almost identical with the Forty Thieves. There are other stories like Sinbad the Sailor. Africans tell many tales like those of Aesop. Many nations claimed Aesop. This was because he was a Cushite of which they were all divisions, so by identity of race he belonged to them all. Tradition said that he was black and deformed. It is very likely that he was a part of the life of Alexandria and the cities of Asia Minor. The great similarity of the old Egyptian

tales and those of the Arabian Nights lay in the
fact that they originated and were the common
property of all the colonies of the widespread
empire of Cushite Ethiopians, of which Egypt
was for many centuries a part.
The ordinary homes of sun dried bricks showed
no small degree of skill. They were generally square of two stories in height with an
open gallery above. There were many latticed
windows. The rooms ranged around three and
sometimes four sides of an open square or court-
yard. In this trees were planted, cisterns and
fountains constructed. The public edifices were
built of stone. The men of Egypt worked at the
loom and carried on the trades. The women
looked after the marketing and frequently trans-
acted the business. This is a custom among all
African nations. The warrior class enjoyed
great privileges. They possessed fully one-third
of the soil exempt from taxation. The husband-
man was attached to the soil, paying rent. The
modern fellah owns no land. The Cushite habit
of India, where the wife died with her husband,
may be seen among the rites of the Cushite
Pharaohs. The tomb of Amen-hotep II, at Thebes,
shows his favorite wives buried with him.

The domestic life of Egypt is described by
Duncker, in his *History of Antiquity* Vol. I, p.
118. "On the tombs five varities of plows can be
seen. There were herds of bullocks, calves, asses,
sheep, goats, cows, and fowl. Butter and cheese
were made. In other sculptures, we see spinners
and weavers at their work. Potters, smiths,

painters, masons, shoemakers and glass blowers, performed their tasks as they worked four thousand years ago.'' There representations of their social occupations, attainments, and all forms of social, political, and religious life are truly marvelous. The pictures referring to rural affairs reveal a state of life at that early day, which may lead us to speak modestly of our own attainments. An Egyptian villa contained all the conveniences of one of Europe at the present day. In weaving and all processes connected with the manufacture of linen, they have never been surpassed. In the making of furniture, musical instruments, vessels and arms they showed great taste and skill.

Among Semitic people herding is highly esteemed. The fact that shepherds and swineherds were the lowest strata of Egyptian society, proves that they were not Semitic in origin. Exodus VIII, 26, savs: ''Egyptians would not eat with Hebrews because they were shepherds, who sacrificed beasts that were an abomination to Egyptians.'' The people of the Nile were primarily agriculturalists which was the basic occupation of all the Hamitic races, coupled with great skill in the arts and industries. The trade of father descended to son. One inscription speaks of the profession of architect in one family for twenty-three generations. This may account for the unequalled genius of the ancient in many lost arts. Intermarriage between the various castes was never forbidden. The domestic tie was strong. The monuments reveal courtesy, kindness and affection as the rule. The homes of the mechanics and husbandmen 4000 years ago were generally of brick, well furnished and better built than the homes of today. In the houses of the wealthy, tables, chairs and beds were elaborately finished and ornamented. Vases and cups were of silver and gold.

The Egyptians were fond of amusements. The jugglers' art was carried to perfection. All the athletic sports were greatly enjoyed. Indoor games were popular. There were ingeneous toys and amusements for their children. Among the higher classes music was the delight of all. Egyptian musicians played upon harps, lyres, guitars, flutes, triangles, pipes, horns, trumpets and drums. The dancing was but graceful and pleasings gestures to music. Ancestor worship and the belief in immortality, caused them to embalm their dead. Their bodies treated five thousand years ago are today in perfect state of preservation. The secrets of their methods are unknown to us. We can preserve the body for only a few weeks. The cost of preparing a mummy in the highest style was twelve hundred dollars. The lowest style was in the reach or all. In the museums of the world we may look upon the faces of the Pharaohs as they appeared four thousand years ago.

The Egyptians were master engineers. The Nile was diverted from its course to build Memphis. Moeris was an artificial lake 450 miles in circumference. It was 350 feet deep, with flood gates, locks and dams. The joints were no wider

than silver paper. Cement still clings to the
casing stones. The Labyrinth astonished Herodotus. It had three thousand chambers, one-half
above, the other half below, the surface of the
earth. The Temple of Karnak covers a square
eighteen hundred feet each way. Travelers are
unable to find words to express its sublimity. It
is a sight too much for human comprehension.
They must have had the knowledge of the principles of the derrick, the lever and the inclined
plane to put into position the monstrous obelisks
and stone animals that stood in rows before the
temples. Greeks appropriated the Doric style of
architecture from Egypt. We shall see in the
chapter on art that Egypt was the originator of
almost all of the designs of Greek decorative art.
Huge statutes were covered with highly finished
hieroglyphics. It seems impossible to tell how
they carved this stubborn material. Our best
modern steel, with difficulty carves even plain
letters in granite.

Amelia B. Edwards in *A Thousand Miles Up
the Nile,* says, ''The distinguishing feature of
Egyptian architecture is it vastness and sublimity. The avenues of colossal sphinxes and lines
of obelisks led to stupenduous palaces and temples elaborately sculptured and containing halls
of solemn and gloomy grandeur, in which the
largest of our cathedrals might stand. The
earliest monuments reveal a considerable degree
of skill which never advanced. Egyptian walls
and ceilings were painted in beautiful patterns
which we still imitate. The great hall of Kar-

nak is the noblest work ever executed by the hand of man. In the doorway of the Hall of Pillars, the columns are the wonder of the world. How was that lintel˙stone raised? Beside it we feel shrunk to the feebleness of a fly. We are stupified by the thought of the mighty men who made them.'' Perhaps not untruly the builders called themselves the descendants of the gods.

The Great Pyramid contains ninety million cubic feet of masonry. It stands on the thirtieth parallel facing the four cardinal points with geometrical exactitude. Beneath the pyramids lie the bodies of Egyptians. Within were sepulchral chambers containing mummies, long ago despoiled of the rich treasures buried with them. So perfectly were they built that after the lapse of tens of centuries the stones are still in position supporting the mountain weight above them. Sayce says that in the pyramid of Khufa, the stones are in exact contact and cemented so perfectly as to seem impossible. Petrie believes that the stones were cut with tubular drills fitted with jewel points. The lines marked upon the stones by the drills can still be seen, with evidence that not only the tool but the stone was rotated. The machinery with which the latter was effected is still unknown. The Egyptian carved the hardests granite, regarded now as impossible to work, as as though it was so much soapstone.

How the letters and figures were elaborately embossed and counter-sunk is astonishing to modern workers in granite. The edges of the inscriptions after forty centuries are as sharp and

beautifully delineated as though the work of yes-
terday. It is thought by some that they must have
possessed the knowledge of electricity. Solomon
truly said, "There is no new thing under the
sun." Sayce asserts, "Those who view Egyptian
art in museums, have but little idea of the perfection of the Egyptian sculptors and painters of
the fifth and sixth Dynasties. The wooden figure
of Sheik-el-Beled is one of the noblest works of
human genius. Pictures in low relief resemble
exquisite embroidery in stone. In statuary they
have never been surpassed. They have excelled
the artists of every age in solemn dignity and
everlasting repose. In the laws of color harmony
Theban painters were as well versed as those of
today."

The blocks of the pyramids weighing from
two and a half to fifty tons were squared and
fitted and levelled with an accuracy that puts to
shame our very best work. Acres of buildings
were put together with an accuracy of measur-
ment equalled only by the optician fitting glasses.
The Egyptians were surpassed only in the plastic
arts by the Greeks. Nude figures are seen as
through a veil. Naked figures can be seen when
the body is clothed. The paintings on the tombs
after the lapse of three thousand years retain
the distinctness of outline and brillancy of color
of recent productions. The lions of Gebel Barkal
Nubia, now in the British museum, are probably
the finest example of the idealization of animal
forms that any age has produced. The Grottoes
of Beni-Hasan contain many pictures character-

ized by remarkable fidelity and beauty. Very
many of the monuments of Egypt have been mutilated and destroyed, not always by Arabs. Some
of the work has been done by Englishmen and
Americans, to the everlasting shame of our claim
to culture.

CHAPTER VII.

EGYPT AND HER MIGHTY PHARAOHS.

M. Chabas regards a space at least of 4000 years, preceeding the first Dynasty as absolutely necessary to such developement as Egypt possessed at the time of the fourth Dynasty. The art of the Old Empire was vigorous and full of original genius but the art of later times was stiff and conventional. The oldest religion had been pure, as proved by the monuments. The reign of Menes began about 3895 B. C. He was a prince of Upper Egypt. The récords of Egypt say that prior to Menes were ten Thinite kings of Upper Egypt, the older of the two countries, as proved by this statement. There were still earlier ages when demi-gods ruled and a vast period when God himself ruled the universe. There is nothing at all in this incongruous with Bible statements. The Scriptures said that there were ten ante-diluvian patriarchs preceeding the Deluge. The Hindu, Chaldean, Arabian, Greek and Celtic chronicles named ten primitive kings. The part of Egyptian chronology, which we cannot understand is that division extending beyond the flood.

Sir J. Gardner Wilkerson in *The Manners and Customs of the Ancient Egyptians* thought that civilization advanced northward from the

Thebaid to Lower Egypt. Hieroglyphics show
that in Upper Egypt were the older cities. Menes
founded Memphis, but This on the Upper Nile was
a royal city, where kings ruled long before the
time of Menes. This was a suburb of Abydos.
Here have been unearthed many relics of the
Old Race. Because of this evidence, Renan asserts that Egypt had no infancy, no archaic period, because her first colonists were civilized in
Ethiopia. Athotis, a successor of Menes, wrote
anatomical facts. A medical papyrus in the
British museum curiously illustrates this fact.
Under the fourth Thinite king a great famine
ravaged Egypt. Mantheo speaks of many wonders and a very great plague under the seventh
king. In the Second Dynasty the worship of the
bull Aphis was introduced at Memphis. Under
another of these kings a law was passed where
women could hold sovereign power.

Dynasty III was Memphite. We read of a
revolt of Libyans showing that Egypt even then
held dominion beyond the Nile. The Rebu, a
dark people, appear on the monuments as kindred of the Egyptians. Dr. Brugsch calls attention to the general absence in the titles of the
kings of the name Ra, which afterwards was essential to throne names. Dynasty IV the first
king was Khufu or the Cheops of Herodotus.
This was an epoch when pyramid building
reached its zenith and was the beginning of the
brilliant era of Egyptian history. We can judge
this by the magnificence of the sepulchers of these
Pharaohs. The kingly power was then supreme.

These rulers were positively worshipped. These were reigns of peace the age before the Old Empire extended itself out over the continents. Khufu built the Great Pyramid and the temple of Isis near the Great Sphinx, which was carved by some earlier monarch. This disproves the charge of impiety against him. Britannica says that the cost of life in building the pyramids could scarcely have equaled the loss in long wars.

Dynasty IV was 3700 B. C. Recent excavations have enabled us to look upon the face of Khufu. He possessed a giant Ethiopian profile. Petrie says of him: "The first thing that strikes us about him is the enormous driving power of the man, the ruling nature which it seems impossible to resist. As far as force of will goes, the strongest characters of history would look pliable in his presence. There is no face quite parallel to this in all the portraits that we know —Egyptian, Greek, Roman or modern." Myers says that these figures standing so far back in the gray dawn of the historic morning mark not the beginning but in some respects the perfection of Egyptian art. It is this vast and mysterious background that impresses us more than these giant forms cast up against it. The ancient Cushite looks at you out of the face of Khufu. Examination of the countenances of any of these first Pharaohs reveals all of the true Ethiopian types and there was more than one of them. Their parallels may easily be found in Ethiopian types around us today. Khufu was author of part of

KHUFU, BUILDER OF THE GREAT PYRAMID.
(From Petrie's "Abydos," Part II.)

.the funeral ritual. His wife was a priestess of Thot.

An ivory statute of a king of the First Dynasty taken from Petrie's *Abydos* shows the flat nose, prognathous jaws, and the long head of the Cushite. Sheikh-el-Beled, in the museum of Gizeh, a supposed overseer of the Great Pyramid is the exact prototype of a modérn mulatto. The Sphinx was the form of the ancient god Horus. This Great Sphinx, the sphinxes at Tanis and the colossi at Bubastis, all represent black, full featured Africans, that are emblematic, says Dr. Dubois, of kings of the earliest dynasties. Under the rulers of the fifth and sixth Dynasties, there was a notable decline in power and achievement. A less careful style of architecture appeared and there was less pains in the excavation of tombs. In the Fifth Dynasty the capital was moved to Middle Egypt. The royal forces at this time were composed chiefly of Ethiopians and their pictures appear largely in the pictured priesthood. Tylor points out that 2000 B. C. Negroes by the tens of thousands were in the Egyptian service, carrying her dominion into Syria and Arabia. After the Sixth Dynasty there is a blank in the records. We have no monuments to guide us.

2400 to 2000 B. C. brings us to the Middle Kingdom. The reigns preceeding it were probably Memphite. The three following were Theban, Egypt always rose in art and achievement when the south was supreme. With Dynasty Twelve came the Golden Age of Egypt. These Theban rulers laid Syria waste. Amenemhat I of Cushite blood ruled beyond Egypt southward as Lord of the Two Lands. All Egypt came under his domination. He extended her bounderies. Sculpture and architecture were revived. The blood that had given Egypt her civilization was again upon the throne. Tens of thousands of acres of marsh were drained and a wonderful system of artificial reservoirs built to hold the surplus waters of the Nile. Theban glory began with the rise of these monarchs. Amenemhat reclaimed 20,000 acres of fertile land. He settled these districts with people from the south. Under these Cushite cultivators the yields of grapes, flax, cotton, peas, beans, radishes, melons and other vegetables were enormous. Under Usurtesen II, the kingdom reached the highest prosperity. The monuments tell of the grandeur of the works and the armies that marched out of the Hundred gated Thebes to foreign conquests. In Dynasty XII Cushites were formidable rivals of Egypt.

The Two Lands were pulling apart, though Ethiopians still sat upon the throne of Egypt. By the Two Lands we mean Egypt and Ethiopia. Ethiopia in those ages extended to the northern confines of Upper Egypt. Amenemhat II and III and Usurtesen I were Ethiopian Pharaohs of this Nubian line. Look at authentic cuts of these kings (see page 209) and you will be satisfied that they were Cushites. During their reigns, the ancient glories of Egypt were restored. No Pharaoh had had a reign so glorious for conquest and works of engineering as Usurtesen III.

On his cartouch was the symbol of the union of
the Two Lands. He was worshipped as a god
in Nubia in subsequent times. Amenemhat III
of the same Nubian line, constructed a vast artificial reservoir, Lake Moeris. Near the lake he
built the famous Labyrinth, the most justly celebrated structure of antiquity. Herodotus who
saw it declared it greater than all the temples of
Greece. He was struck dumb by the magnificance
of its three thousand apartments. The domestic life of this age excites our admiration. We
read of no expeditions into Nubia. These monarchs seemed anxious to build up the country.
    1700 B. C. finds Egypt invaded and con-
quered. Dynasty XIII brought another blank in
the monumental records. Egypt had broken into
two really separate kingdoms. This enfeebled
the country for the conquest of the Hyksos. During their stay, the native princes at the south
maintained themselves. 2080-1525 B. C. these
Shepherd kings ruled over Egypt. They were a
barbaric and nomadic race from Asia which destroyed the temples and left no monuments standing in Egypt. Those who contend that the origin of the civilization of the Nile was from Asia
should note that under these Asiatics, Egypt entered into the darkest period of her history. The
Shepherds were expelled from Egypt by Aahmes,
a mulatto and a Theban. He was the Amoisis of
the Greeks and king of the north and south. He
secured the favor of the Cushites by marrying
Nefruari, the black princess of Ethiopia, famous
for her dusky charms, wealth and accomplish-

ments. The marriage of the Pharaohs to black
princesses was frequent and seemed to establish
the legality of the claim of descent from the black
god Amen-Ra, whom the ancients represented as
Cush of Ethiopia.
Nefruari or Nefertari was by the inscriptions,
the most venerated figure of Egyptian history.
She was a queen of great beauty, strong personality and administrative ability. Her son, Amenhotep the Amenophis of the Greeks, reigned
jointly with her for many years. Mariette discovered in 1850 the mummy of Queen Aahotep,
the Nubian mother of Aahmes. The ornaments
now preserved in a museum near Cairo are of such
marvelous workmanship that modern jewelers
confess their inability to even imitate them. Under
Aahmes Egypt again became supreme. The de-
cayed and ruined temples were restored to their
ancient richness and splendor. In a few years
she had regained what had been lost in the five
Centuries of rule of the Hyksos. The country
became covered with edifices and new roads were
opened for commerce and trade. Aahmes founded
an empire that lasted 1500 years, a period rich
in its records of history and growth for Egypt.
As late as 663 B. C., Psamtik, a Pharaoh of Libyan origin strengthened his claim to the Egyptian throne by marriage to an Ethiopian princess, the daughter of Sabako. The father of the
great Ramses II followed the same procedure.
Dynasty XVIII, 1500-1300 B. C. Egypt attained
the summit of her power. She became the
arbitress of the whole world. Sayce says that

they returned with new rolls of conquered provinces and with the plunder and tribute of the
east. Amenophis I, son of Aahmes and Nefertari,
carried on the Ethiopian wars. Ethiopia was
breaking away from Egypt. His son Thotmes
I, subdued Phoenicia and Syria. His daughter,
Hatasu, called herself daughter of Amen and his
incarnation. She had a strongly mulatto countenance. The name of her father occurs at Meroe.
His son Thothmes I ordered offerings made to
the gods of the south. He sent out expeditions to
Khent-hen-nefar, probably the country known
today as the western Soudan. He was called
sovereign of the Two Lands. He was the first
of a long line of conquering pharoahs. The astonishing resemblance of the art of the Fourth,
Twelfth and Eighteenth Dynasties, the great
periods of Egyptian history lies in the fact that
they were dynasties that were purely Ethiopian.
They represented the best genius of the race that
had given Egypt her civilization. When they were
out of power her culture always declined.

The great Thotmes III was of all the Pharaohs,
unquestionably the greatest. During his long
reign of fifty-four years, the country was covered
with monuments and became the center of trade
and intercourse. Sayce says that countless
treasures flowed into Egypt and Thebes became
the capital of the world. Thotmes created a considerable navy upon the Mediterranean and was
absolutely supreme upon its waters Monuments
of his reign have been found in Algeria. In the
Hall of Ancestors, Karnak, Thotmes III, may be

seen making offerings before sixty-one of his ancestors. This will give us some idea of how many Ethiopian monarchs had sat upon the Egyptian throne. He called himself the royal son of the land of the South. He erected in Nubia many more edifices than any other monarch. There he appears worshipping the' gods of the south. From his expeditions into Asia he returned with enormous spoil. He was undoubtedly, the Alexander of Egyptian history. He conquored the known world. Thothmes III carved the names of 628 vanquished nations and captured cities on the walls at Karnak. Syria, Mesopotamia, Arabia, Armenia, Abyssinnia and Nubia were parts of his domain.

This Pharaoh was also a magnificent builder. His works are almost numberless. One being a portion of the temple of Karnak, the most magnificent ruin in the world. During the reign of Thotmes III, Mycenaean culture was at its zenith. Sayce shows that he established royal botanical and zoological gardens, stocked with curious plants and animals which he brought back with him. Year after year tribute and taxes of every kind came regularly to the Egyptian treasury from the towns of Palestine, Phœnicia and northern Syria. From Cush and Punt came offerings. He received also the tribute and homage of the Assyrian and Chaldean kings. This was without doubt the Middle Ages when the Cushite race ruling from Thebes as a center, sought to follow and hold the old lines of the more ancient Cushite empire of Ethiopians, that in the ages of

Amen-Ra and Osiris had covered three worlds. In an earlier age, the central seat had been the primitive Meru. In the latter days of the Egyptian empire, the priestcraft and soldiers retired and set up a new capital at Napata; but the days of world empire were over, which empire had lasted, some authorities say, for six thousand years.

The next king of this dynasty was Amenhotep II, the son of Thothmes III. The Egyptians under his lead captured Nineveh. He brought back the bodies of seven kings that he had taken in battle. He put up their heads as trophies on the walls of Thebes. A new strain of Ethiopian blood appears in this line through the Nubian queen, Metuma, about 1400, B. C. Her son, Amenhotep III, the Amenophis of the Greeks, covered the banks of the Nile with monuments remarkable for their grandeur and perfection. He was the Memnon of the Iliad, who came to the relief of Troy. There he is called the black prince. He built monuments inscribed with his name. At Sulb, he and his wife, Tai, appear making offerings to Amen-Ra. He built the great temple at Luxor and the colossi at Thebes and was called by the Greeks the miracle working Memnon, who each morning with musical sounds greeted his mother. His rule extended from southern Ethiopia to Mesopotamia. He seemed to have wished to make the Soudan prosperous.

Thotmes III, Amenophis III and Amenophis IV were in appearance unmixed Negro types. Darwin was struck by the extremely Ethiopian

characteristics of the statute of Amenophis III.
We will pause here to glance at a son of Amenophis who in our day has aroused universal interest. Tut-ankh-amen was born 1350 B. C., long
before the days of Athens and Rome. His tomb
was discovered in a limestone cliff in the Valley
of Tombs about five miles from ancient Thebes.
It had practically been unmolested for thirty
centuries. Here were the tombs of the other
Pharaohs of the 18th, 19th and 20th Dynasties.
All had been ruthlessly pillaged. Every effort
had been made to conceal the spot. Herbert Car-
ter, for thirty years had searched for the tomb.
He found it in 1922. He knew by the seals on
the door that it had been undisturbed. He sent
at once to his generous patron Lord Carnarvan,
and sought the aid of the world's greatest Egypt-
ololists.

One of the first visitors to enter the tomb was
Professor Breasted. He said: "It is a sight I
never dreamed of seeing—the antechamber of a
Pharaoh's tomb, filled with the magnificent equip-
ment which only the wealth and splendor of the
imperial age of Egypt could have wrought or
conceived. In quality it is an astonishing revelation of the beauty and refinement of Egyptian
art—beyond anything I had imagined." The first
room of the tomb entered contained statutes, cas-
kets, chests, beds, chairs and chariots all beautifully carved and decorated. On the lid of one
chest were hunting scenes. The beauty and min-
uetness of the details of the painting excels the
finest Chinese and Japanese art. Still more valu-

able articles besides these which filled the room
had been plundered. The kings robes were elaborately decorated with beads of gold. There was
a beautiful amber necklace. His sandals of
leather were inlaid with gold. The king's throne
was one of the finest specimens of Egyptian art
ever found in a tomb. It was covered with gold
and silver and inlaid with sparkling gems. Several very beautiful alabaster vases were found.
Perfumes 3000 years old still gave forth a pleasant odor. Behind this chamber was another
packed five feet high with inumerable objects.

Harold M. Weeks says, ''This imperial age or
first empire, now shines out as one of the world's
most astounding epochs. It is needful only to
point out that objects in Tut-ankh-amen's tomb
have been valued at such sums as $10,000,000
(though it is futile to price the priceless), and
then to remember that Tut-ankh-amen was but
a weak declining star compared to the other brilliant Pharaohs of the Eighteenth Dynasty con-
stellation.'' At this age the nations of Asia were
pouring tribute into Egypt. These nations remembered the terrible power of Amenophis and
trembled. From the statutes and the wall paintings, the king of this tomb was black. This may
have had something to do with the hasty closing
of the tomb. His name ended with Amen the
black god of the Soudan and Egypt. With his
name the Egyptians began and ended their
prayers We of the Christian world, through the
Hebrews have appropriated it and use the title
of the great Amen at the close of our petitions.

During the Hyksos invasion, the native royal family of lower Egypt took refuge in Ethiopia. Alliance with Cushite princesses was common. Moses, says Giekie, only followed their example. Amenophis IV. tried to establish a new religion. Open war broke out between him and the priests of Amen. In enforced flight he retired to a new capital. Weakened by this strife he lost his hold upon the Asiatic provinces. The close of his reign found Egypt shorn of all that had been won by his predecessors. His successor speedily made peace with the priests of Amen and was permitted to be buried in the royal burying ground. Dynasty XIX, 1300 B. C. brings us to Ramses I and Seti I who restored the waning glory of Egypt. He strengthened his claim to the throne by marrying princess Tai, granddaughter of Amenophis III. Remeses II, the son of this marriage became the legitimate king. He was the Sesostris of the Greeks. He reigned sixty-seven years. The temple of Abydos records the names of sixty daughters and fifty-nine sons. He built two magnificent temples in Nubia and part of the temples of Karnak and Luxor. Around his name, says Lenormant, clustered the lustre of his predecessors. We know he subdued Syria, Mesopotamia, Assyria, Media, Persia, Bactrina and India even to the Ganges, the Scythians and the inhabitants of Asia Minor. All of these regions were anciently Cushite. He returned after nine years loaded with captives and spoil.

Great changes were taking place in world populations. The emigration southward had begun that made the modern Persian nation, Armenians, Turo-Scythic populations were pouring down upon Greece. ·The old Cushite colonists of the great belt that had once stretched from India to Spain became restless and chaffing under the inroads of these barbaric hoards they began a movement southward—an attempted return to the regions of their origin. Egypt strong, fully populated, did not feel inclined to receive them. As these new infusions entered and changed the life and ideals of Mesopotamia, Syria, Asia Minor and the Ægean, their attitude toward Egypt became more hostile. These conquered nations revolted and the Egyptians were driven back to almost the valley of the Nile. Remeses III was the last of the heroes, when he assumed the crown Egypt was surrounded by enemies. The Libyans had established themselves in the western portion of the Delta. They attacked Egypt but were repulsed. The successors of Remeses were insignificant soveregins; the high priests of Ammon at Thebes usurped their power and 1100 B. C. set aside the heirs and seized the throne. They did not long retain this dignity.

The Tanites 1090 B. C. succeeded in expelling the priests of Ammon and established dominion over Egypt. They reigned one hundred years. They were succeeded by the Bubastes of Lower Egypt. With the Tanite dynasty, the high priesthood which had been so powerful from early ages, with the royalty, retired to Ethiopia and set up a rival state at Napata. Azerch-Amen, King of Ethiopia starting from Napata invaded Egypt, traversed the whole length and penetrated Palestine at the head of an army of Ethiopians and Libyans. 800 B. C. Pianki made the Thebaid a simple province dependent upon Ethiopia. The people of Egypt favorably received his accession to the throne at Thebes. They were better disposed toward an Ethiopian king than one from the Delta. 693 B. C. Tarkaka conquered the whole Nile valley. Thebes welcomed him with enthusiasm. Priests opened the gates of Memphis. He fixed his capital at Thebes. Strabo said that Tarkaka rivalled Remses II in his conquests, which extended westward to the Pillars of Hercules and eastward to the Assyrian domains. With the wrestling of Egypt from Ethiopian conquerors, the old empire died.

670 B. C. in the twenty-third year of his reign, the Assyrians drove Tarkaka out of Egypt. His successor Tanut-Amen determined to wrest Egypt from Asia. Thebes and Memphis opened their gates and even Tyre sent help, but the Assyrians returned and executed a terrible vengence. 660 B C. Psammeticus, of Libyan orgin, threw off the yoke. He married an Ethiopian princess as so many Pharaohs that had preceeded him. This prince of the final line of native sovereigns gained the throne by aid of Greek mercenaries. He threw open the door of Egypt to foreigners, especially Greeks. Greek travelers visited the cities of the Nile. The Greek colony of Naucrates was given special privileges. He entrusted some of the highest offices of Egypt to foreigners. The military class because of this

emigrated to Ethiopia. Psammeticus humbled
his pride and sued for their return but these two
hundred thousand preferred Ethiopia. 343 B. C.
the last native dynasty ceased, with the flight of
Nektanebos with the treasury of Egypt to Ethiopia, upon the approach of Persian conquerors.
Persia did not enjoy sway over Egypt very long,
her sceptre soon passed to Alexander.
332 B. C. Egypt was glad when the empire fell
to Alexander the Great. He was welcomed in
Egypt as a deliverer. 331 B. C. he visited the
oases of Ammon in the Libyan desert where he
was recognized by the priests as the son of Amon.
In the winter of the same year he founded the
city of Alexandria. Ptolemy I, 306 B. C., raised
Egypt again to first rank. Alexandria became
the foremost city of the world as a center of
commerce and culture. The famous museum and
library attracted to Alexandria men of science
and letters from all parts of the Hellenic world.
Under his successors Egypt prospered greatly.
Philadelphus is said to have suggested the prep-
aration of Manetho's Egyptian History from
native sources. The line of Ptolmies ended with
Cleopatra, who through her influence over Caesar
managed to preserve the nominal independence of
Egypt. At her death the land of the Pharaohs
became a Roman province. Christianity was
early introduced and at first was severely per-
secuted. 391 A. D. it became the state religion.
639-641 A. D. Mohammedan Arabs conquered
Egypt. Cairo became the capital and a great
center of religion and learning.

So we might continue on down the line of changing sovereigns to modern times, but that is not the purpose of this book, which seeks only to follow the more ancient traces in Egypt of the ancient Cushite empire of Ethiopians. Diodorus Siculus said of the work of the closing Ethiopian dynasty, that there were numerous canals built and embankments, intended to keep the towns above the level of the Nile. Hosea, king of Israel, sent presents to Shabaka. Amen-Iritis his sister was a woman of rare intelligence and superior merit. She was three times regent of Egypt under three sovereigns of the Ethiopian dynasties, showing the respect the Ethiopian had for his womankind. Amen-Iritis was very popular at Thebes. Shabaka abolished capital punishment and substituted hard labor. At Luxor he appears making offerings to the gods of Thebes as a native sovereign. Tarkaka in 693 built the great temple of Gebel Barkel. Many of the reliefs of the pyramids present the Ethiopian rulers as Lord of the Two Lands, with the throne titles Amen and Ra. They wear the same symbols upon their heads. We read the names Ankh-Ka-Ra, Alu-Amen, Amen-Ark-Neb, showing that for ages Nubia and Egypt were ruled as one land, ages far earlier than the period marked in the average history as the Ethiopian dynasty.

The original inhabitants of Asia Minor, of the South Caspian and the basin of the Mediterranean were closely related to Egypt. They had the cranial formation of Upper Egypt. In Egyptian war scenes there appeared very strangely formed

and remote nations, that because of distance had
lost the ancient race type. We see red hair, blue
eyes and tatooing on the legs like the ancient
Scythian. These may not have been aliens but
northern branches of the Cushite race. The extended conquests of the Egyptian kings do not
seem at all impossible when we remember that
they were recovering and reclaiming regions anciently their own. We know by the records that
Amenophis (Memnon), seized the whole coast
of Arabia, Libya and Ethiopia. In the Iranian
histories he had extended his conquests to far
Bactrina. Amenophis subdued the Scythic nations in the Caucasus. He marched into Colchis
which was Ethiopian (Her. II, 104) and marched
as far as the Don. These were but old Cushite
dominions. The passage of Hercules represents
the early colonization of Western Europe by the
race. Other ancient records tell us that the Ethiopian Cymandes led an immense army to conquer
the Bactrians. The triumphant arms of Osiris
reached from the sources of the Ganges to the
Danube in Europe. Western Europe had its
legends of the passage of Bacchus and Dionysus.

CHAPTER VIII.

ARABIA AND HER ANCIENT RACES.

Arabia was once a portion of the ancient Cushite empire. Some authorities claim that it was the original seat of Ethiopian culture. The ordinary encyclopedia and historical book give but little light upon the early race life of Arabia. When our research has gone deeper we will find that the true ethnic story of Arabia, Asia Minor and India have not yet been told. Recent books have rewritten the history of ancient Greece, as the findings of archaeology reveal other races and other sources for the civilization of Hellenic lands. The history of Arabia needs rewriting. This chapter is a contribution in that direction; the sum total of the careful investigations of scholars and investigators whom we can trust. The ancients gave Arabia a triple division. Petrea the stony, Deserta the desert, and Felix the happy. They did not assign to these any very distinct boundries and much of the real surface of Arabia is unknown to us today. Yemen includes the whole southwest quarter which possesses many advantages in climate and soil. Here existed to almost our times the late flowers of a rich primeval civilization, which did not spring from the Semitic race, which is in possession of Arabia today.

Arabia Deserta, is the land of the Semitic
Arabian for we find two races incorporated in
the term Arabian. The ancient Adites and Tha-
mudites were of Ham. The ancient inhabitants
of Arabia Petrae were of the "Anu" of the "Old
Race" of Egypt. The Semitic Arabians trace
their descent from Heber of the race of Shem.
Deserta had the Euphrates for its eastern boun-
dry. The inhabitants live a wandering life, having no cities or fixed habitations, but wholly
dwelling in tents. These are called Bedouins.
When the Scriptures spoke of Arabia it referred
to a smaller territory than the vast region we call
Arabia today. Hebrews spoke of Kedem as the
land to the east of them. Arabia Petrae lies
south of the Holy Land. In this region dwelt the
Edomites, Amalkites, Cushites and other tribes.
Arabia Felix lay still farther south being bounded
by the Persian Gulf, the Red Sea and the ocean.
This country abounded in riches and especially
in spices and is now called Hedjaz. It is much
celebrated because the cities of Mecca and Medina
are situated in it.

Having never been really conquered, Arabia
has known no changes saving those of nature.
There the deserts and mountains have always
secured them from conquest. Nejd the central
plateau is an important region regarded by the
Arabians as the stronghold of their cherished
institutions and traditions. Nejd is the favored
land of the date palm of superior species. It is
the special pride and ornament of the country.
The coffee plant is highly prized. This central

highland is surrounded on all sides by a broad desert belt. In general features, Arabia resembles the African Sahara of which it is but a continuation. Its general characteristics are African. Arabia roughly summed up is composed of one third coast ring and mountains, one third central plateau which is tolerably fertile, and one third desert circle. Throughout the highland of Nejd, though the days are hot, the nights are cool and pleasant. Here epidemic diseases are rare. It is very hot below in the plains. Sayce says that the divisions of "sandy," "stony" and "happy," so familiar to the Greeks and Latins is unknown to the Arabians of today. This is because they were terms used by the earlier Cushite Arabians.

Arabia was originally settled by two distinct races, an earlier Cushite Ethiopian race and a later Semitic Arabian. The Cushites were the original Arabians and dwelt there before Abraham came to Canaan. Ancient literature assigns their first settlement to the extreme southwestern point of the peninsula. From thence they spread northward and eastward over Yemen, Hadramaut and Oman. A proof that they were Hamites lay in the name Himyar or dusky, given to the ruling race. The Himyaritic language, now lost, but some of which is preserved, is African in origin and character. Its grammar is identical with the Abyssinian. The Encyclopedia Britannica in its article on Arabia says, "The institutions of Yemen bear a close resemblance to African types. The inhabitants of Yemen, Hadramaut, Oman and the adjoining districts, in shape of head, color, length and slenderness of limbs and scantiness of hair, point to an African origin." The first inhabitants of Arabia were known to the national traditions as Adites. The Scriptures called Ad a descendant of Ham. /

These Cushite Arabians were given to a settled life and not to the wandering habits of the Semitic Arabians. They were fond of village life, society, the dance, and music. Among the cities the most ancient and populous were in "Happy Yemen." Like the Cushites of Egypt, here was the marvelous reservoir of Marib constructed by the Himyaritic kings. Their descendants of today are good cultivators of the soil, traders and artizans and averse to pastoral persuits. All of these traits distinguish them from the Semitic race. They have much more to do with the African coast than the Asiatic. Marriage with extreme facility exists between all classes of southern Arabia and the African races. There is the absence of any caste feeling between these Arabs and the still darker natives of Africa. All of this points to a common origin. Keane thinks that these people of southwestern Arabia, at a remote period found their way across the narrow strait of Bab-el-Mandeb and secured a permanent foothold on the Nubian steppes. These Himyaritic Arabians call themselves Æthiopians still in diplomatic and elevated circles.

Arabia in the average book is described as a dreary barren waste, the home of the Semitic Arabian. In the most sterile regions we do find this race. They are a nomadic people wandering from pasturage to pasturage, as their ancestors have done from time immemorial and as they shall probably do to the end. The Arab despises agriculture and the customs and restraints of civilized life. There is constant resistance among them to anything like regal power or organization. There is some similitude between them and the Cushite Arabians for they have long lived in proximity; yet there is rivalry and the enmity that would spring from difference in race. The Semitic Arabians are compelled to a pastoral life because they occupy the most waste portions of the plateau. Their condition involves them in constant quarrels over wells and pasturage. This caused the separation of Abraham and Lot. Extreme want makes them plunderers of caravans. They are utterly ignorant of writing or books. This division of the inhabitants has no remembrance of the ancient geography of Arabia, because they were not then the inhabitants. The only authority that they recognize is that of an elder.

These Arabs trace their descent from Heber, from whom the line of Abraham descended. Abraham's son Joktan became the first king of the country. According to Herodotus their original home lay between Colchis and the Medes. They lived in Arabia without mingling until Ishmael, the son of Hagar settled among them. Some of these Ishmaelites applied themselves to traffic and husbandry; for Hagar was Hamitic. It was from this class in later days arose the Mohammedan conquest. The tribe of Koreysh claimed to have descended from Ishmael through Hagar. They were intimately connected with the southern Cushite tribes that were the originators of the idol worship of the Kaaba at Mecca. The great majority of the Ishmaelites lived a life like the modern Bedouin, who too traced back to Ishmael. Their domains stretched from the Persian Gulf to the Red Sea. Their hand was against every man and every man's hand against them. These Arabs will not marry with the settled tribes or with Turks or Moors. The third division of pure Semitic Arabians probably sprang from the children of Abraham and Keturah. In prodigious multitude they cover Syria, Mesopotamia, Palestine, Egypt, and a great part of Africa.

These Semitic Arabians are quite unlike in nature to the Cushite and Hebrew stock, which in early ages must have been deeply permeated with Ethiopian blood. This made the Jew more gentle than the fierce nature of his wilder unmixed Semitic brethren. This intermingling of Hebrew and Ethiopic blood could easily have taken place in the four hundred years of the Jewish exile in Egypt, and later in Canaan they intermingled with the original inhabitants who were Cushite. Let us examine the nature of the pure Semitic race. Sayce describes their life as full of danger and distress. Our private citizens possess more solid and pleasing luxuries than the proudest emir, head of ten thousand horse. The care of the sheep and camels is abandoned to the women, while under the banner of the emir the men practice the use of the bow, javelin and scimeter.

The dignities of sheik and emir descend in an order that is loose and precarious. If an Arabian prince abuses his power, he is quickly punished by the desertion of his subjects. The natural state of the nation is free, each of her sons disdains submission to the will of a master. Caravans from the remote times of Job and Sesostris have been the victims of their rapacious spirit. They pretend that the riches of the earth and the fertile climates were given to the other branches of the human family and that they must recover the portion of their inheritance of which they have been unjustly deprived. The caravans that traverse the deserts are ransomed or pillaged. The temper of a people thus armed against mankind is doubly inflamed by this domestic license of rapine, murder and revenge. Each Arab might point his javelin against the life of his countryman with impunity and renown. The jurisdiction of the magistrate was impotent. The recital in prose or verse of an obsolete feud was sufficient to kindle the same passions among the descendants of the hostile tribes. They would wait whole months and years for the opportunity of revenge. The refined malice of the Arab refuses even the head of the murderer, substitutes the innocent for the guilty person and transfers the penalty to the best and most considerable of the race by whom they have been injured.

The bitter hardships of the son of Abraham, cast out without succor, seems to have accentuated the evil of his nature. Sayce reveals a better side of Abraham showing in their hospitality. This ferocious Arab, the terror of the desert, embraces freely without inquiry, the stranger who, dares to confide in his honor and enter his tent. He is kind and respectful. He shares his wealth or property with his guest and dismisses him with gifts. Though disdaining law he proudly indulges the impulse of pity and alms. Thus everywhere over the earth where we find people crowded back by climate or conquest to bleak and barren districts we see the change of human nature from gentleness to ferocity. Columbus found a peaceful and gentle people in America.

The foregoing description of Arabia and Arabians found in *Ancient Empires of the East,* is not sufficient to give us a clear idea of Arabia and Arabians. It is a true and faithful account of the Semitic branch but does not account for other conditions and races there. Palgrave's expedition to Arabia in 1862 found beside wandering Bedouins and wastes, a rich and beautiful country. Arabia is a vast region. Baldwin reports that he found throughout almost all his journey a settled and civilized country, with cities, towns, villages and a settled government. All of this was the legacy of the earlier culture. In these regions the Bedouin or later Arab counted for nothing. He found central Arabia an extensive, fertile tableland, surrounded by a circle of desert waste. Here were settled nations of the Cushite Arabian stock. Here they had developed for thousands of years the noble breed of Arabian horse. Naturalists agree that Arabia is the genuine and original home of the horse. Here it attained its highest perfection, not perhaps in size, but in form, symmetry and beauty. For endurance, docility and speed for incredible distances these horses have no equals. Sayce says, that the Barb, the Spanish and the English breed are all built on the foundation of the imported Arabian horse.

The development of the camel is Arabian. It does not appear on any of the Egyptian monuments. The Bedouin has superstitious love for the pure horses of Arabia. A female is rarely sold. These horses are educated in the tents among the children of the Arabs. This trains them to habits of gentleness and attachment. Their senses are not blunted by abuse of spur or whip. As they feel the touch of the hand or stirrup, they dart away like the wind, if the rider is dismounted in the rapid chase, they instantly stop till he has recovered his seat. They disappear before the enemy like the mist. In the sands of the deserts of Africa and Arabia the camel is a sacred and precious gift. The driest thistle and the barest thorn is all the food they require. Nature has formed cisterns within the camel. He can lay up a store of water that will last him from twenty to thirty days. The value of the camel to the Arabs and Oriental nations is inestimable. They regard it as a peculiar gift of heaven to their race. They were called the "ships of Persia," so dependent was commerce upon their instinct to cross the trackless wastes. A dromedary can cover ten times as much ground as a horse. Every part of the camel filled some Arabian need. To the Cushite race belonged the oldest and purest Arabian blood. They were the original Arabians and the creators of the ancient civilization, evidences of which may be seen in the stupendous ruins to be found in every part of the country. At the time that Ethiopians began to show power as monarchs of Egypt about 3000 to 3500 B. C. the western part of Arabia was divided into two powerful kingdoms. In those days the princes of Arabia belonged wholly to the descendants of the Cushites, who ruled Yemen for thousands of years. Zohak, celebrated in Iranian history was one of these famous rulers. These Arabians hid the sources of their commerce and the Greeks had of them only cunning stories that the Arabians put in circulation about their country. Much of the rich commerce of India, the treasurers of Africa, crossed between Yeman and Syria avoiding the tedious navigation of the Red Sea. Strabo, Pliny, Diodorus and Ptolemy tell us that in very early ages, Yemen reached a high state of civilization. Arts and commerce flourished and wealth was accumulated, literature was cultivated and talent held in esteem. The national writings that survive to this day, tell the same story. This culture had declined before its extinction in the seventh century.

The *Encyclopedia Britannica* (Vol. II, p. 222, 223) says, "The first dawning gleams that deserve to be called history find Arabia under the rule of a southern race. They claimed descent

from Khatan. They were divided anciently into
several aristocratic monarchies. These Yeman-
ite kings descendants of Khatan and Himyar
'the dusky,' a name denoting African origin,
whose rulers were called 'Tobba,' of Hamitic
etymology, reigned with a few dynastic interrup-
tions for about 2500 years. They demanded the
obedience of the entire southern half of the peninsula and the northern by tribute collectors. The
general characteristics of the institutions of Yemen bore considerable resemblance to the neighboring one of the Nile Valley." One of its monarchs subdued the whole of central Asia, reach-
ing even the boundries of China. Another made
conquests in Africa. Their chroniclers appropriated the glories and some of the exploits of
the early kings of Ethiopia, because Arabia,
Egypt, Chaldea, and India were colonies of the
Cushite empire. Ethiopia was mother of them
all and her rulers under various titles were their
rulers. Modern histories speak of the Semitic
conquest of Babylon as early as 4500 B. C. which
is erroneous unless they explain that these Arabians were Cushite Arabians, another division of
the race of the black Sumerians. The line of
Sargon 3800 B. C. was of the same race. Each
one of these early Arabian conquests was of African Arabs.

While the sceptre of Yemen was outstretched
far over the length and breadth of the land and
the genuine or African Arabs formed a complete
and dense circle all around, the deserts of
Arabia remained the stronghold of a different

race, wild, ferocious tribes, less susceptible to
culture, but of a far greater energy. This race
was the Semitic Arabian, that had come into the
land from the north. They spoke a language akin
to the Syriac and Hebrew. Unlike the African
Arabians they had little disposition for agriculture, architecture or the fine arts. Their instincts
led them to a nomadic, pastoral life. History has
left unrecorded the exact date of their arrival and
the period that they remained tributary, though
often refractory, to the kings of Yemen. In the
fifth century of the Christian era, a late date, a
leader arose who broke off the bonds of Yemen.
He slew the tax gatherer and raised the banner
of revolt. He was assassinated and in the sixth
century they had narrowed the boundries of the
earlier Cushite Arabian monarchies, and both
northern and southern communities were coming
under the growing power of the tribe of Koreysh.

The Koreysh figure as the descendants of Ishmael. In their artificial annals, says Britannica,
the Yemenites or genuine Arabs appear under a
cousinly character. On all these points Mohammedan annalists are equally positive. All other
trusty testimony is adverse. Their falsifications
have found favor with our European writers.
Baldwin in *Prehistoric Nations*, pp. 76, 77, says
that the Semitic Arabians and later Mohammedans confused and altered the earlier Arabian history. They sought to bring upon themselves the
glory of the Cushite Arabian name. They have
appropriated the names of the old Ethiopians,
whose career had long since closed before the en-

trance of the Semites into Arabia. Mohammedan writers give but vague pictures of the conditions of their country. They were not a literary people and their first attempts were after the death of their prophet. The times of Mohammed were becoming ancient when these men wrote. They had entered Arabia after the extended empire of the Cushite Arabians had declined and disunited. The Semitic Arabian lived a rude nomadic life in obscurity until 700 A. D., Arabian civilization extended back behind them for thousands of years.

To sum up, 3000 to 3500 B. C. Arabian civilization equaled that of Egypt and Babylon. The ancient glory had departed prior to the rise of Assyria. The same wave that entered Arabia from the north had become predominant in Assyria, which from its monuments had in its origin been Cushite. The fierce nature of the Semitic Arabian and of the children of Esau, whom Abraham had said in blessing their father, "they shall live by the sword," showed in the merciless tortures and cruelties of the later Assyrians. The first Adite empire of Arabia was overthrown 1800 B. C., so long ago that the cause now is mythical. The ancient chronicles speak of a "Flood of Arem," which dispersed the families of Yemen over the northern part of Arabia. This flood destroyed Mareb the ancient capital. Lenormant says in the *Ancient History of the East,* Vol II, p. 306, "The Jokanites were subject to the Cushites until the end of the second Adite empire. We may be sure the Sabaeans, who at first

let them in peaceably made a stout resistance.
The Cushites were their superiors in knowledge
and civilization.'' It had been a Cushite principle to mete out equal justice to aliens. For
many years the Semites lived subject to the laws
of the Sabaeans, silently increasing in strength.
They accepted in part the language, manners and
institutions of the Cushites. At last they rose
and overthrew those who had given them the
light.

None of the ancient empires were able to sub-
jugate Arabia. Bravely for thousands of years
she maintained her freedom. When the second
Adite empire was overthrown, masses of the Sabaeans emigrated to Abyssinia. Ghez is a living
relic of the ancient speech of Yemen. These
Cushites clung long to their faith and peculiar
institutions. Alexander the Great, hearing of her
rich treasures, desired to pit his great strength
against her, but death interrupted his plans.
Ælius Gallus, Roman prefect of Egypt, undertook an expedition against Yemen, with an army
of ten thousand infantry and fifteen hundred
horsemen. He crossed the Red Sea but his soldiers, disorganized by the intense heat, were incapable of laying seige to Mareb. The old Cushites of Yemen stoutly maintained their independence, when other dominions were forced to yield
to Rome. After the Mohammedan conquests,
which exhausted the Arabians, they were easy
prey for the Turks. Thus came the fall of that
empire, as Assyrians, taught and inspired by an
earlier culture, which carried the arms, language

and institutions of Arabia over half of the old
world, ''from the banks of the Indus to the shores
of the Atlantic, from the mid-African desert with
its burning sands to the green vineyards of pleasant France.'' This later flower of Semitic culture
was grafted upon the old Cushite root. The later
lines of conquest following the identical pathways
of the ancient Cushite empire of Ethiopians.

CHAPTER IX.

THE MARVELOUS ARABIAN CIVILIZATION.

Arabia was one of the earliest colonies of the ancient Cushite Empire of Ethiopians. Baldwin claims that it was the original land of Cush. ! He says, "In the oldest recorded traditions, Arabia is the land of Cush, the celebrated Ethiopia of very remote times." He continues, "In ages older than Egypt or Chaldea, Arabia was the seat of an enlightened and enterprising civilization that went far into neighboring countries. At that time Arabia was the exalted and wonderful Ethiopia of olden tradition, the center and life of what in western Asia was known as the civilized world. Traditions of the ancient world rightly interpreted can have no other meaning. In the early traditions and records of Greece, Arabia was described as Ethiopia." Arabia was only separated from old Ethiopia by the Red Sea. We would decide that the "Old Race" of the Upper Nile early sent colonies across the sea, which built up the cities and communities along the opposite Arabian coast. This happening before the founding of Memphis or the colonizing of Chaldea.

The Scriptures unite Arabia with the most intimate dealings of God with men. Here says the *Cyclopedia of Biblical Literature,* were trans-

acted the marvelous panorama of the life of the
Patriarch Job, who was described as one of the
greatest men of the east. To this land Moses
escaped after killing the Egyptian. Here he lived
(put to school as it were) among the Midianites,
descendants of Cush. Here he married a daughter of Ethiopia, here he saw the burning bush
and here he talked with God. Here Elijah was
fed by the ravens. In Arabia was the scene of
all the marvelous displays of divine power and
mercy that followed the deliverance of Israel
from Egypt and accompanied their journeyings
into the Promised Land, and here Jehovah manifested himself in visable glory to his people. Here
today in the desert of Sin, manna still forms a
tiny cereal upon the rocks. It was out of this
region that God selected the race through which
in two religions, one supreme God should be revealed to the world, the Hebrews and Mohammedans spring from the same race.

These primitive Semites were a north Arabian
race. Southern Arabia was occupied by the older
and more civilized Ethiopian race. Gibbon speaks
of Sabaeans in north Arabia, if they were it was
families that had passed northward after the
Flood of Arem, which dispersed the families of
old Yemen over northern Arabia. These people
were advanced in civilization. The fact that the
father-in-law of Moses could show him defects
in his administration of government, proves that
he was in possession of an older and more seas-
oned form of law. The Scriptures tell us that
Moses harkened to the voice of his father-in-law

and did all that he said. There is marked similarity between the Jewish law and the code of Hammurabi, which was the essence of the old laws that for thousands of years had ruled the Cushite race. The Jewish law maker was thus placed in close contact with the race which in earlier ages had possessed the revelations of God in law and equity. This is why the code of Hammurabi, though it preceded Jewish law by many ages, yet in many features was the same code.

Arabia possessed many products in ancient days, that were coveted by the rest of the world. Nothing then was considered more costly and desirable than frankincense and myrrh, which were Arabia's fabled products. It was by this commerce that she amassed her fabulous wealth. The treasures of Africa were conveyed over the peninsula to Gerrha. Joined by the pearls of the Persian Gulf, this commerce was floated on rafts to the mouth of the Euphrates. Diodorus Siculus says, Bk. II, ch. 3, "The perfumes of Arabia ravished the senses and were conveyed by the winds to those who sailed near the coast. Having never been conquered, by the largeness of their country, they flow in gold and silver; and likewise their beds, chairs and stools have their feet of silver; and all their house stuff is so sumptuous and magnificent that it is incredible. The porticoes of their homes and temples, in some cases are overlaid with gold. They have enjoyed a constant uninterrupted peace for many ages and generations." Archaeological research has proved these assertions to have been true of the southern Arabians of the Hamitic race. Pliny said of these Arabians that they were the richest nations in the world. The harbors of Oman and Aden were laden with the precious cargo of perfumes. Agatharchides declared, "The Sabaeans surpass in wealth and magnificense not only the neighboring barbarians but all the nations whatsoever. As their distant situation protects them from foreign plunderers, immense stores of precious metals have been accumulated among them, especially in the captial. They have curiously wrought gold and silver drinking vessles in great variety, couches and tripods with silver feet; an incredible profusion of costly furniture in general; porticoes with large columns partly gilt and capitals ornamented with gold fretwork set with precious stones; besides an extraordinary magnificence reigning in the decorations of their houses, where they use silver, gold, ivory and the most precious stones and all other things that men deem valuable." (*De Mari Erythraeo*, 102.) This civilization was one that rose and perished long before the day of the Saracens.

From Baldwin's researches we learn that Strabo, Pliny, Ptolemy, as well as the Hebrew writers speak of the great cities of Arabia, that no longer exist. So far back does this ancient civilization extend that from the great length of time its literature has disappeared. The monuments of these Himyarites were inscribed with an obsolete and mysterious alphabet. The present Cufic letters were invented on the banks of the Euphrates, Gibbon tells us. The present inhabitants cannot explain the ancient ruins. They owe their origin to very remote antiquity. At Mareb is the Great Tank, so famous in Arabic tradition. The history of its origin was lost before the age of Solomon. Then the solid and vast embankment was going to decay. The ancient city of Saba was in ruins before the time of Christ. Throughout Yemen are to be found gigantic ruins which bewilder the beholders, who cannot understand how they were raised by human hands. They were built by the same race that reared the columns at Belbec and Karnak. These original Arabians were spoken of by later Arabs as Adites, Men of Ad, giants of old.

Lenormant in his painstaking researches found that Cushites were the first inhabitants of Arabia and were known in the national traditions as Adites. These descended from Ad, a grandson of Ham. His sons were Shedid and Shedad. To them was attributed the Shepherd invasion of Egypt. It was recorded in the traditions that one of them built a palace of superb columns surrounded by a magnificent garden. He tried to imitate the celestial paradise and God took him away. The Adites were depicted as men of gigantic stature. Fanciful tales like the Arabian Nights exist in Arabian legends, springing from the same source as those of the Egyptian manuscripts. Lenormant says, "We may perceive in all this the remembrance of a powerful empire founded by Cushites in very early ages. We find traces of a wealthy nation, constructors of great buildings, with an advanced civilization like that of Chaldea. This must be true as everywhere we find traces of Cushites in Arabian literature and their brothers the Canaanites." (*Ancient History of the East*, Lenormant, Vol. III, Arabians, p. 296.)

Alexander the Great said that Arabia was inferior to no country of the earth. He referred to the once famous town of Oman, which had been a harbor of the ancient commerce. It was in the day of Alexander a wilderness. His estimate of these Cushites was, "Taking them all in all, they are the richest nation of the world." Alexander lived in the declining days of Ethiopian power. Himyar was the son of Seba, the son of Cush. These were the people of Yemen and the Sabaeans of the Greeks. Lenormant called them related to the Accadians of Shinar and the Ghez of Abyssinia. Himyar became the head of the dynasty of Himyarites. These Cushite Arabians were a fine race of remarkable stature and dark complexion. The Semitic Arabians are brown, thin, small, well formed and of opposite traits from the Cushite Arabian. The Omanee kingdom attained a latter great splendor at the beginning of the Nineteenth Century. The conquering Mohammedan tribes of the north in idol-destroying mood have effaced all the pagan temples that once covered Arabia. Several enormous stone circles like those of some parts of Europe, built as a form of primitive religion, still remain.

At Hagerein, Gen. E. T. Haig saw the ruins

of once fertile districts under the weight of sand
that had overwhelmed them. There were ruins
of once lofty square buildings. The ground lies
strewn with fragments of Himyaritic inscriptions
and pottery. Wherever he found ruins they were
on elevated spots. The centers of civilization in
the valleys must have been buried very deeply.
Arabia, just as once fertile spots of the Sahara,
has been overwhelmed by the sand. At Al Azorem
are many ancient stone monuments on slightly
elevated ground. The old Cushite stones of crom-
lech type abound. They are decorated with geo-
metric patterns, which are like the Cushite decorations of Rhodesia in Africa and those of Asia
Minor. There were buildings surrounded by
stone walls. Welsted uncovered at Nakab-el-
Hajar a massive wall, thirty or forty feet high
flanked with square towers. On the face of the
building he found an inscription in the ancient
Himyaritic writing, which is a form of the primitive African language and has no relation to the
Semitic tongues.

In Yemen appears another evidence of Cushite
occupation, the terracing to be found on all ancient Hamitic sites. In one district the whole
mountainside was terraced from top to bottom.
Gen. Haig saw in this district everywhere above,
below and around, endless flights of terraced
walls. One can hardly realize the enormous
amount of labor, toil and perseverance, these represent. These walls were usually four or five
feet in height, but toward the top, they were sometimes as high as fifteen to eighteen feet. Agri-

culture among these indefatigable people was brought to the highest degree of perfection. They constructed immense dikes, forming permanent reservoirs, which irrigated the lowlands in dry weather. The Semitic Arabian abhors agriculture. It is by these differences in traits that we can unerringly detect race. When the Israelites first appear in the light of Bible history, they were keepers of flocks. Pastorals do not originate culture. The nature of their life renders it impossible. Nomadic people have been the invincible opponents of culture.

A primitive form of religion called Sabaeanism spread all over the Arabian provinces in the ear-lier ages. We find a gross form of Sabaeanism among the Turanian nations mixed with magic, but this religion in Arabia was without images, idolatry or priesthood. Once this religion was spread over the whole primitive world wherever Cushites were established. They addressed worship to the stars from high places. It was probably from this observation of the stars, that the science of astronomy first developed among them. To this use was put the tops of the pyramids. The pyramids of the ancients were built by this race for sacerdotal purposes. In India, Egypt, Rhodesia, in West Africa and western Europe this worship from high mountains was slow to die out. The ancient inhabitants of Arabia Petraea and Yemen believed in one god and a future life. Dead ancestors were cannonized and worshipped by their families. This one custom marked the race of "Anu" one of the names of the "Old

Race" of the Upper Nile. The people that by the traditions of Western Europe settled old Gaul, Ireland, Spain, and ancient Thrace.

Myers tells us in his *Ancient History*, that just as the "Oddessy" of Homer mirrored the trade voyages of the prehistoric Greeks, so the marvelous tales of Sinbad the Sailor pictured the adventures of the Cushite Arabian sailors upon the seas. The ships of these Ethiopians in the early ages of their dominion covered the ancient world. It was from this branch of the race, that the early race of India gained the knowledge that appears in Sanskrit books, that contain maps upon which we can trace the outlines of Western Europe and the British Isles. These books portray knowledge of ages prior to 2000 B. C. The Phoenicians in later times only followed courses that their Cushite cousins had pursued in earlier ages. They learned geography from their wide conquests and extended trade relations. The Portugese found maps and charts in their possession when they first came in contact with them on the coasts of East Africa, which were original and authentic. Some showed routes extending to the new world long before the age of Columbus.

One early Portugese map, gained from these Arabians marks South America, Western Africa and Southern Europe, as three ancient centers of civilization. The remains of primitive American nations give forth relics proving ancient Cushite communication. Before the arrival of the Portuguese, Arabian navigators had kept this knowledge secret. With declining Ethiopian power the links of this great chain had been broken to the Americas but they still kept up the ancient lines of trade with the nations peculiarly Cushite, India, Chaldea, South Africa, and Western Europe. By caravan routes they crossed deserts and delivered merchandise to the North African colonies, which in ages earlier than Phoenician dominion had been Cushite Ethiopian nations. To sum up we must decide that the meager information of the average historical book is very misleading as to who were the original Arabians and the giving of the right credit to the race which was responsible for the earlier so-called Arabian conquest of Babylonia. The later spurious stock, the Semitic Arabians appeared there in comparatively modern times. They were a pastoral, warlike people who in their mode of life, their food, their dress, their traits, manners, customs, and government were wholly unlike the original Arabians.

Through the ages these differences have remained unalterable. The riches to be gained as carriers induced some of the Semitic Arabian tribes from the more wild life to the service of bearers of the rich ancient commerce over the deserts. Having to constantly change their residence these Semites live in movable tents. These are divided into two parts one of which is for the women. The tents are arranged in an irregular circle, the space between being reserved as a fold for the cattle at night. As they have no land belonging to themselves they change their abode as often as they please. Col. Capper thus describes an Arab encampment, "From this hill, we could see at a distance of about three miles an Arab encampment, an immense body. There were nearly twenty thousand of them including women and children. They demanded and received tribute from us and promised a protecting guard until we were past all danger of attack from their detached bands." Those too poor to own a tent sheltered themselves under a piece of cloth suspended from poles Their tents are of coarse black material woven by the women from goats' hair.

The primitive nature of the Semitic Arabian is to be seen in the religion of Mohammed, in the presentation of his gospel, at the point of the sword; as Gibbon says, if they professed the creed of Islam they were admitted to all spiritual and material benefits. His apostles united the professions of merchant and robber. The distribution of the spoil was regulated according to Mohammed by divine law. From all sides the roving Arabs were allured to his standard by this combination of religion and plunder. In one incidence seven hundred Jews were dragged in chains to the market place of the city and descended alive into the grave prepared for their execution and burial; and the Apostle beheld with an inflexable eye the slaughter of his helpless enemies. In 628, the town of Khaibar surrendered, the chief of the tribe was tortured in the presence of Mohammed, to force confession of his hidden treasure.

Gibbon looks on the other side of Mohammed's character. He seemed endowed, whether he was an imposter or enthusiast, with a pious and contemplative disposition. He despised the pomp of royalty; he observed without effort or vanity the abstemious diet of an Arab and a soldier. The interdiction of wine arose and was confirmed by his example. The freedom of divorce was discouraged and adultary made a capital offense. During the twenty-four years of his marriage to his first wife, he abstained from polygamy. At her death he placed her in the rank of the four perfect women. The triumphant banners of Mohammed after his death waved over the cities of the Euphrates. ˙Persia was reduced. Turning to Syria, his followers invested Damascus, which fell; then Jerusalem, until all Syria bowed under the scepter of the caliphs. Greek rule had become odious in Egypt and it was gladly exchanged for the rule of the Saracens. The Greeks retreated from Upper Egypt and made their last stand at Alexandria. After a siege of fourteen months the Saracens prevailed. Mohammed's standard was set up on the walls of the capital of Egypt.

Let us examine the passage of the Semitic Arabians across Africa. Was his influence for the making of civilization? They burned the priceless collection of books that made up the Alexandrian library, in which were locked up the secrets of the lost arts and the knowledge of the origin of civilization. So great was the number of books that six months were needed for the consumption of this precious fuel. Every scholar with pious indignation has deplored this irreparable shipwreck of the learning and genius of antiquity. Many

Africans and Moors helped to make up the numbers and strength of the armies of the Saracens. After successive expeditions, the arms of Hassan reduced and pillaged Carthage. Greeks and Goths who came to the aid of Carthage were defeated and the city given to the flames. This ancient Metropolis of Africa was destroyed, all but the broken arches of an aqueduct. The Moors under the standard of a queen attacked the invaders with an enthusiasm equal to their own and the Arabians were driven back to the confines of Egypt. In later expeditions the blood of the Moors and Semites was insensibly mixed.

Moor and Arab attacked Spain then under the crumbling domination of the Goth. They landed at the Pillars of Hercules. The royal city of Toledo fell. Their conquest spread northward. A table of emerald, Gothic spoil from the Romans, was sent to the caliph at Damascus. In 712 A. D. 10,000 Arabs and 8,000 Africans passed over from Mauritania into Spain. The ports were thrown open to the vessels of Syria and the Goths were pursued to Gaul. Spain imbibed in a few generations the name and manners of the Arabs. This need not be surprising for in Spain was the basic blood of the Cushite, that ran in the Moor and the Cushite Arabian, who as natives of Yemen and other Cushite centers of Arabia, represented the proudest and noblest of the Arabian tribes. From this combination of conquerors sprang a most prosperous era of wealth, cultivation and populousness for Spain. Those who were willing to pay a moderate tribute were allowed freedom of conscience in religious worship. Where it payed the Moslem practiced moderation.

A glance taken over the vast empire of the Semitic Arabians finds them extended from the confines of Tartary and India to the shores of the Atlantic. The laws of the Koran were studied with equal zeal at Samaracand and Seville. Hindu and Moor embraced as brothers on the pilgramage to Mecca. Yet this does not seem strange for the Moor and Hindu in race were brothers. Forty-six years after the flight of Mohammed from Mecca, Arabian arms appeared under the walls of Constantinople in seige of the city. The solid and lofty walls were guarded by numbers and discipline. For six summers they made an attack with a retreat. This revived the reputation of the Roman arms and cast a momentary shade over the glory of the Saracens. Persia and Syria revolted. 717 A. D. the attack was made on Constantinople by 120,000 Arabs and Persians. A huge armada approached from Egypt and Syria. Entering the harbor they were assailed with Greek fire and the Arabian arms and vessels were involved in flames. In a later attempt the Egyptian ships deserted to the Christian emperor. The arms of Arabia retired after almost incredible disasters.

The deliverance of Constantinople sprang from the terror and efficacy of Greek fire. The skill of a chemist defeated fleets and armies, a distant forerunner of the gases of the world war of our day. Its composition was guarded by the Greeks with zealous care. It was the invention of a Cushite Arabian but was bought by the emperor and it filled the Semitic Arabs with superstitious terror. The secret of Greek fire was finally stolen by the Mohammedans and returned upon the heads of the Christians in the holy wars of Syria and Egypt. This Arabian invention effected a revolution in the art of war and in the history of mankind. Turning for a survey of the onward sweep of the Saracens of the west, we find them invading Gaul (France). Here we find Goth, Gascon and Franks assembled under the standard of the Duke of Iberian (Cushite) Aquitaine. He repelled their first invasion. In a second engagement the Arabs conquered and overran Aquitaine They stripped the churches of their ornaments and delivered them to the flames. Their invasion formed the groundwork of many a weird tale of chivalry.

Had they not been checked, instead of the Bible, interpretations of the Koran would today be taught at Oxford. To a circumcised people would be demonstrated the revelations of Mohammed. Christendom was delivered by the genius of one man. Half the kingdom was in the hands of the Saracens when Charles Martel, Duke of the Franks aided by the Germans met the enemy in the center of France. At the close of seven days of fighting the leader of the Saracens was slain. The tribes of Yemen, Damascus, Africa and Spain were provoked to turn their arms against one another. A hasty and separate retreat was made the spoils being left in the tents. The victory of the Franks was complete and final. Aquitaine was recovered by the arms of Eudes. Thus the ancient Franks saved the Christian world. Arabia at this time was convulsed with the massacre of the warring factions claiming their right of succession to the authority of Mohammed. The chair of Mohammed was disputed by three caliphs. At Bagdad they aspired to emulate the magnificence of the Persian kings. $150,000,000 was exhausted in a few years by the children of Caliph Almansor. His grandson showered a thousand pearls of largest size upon the head of his bride. Barges and boats of superb decoration were seen on the Tigris. In the palace were 38,000 pieces of tapestry, 12,500 of which were embroidered with gold.

Here was a perfect setting for the stories of the Arabian Nights, Gibbons continues this description, "A hundred lions were brought out with a keeper to each lion. Among the other spectacles of rare and stupendous luxury was a tree of gold and silver spreading into eighteen large branches, on the lessor branches sat a variety of birds made of the same precious metals, as well as the leaves of the tree. While the machinery effected spontaneous motions, the several birds warbled their natural harmony." In the west the Caliphs of Cordova supported an equal pomp. The hall of audience was incrusted with gold and pearls. The caliph was attended to the field by a guard of 12,000 horse, whose belts and scimeters were studded with gold. Luxury terminated the progress of the Arabian empire. 786 A. D. Harun, the most powerful and vigorous monarch of his race, ascended the throne. He was the perpetual hero of the Arabian tales. He swept the surface of Asia Minor. The ruin was complete, the spoil was ample, 823 A. D. the islands of Crete and Sicily fell and the cities of the age of Minos became thirty.

846 A. D. a fleet of Saracens from the African coast entered the Tiber and approached Rome. Her gates and ramparts were guarded by a trembling people. The costly offerings were torn from the altars. The Arabians divided their forces to pillage the neighboring towns of Fundi and Gaeta, and this division saved the capital from the yoke of the Prophet of Mecca. 838 Saracens advanced again upon Constantinople. A domestic traitor after fifty-five days of fruitless fighting pointed out the weakest part of the wall. Constantinople fell, the Arabs satiated with destruction then returned to Bagdad. Quarter was seldom given in the field. Those who escaped the edge of the sword were condemned to helpless servitude or exquisite torture. As the Arabian conquerors mingled with the servile crowds of Persia, Syria and Egypt, they lost the free-born virtues of the desert. Therefore the mercenary forces of the caliphs were recruited from the north. Mutasm introduced into the capital fifty thousand Turks. His son was cut in seven pieces by their swords. In three years they created, deposed and murdered three commanders of the faithful. Then Abbasids curbed and divided their power.

Near the end of the ninth century an imposter

arose. He relaxed the duties, ablution, fasting and pilgrimage. His twelve apostles dispersed themselves among the Bedouins, a race of men whom Abulfeda called equally devoid of reason and religion. His subjects were ripe for revolt disclaiming the title of the house of Abbas and abhorring the worldly pomp of the caliphs of Bagdad. 107,000 fanatics took and pillaged the cities of Racca, Baalbec, Cufa and Bassora. Bagdad was filled with consternation. The city was taken. They stormed and trampled upon the most venerable relics of the Mohammedan faith. Their sect was finally broken into sections but they were a second visible cause of the fall of the empire of caliphs. A third cause was the unweildness of the empire resulting from its magnitude. The provinces of Syria and Egypt were twice dismembered by Turkish slaves. The sons of the caliphs were educated in the vices of kings. 1000 A. D. Persia became free and her language and genius revived. Radhi the thirty-ninth of the successors of the Prophet was the last to represent the wealth and magnificence of the caliphs. After him the lords of the eastern world were reduced to abject misery. The treasury was no longer replenished by the spoil and tribute of nations. The African and Turkish guards turned their swords against each other. The chief commanders imprisoned or deposed their sovereigns. 945 A. D. the caliph was dragged from the throne to a dungeon. His palace was pillaged and his eyes put out.

In this school of adversity the caliphs went

back to the rigid virtues of the more primitive times. Sometimes through the division of their tyrants the Abbasids were restored to the sovereignty of Bagdad. Their misfortunes were embittered by the triumphs of the Fatimites, claimed progeny of the daughter of Mohammed. Rising from the extremity of Africa, they put an end to the authority of the Abbasids. In the declining age of the caliphs the arms of the Byzantine empire extirpated the nest of the Arabian pirates upon the island of Crete. 963 A. D. and 969 A. D. was the most splendid period of the Byzantine annals. Roman arms were carried into the heart of Syria. The reign of Caesar and of Christ was restored at Antioch the ancient metropolis of the east. At Aleppo they found in the stately palace outside the walls a magazine of arms, 1400 mules and three hundred bags of silver and gold. A hundred cities were reduced to obedience. Greek ardor was quickened to seize the virgin treasures of Bagdad but they had already been dissipated by the avarice and prodigality of the domestic tyrants. The fears of Bagdad were relieved by the retreat of the Greeks. Hunger and thirst had guarded the deserts of Mesopotamia. The emperor laden with oriental spoils returned to Byzantium. The Moslems purified their temples and overturned their idols but the old days of glory were fled. 1538 the claim to the caliphate passed to the Ottoman Turks. Their sultan called himself head of the Mohammedan world.

CHAPTER X.

THE RICH ARABIAN LITERATURE.

Gibbon speaks of the times of ignorance that preceeded Mohammed. This is true if we speak of Semitic Arabia, but later research has revealed a different source for the literature of the land. *Britannica* says of Arabia (Vol. 2, p. 230), "Arabia if poor in monuments is superabundantly rich in manuscripts. There are verses inscribed to the kings and heroes of Yemen dated a thousand years or more before the Christian era. We find undeniable specimens of at least two full centuries before Mohammed, of poems which in vigor and polish yield to few composed in Arabic or any other tongue. At this early date we find metrical and rythmical laws simple, yet susceptible to the highest art, with a scansion of almost Horatian elegance and variety, that Pope himself might have admired but could hardly have imitated." The nations of Arabia that were nomadic were tardy in the arts of peace. Before the time of Mohammed they had no literature. The times of the prophet were growing ancient when his deciples wrote. To whom then would we attribute this earlier literature of Arabia? Let us go deeper into research to find out.

Oriental histories say that the language spoken in the more ancient times was wholly different

from the Arabic of Mohammed. The fragments
of verse composed at least a thousand years before Christ were in the ancient Himyaritic tongue
and the language of Yemen glorifying its heroes
was the same Himyaritic dialect. In the days before Islam, not far from Mecca at Okad, was held
a national meeting like the Olympaids of the
Greeks. It was an annual fair, frequented by
men of all conditions from every quarter of Arabia. It lasted thirty days, preceeding the annual pilgrimage, which itself was taken over by
Mohammed from the earlier life. As well as the
exchange of corn and wine, there was the enjoy-
ment of eloquence and poetry. We may read in
our own language the seven original poems which
were inscribed in letters of gold and suspended in
the temple at Mecca. In the Fourth and Fifth
Centuries A. D. poetry had become a refined art.
The metrical contests were firmly established.
The most renowned poets crowned at these festivals were Antar, Amur-El-Kais and Tarafah.
This Arabian Olympiad was abolished by the ignorance and fanaticism of the first followers of
Mohammed.

Let us examine this fair that had sprung out of
the culture of the earlier Cushite Arabian races.
Horse races, poetical recitals, and every kind of
amusement, was used to offset the weightier commercial transactions of an open fair. It had the
proportions of a national exhibition. Here the
best masters of art met for the purpose of recit-
ing their compositions and receiving the reward.
Metenebhe was esteemed by many as the greatest

Arabian poet. In range of thought and excellence of diction he surpassed all. Toghrai furnished Tennyson with his model for *Locksley Hall.* Ebn Farigh composed poetry that has never in its kind been surpassed or even equaled by the poets of any land. We find in the annals Noseyyeb, a Negro who was master of descriptive poetry. This is the estimate of the Arabian poets by the literary critics of high repute of other lands. Many European writers drew their inspirations from romances and legends like the Exploits of Antar, and the Arabian Nights, which have become a part of the real literature of the world.

The culture of the Saracens and Islam arose and flourished from ingrafting of Semitic blood upon the older Cushite root. The mingled language was distinguished for its richness, softness and high degree of development. By the spread of Islam it became the sole written language of all southwestern Asia, eastern and northern Africa and for a time of southern Spain, Malta and Sicily. Arabic writers of the Semitic division, wrote so late, that from religious prejudice and lapse of time they were incapable of being faithful historians of the older Cushite civilization. In their versions those old cities of the Adites and Thalmonites were enterprising rich and powerful. They represented them as of wonderful magnificence, but Mohammedan ardor, as Baldwin points out, executed upon these cities miraculous judgments, because of unbelief in Islam, which did not then exist. ''These are but faint and confused recollections of a civilization that had de-

caying monuments, ruined cities, and mysterious
antiquities before the time of Khatan which itself was ancient. These wonderful creations disappeared, not in fiery wrath from heaven but under the influence of thousands of years of time
and change." (*Prehistoric Nations,* Baldwin, p.
104.)

The Koreysh to whom many European and
American writers delight in dedicating the Arabian genius have carefully, too carefully, built
up the family tree that includes Mohammed himself and in their annals the Yemenites, the genuine Arabs of genius, appear as cousins and descendants of Heber. On these points all Mohammedan annalists are equally positive and that we
should accept these falsities, the fruit of vanity
and ignorance, *Britannica* says, is surprising.
Mohammedan chroniclers adopted much from the
Jewish records, their country at that time was
full of the Jews dispersed by the conquest of their
own lands. They conceal the facts of their own
late appearance in Arabia by childish fictions.
Saracen conquest was directly represented by the
tribes of Mustareb origin, but the civilizing influence sprang from the accompanying arms of
the old culture, the ancient aristocratic tribes of
Yemen. Nations in the south, east and north, of
the same ancestry had sunk to half vassalage to
Persian or Byzantine authority. In their hands
had been the custody of the temple of Mecca
which was seized and forever after held by the
Koreysh who thus gained religious preeminence
by possession of the treasures of gold, silver,

jewels and other offerings gathered by pagan piety of Cushite Arabians. The Semitic Arabian race has not been noted for any creative or constructive qualities and until united in conquest with the more ancient Cushite race was wholly destructive. Mohammed took over a primitive Cushite pilgrimage to Mecca.

Myers says, "The poetry of the Arabians was wholly original. It was the natural and beautiful expression of Arabic genius." The fanciful imagery of the Arabian poetry and the legends were very much like the literature of the same type in India. It showed in the superior development of the speech of Islam, the lustre of the empire of the caliphs, and in the knowledge of the arts and sciences carried to western Europe by the Saracens. This rich Arabian language was the union of the dialects of northern and central Semitic Arabians and the Himyaritic of southern Arabia. This can be proved by the similarity of the roots. The languages had so overlapped that the Cushite inhabitants of Palestine, who were called Samaritans, could converse with the Hebrews. Christ talked with the Samaritan woman at the well. Constant trade relations had unified the tongues. Moses in earlier days had been able to converse with the Ethiopian daughters of Jethro. Gideon and his servant went down to the camp of the Midianites, who were Cushites, he overheard their conversation and understood it. The Queen of Sheba, who was Ethiopian, was able to converse with Solomon. The Ethiopian treasurer of Queen Candace was reading a Hebrew version of the Scriptures, when Peter was told by the Spirit to preach to him Christ crucified.

Students of philology know that there was great dissimilarity between the Hebrew of later times and the Arabic; for the language of the Israelites underwent a change during the captivity in Babylon. After the exile, the Hebrews spoke Aramaic. The order of Hebrew letters and Arabic are different. The Arabic of the earliest form have that of the Himyaritic alphabet, and are strikingly like this Ethiopian language in form. Thus we see how easy it is for superficial scholarship to have made the mistake of blending under the same name Arabian, two distinct races, to have failed to recognize the blending of two languages, to have failed to perceive the earlier ancient Cushite civilization. Even the Hebrews were introduced to the art of building cities and to a settled life by the Cushites and Canaanites. The Semitic race was always nomadic, never becoming settled traders, unless mixed with Hamitic blood. In the dispersion of the Hebrew family they scattered to Arabia, Africa, and to the east. Arabia is densely populated with a free black population. They have so intermixed with Semitic Arabians that a fair skin is the exception. In Arabia because of the old high Ethiopic culture no prejudice whatever exists against black and Arab alliances. There is no social or political bar between African and Arab. A Negro may become the highest official or ruler if his talents allow.

We must decide from these evidences, that out of the bare life of the Semitic Arabians could not have sprung the abundant roots and rich variety of the perfected Arabic tongue; but these additions were but budded growth from the rich ancient Cushite Arabian life. It seemed a language most perfect as "a vehicle for impassioned and sublime appeals, for artless simplicity and philosophic subtilties. The genius of the Arab constantly flowered in poetry of highly artistic form, delicate descriptive poems and novels in verse." This was the Arabian heritage of splendor from the magnificence of Cushite Arabian days which the prodigality of the later caliphs sought to imitate. The tales of genii, fairies, and enchantments passed into the poetry of the west. We might think this addition to western barbarism of little worth but the images and fancies of powerful immagination have given the world the fuel for the fires of art. The warlike Arabian, as the earlier cruel Assyrian, embibing an older culture, by conquest scattered widely for later ages the precious cultural seeds of the ancient Cushite empire of Ethiopians.

The *Arabian Nights Entertainments* filled Europe in 1717 with wonder and delight. Few books have been translated and read among so many nationalities as these tales, which were the gateway into fairyland of our childhood. They were a collection of tales from the widespread colonies of the Cushite race. The richest of the tales came from India, the cradle of story and fable. Many were from Bagdad the royal city of the eastern caliphs. They are fanciful pictures of the decadance from a higher and more perfect civilization.

The *Arabian Nights* will always be one of the most wonderful books of the world and is an addition to the world's imperishable literature. The Arabian writers were remarkable for their sublimity of conception, power to stir the heart, and the intensity of love and hate shown in their creations. This literature carried westward by the Saracens had a powerful influence in moulding the forms of poetry and letters of Europe. Arabian ideals and philosophy rule all the ecclesiastical life of Persia, Turkey and all of the eastern lands that have come under Mohammedan sway.

The Arabians brought to Europe not only poetry but astronomy and mathematical science. They gave Europe the nine digits, the Arabian figures to ten, and algebra. The oldest mathematical book, 1700 B. C., contains some problems similar to algebra. The book was written by the Ethiopian Aahmes. We find a little of the study among the Greeks, but the Arabians brought it up to the importance of a science. In the tenth century they left the Greek masters behind and reached the limits of spherical trigonometry and solved quadratic and even cubic equations. What the later Phoenicians were in navagating the Mediterranean, the Sabaeans had been in the Indian Ocean. They created the knowledge of geography in the Middle Ages, which they had gained from the commercial activities that had nourished the ancient cities of Babylon, Tyre and Sidon. Lucian thought that the Arabian Cushites were the first who invented astronomy, being led to the science by their cloudless skies and favorable climate and by their surprising intellectual sagacity, subtility and force.

With the knowledge gained from the earlier civilization, the Saracens made their own scientific additions. In the earlier days no Greek poetry, orations or history were ever translated into Arabic. Arabian immagination and reason did not need such assistance. For a period the studies of the Mohammedans were confined to the interpretation of the Koran and the eloquence and poetry of their native tongue, but the later caliphs collected the knowledge of other seats of ancient culture. With comparatively rough musical instruments, they carefully elaborated a musical scale. Their book of songs contains a hundred airs, each esteemed a masterpiece by competent judges. As a people continually facing death in battle, the medical art became highly esteemed. They were the first to make medicine a true science. They invented the probang, a valuable surgical instrument. To them must be credited the lancet and the couching needle. Arabians were the first to develop chemistry and they first prepared prescriptions for the mixing of drugs. From them have come down to us most of the medical recipes of today. For whatever resources chemistry availed itself up to a recent date, we are endebted to Arabic research. The real scientific development of medicine must be credited to their genius.

In the great cities of Bagdad, Cairo and Cordova, centuries before Europe could boast of anything beyond cathedral or monastic schools, great

Arabian universities were drawing together vast throngs of eager young Arabians; and creating an atmosphere of learning and refinement. Students from all parts of Europe in the Middle Ages, studied mathematics and medicine in the Arabian schools. The famous university of Cairo has at the present day an attendance of several thousand, a survival of the great days of Arabian Islam. Their libraries and schools were visited by many Christians, especially in Spain, who helped to introduce their learning into western Europe. In geography, history, philosophy, medicine physics and mathematics, the Arabians rendered important service to science. They are considered the founders of modern experimental science. They devised the duo-decimal system of notation and gave Europe this indispensible instrument of calculation. The Arabian architect developed a new striking style of edifice, which has been preserved at Cordova and Granada in Spain. This style has given modern builders some of their finest models. The temples of India, perhaps unsurpassed in beauty anywhere in the world, are the result of Arabian genius unfolding in Mohammedan art.

The rival schools of the Arabian empire, investigated in the eighth, ninth, and tenth centuries, every nicety of grammar. The grammatical treatise of the celebrated Ebn Malek is even now a standard work in the hands of our professors. The practice in the earlier days of suspending in gold letters' the poems of the highest merit that won the premium, in the temple of Mecca, had brought to the highest point the passion for perfect results in literature. To Hereeree must be credited the absolute mastership of language, combined with exquisite taste in the use of the subtlest refinements of both rhetoric and grammar. His Makamat of the eleventh century, though it has many imitators has never yet had a rival. Great libraries existed at Bagdad, Alexandria and Cairo. In every city the productions of Arabic literature were copied and collected. The royal library of the Fatimite caliphs contained over one hundred thousand manuscripts, elegently transcribed and splendidly bound. The Omayyads of Spain had formed a library of six hundred thousand volumes. Everywhere the Arabians of the tenth century conquered, they became the preservers and distributers of knowledge.

Romances and stories of a biographical character were very popular among the Arabians. Antar the Lion, 525 A. D. was the story of the life of one of the most renowned poets of those crowned at the contests at Okad, which in the earlier days were more greatly attended than those of Thebes. Antar was a black poet who had killed a man who had failed in respect to a woman. He had a purely African face, his mother being a black slave. He married a princess of one of the noblest and purest tribes. By deeds of heroism he became protector of his people and the pattern of chivalry. His fame spread across the Arabian peninsula and throughout the Mohammedan world. Like the Homeric legends his deeds were recorded in poetic form. The romance of Antar was a source of wonder and admiration for hundreds of years to millions of Arabians. He was the father of knighthood, champion of the weak and oppressed, protector of women, impassioned love poet. It was from the tales of Antar that Europe received her inspirations for romantic chivalry, so common in the twelfth century in Italy and France. How Cushite ideals have colored all the life of the ages.

This national classic, Antar the Lion, the Arabian Iliad, is of great length in the original, being often thirty or forty manuscript volumes. Portions of it have been translated into English, German and French. The original book puports to have been the delight of all Arabians. Every wild Bedouin of the desert knew much of the tale by heart and listened to its periods and poems with quivering interest. Compare this with our poetical apathy today. Every coffee house in Aleppo, Bagdad, or Constantinople had a narrator who nightly recited it to wrapped audiences. The united sentiment of the east has been that the romance of Antar, is a book that has reached the highest summit of literature. One Arabian author has said that the Arabian Nights, is for the amusement of women and children, but that Antar is a book for men. From it they learn eloquence, magnanimity, generosity, statecraft and bravery. Mohammed a foe to the ancient gatherings that fostered poetry, instructed his disciples to relate the traditions of Antar to their children. There is nothing surprising in this recognition and adoration of Antar when we understand that his race was the basic blood of Arabia. The Saracens also carried westward knowledge of irrigation, rotation of crops, fertilizers and the art of grafting and producing new varities of plants and fruits. This knowledge came directly from the Cushites of the southern and western coasts, who were peculiarly agricultural. From these came cotton, flax, hemp, buckwheat, rice, sugar cane and coffee. Others of our vegetables trace to the same source including asparagus, artichokes, beans and such fruits as melons, oranges, lemons, apricots and plums. To prove that these plants originated among Cushites, wild specimens which only grow where the plant originated, can be found across the Soudan. The Arabs excelled in manufactures. The industrious Arabs led the way by their inventions and skill to most of the complicated manufactures of our time. In metallurgy their art in tempering and enamelling became justly famous. No sword blades ever ranked higher than those of Damascus. It was also famous for its brocades, tapestries and the damask of our day which still preserves the name of the city. No coppersmiths excelled those of Bagdad.

Cordova was famous for leather, Toledo for armor, and Granada for rich silks. Specimens of their skill in porcelain yet remain in Spain and Syria. The smiths of Oman were unexcelled in gold and silver workmanship. Arabian craftsmen taught the Venetians how to make crystal and plate glass. The work of these potters and weavers was the admiration and despair of the craftsmen of Europe. The words morocco, gause from Gaza, and cordovan, still in use in our times attest their cleverness in preparing and dyeing leather. They seem to have introduced the pointed arch into Europe, swelling domes, vaulted roofs, arched porches and minarets were characteristic of Arabic architecture. The pendulum and semephoric telegraph, if not invented, were introduced by them into Europe, as was the manufacture of silk and cotton, and an invention of the highest importance—the mariners compass. They knew the lost secrets of dyeing. As early as 706 A. D. writing paper was made at Mecca, whence it spread through the Arabian dominions to the western world. They claim the invention of gun-powder as far back as the eleventh century.

To sum up, the literature, art and science of the Arabs formed a connecting link between the civilizations of ancient and modern times. "To them," says *Britannica*, "we owe the revival of learning and philosophy in western Europe and the first awakenings of the critical and inquiring spirit, that rescued western Europe from the lethergy of monkish ignorance and from ecclesiastical bigotry. To them is due the credit for most of the useful arts and practical inventions laboriously perfected by later nations. Widespread was the empire of the Arabs' sword but wider and more durable was the empire of the Arabs' mind." (*Britannica*, V. 2, Arabia, p. 232.) Today among the Bedouins there are no schools. Utterly ignorant of writing and unacquainted with books they trust to memory or imagination.

Their assertions as to the past cannot be trusted
Yet many a modern history of Arabia is built
upon no more solid foundation. It is doubtful if
Mohammed could read or write. Their genealogies cannot be depended upon, by the real seeker
after truth.

Let us glance at Arabians living today in fixed
habitations, as their ancestors have done in Arabia from time immemorial. There is rivalry and
enmity between these Cushite settlers of today
and the Semitic division that under various
forms has never ceased down to our times. Even
in the desert the children of these settled Arabians are taught to read and write and calculate. In
the towns education is general. The possession
of written records, the habits of order and reflection, enable the settled Arabs to retain a more
accurate knowledge and nicer distinction of pedigree and race. It was their idols that Mohammed
cast down in the Kaaba at Mecca, which had belonged to the kings of Yemen. To the Arabian
of the old unsettled nomadic life we must give the
credit of Saracen conquest. These tribes went
forth at first unarmed comparatively, spurred on
by religious zeal. They bore westward and eastward over the oft recrossed highways of the old
Cushite empire the latest impulses of that race
that in earlier ages had originated civilization
for the world. On the crest of the conquering
arms rode the princes of Yeman not one whit
less in valor but carrying the genius that fully
developed in the lifting of a headlong campaign
to the status of a culturing conquest.

CHAPTER XI.

THE STRANGE RACES OF CHALDEA.

The foundations of ancient Chaldea, were laid as early as those of Egypt. In fact they were the sister colonies of a parent state. The earliest civilized inhabitants were Sumerians. 5000 B. C. the land was full of city-states. The Sanskrit books of India, called Chaldea one of the divisions of Cusha-Dwipa, the first organized government of the world. These Sumerians were the inventors of the cuniform system of writing, which was later adopted by their Semitic conquerors. In the later days their language was still cultivated in the ritualistic services until the time of Alexander the Great. It is thought that this civilization originated from southern Susiana. The pictoral hieroglyphics which made the cuniform characters were probably invented in Elam. In Babylonia however this culture underwent a rapid development. The northern division of Babylon was called Accad, comprehending Babylon, the southern Sumer, including Erech and Ur. North of Accad were the Semitic tribes which so largely made up the blood of Assyria in later days. The Babylonians were further mixed by Elamite and Cassite conquests.

What was the original race of these Sumerians, Cassites and Elamites? Recent explorations upon these sites is giving much light upon the subject. The finds prove that the records and traditions of antiquity were in perfect accord with these new discoveries. The history of Babylonia like that of most nations begins with myth; but we are beginning to realize that a deep significance lies beneath age old myths. Ten kings appear in the primitive annals, corresponding with the ten patriarchs of the Hebrew Scriptures and the ten rulers of Egyptian chronology. Enormous cycles of years accompany their reigns, so do they in the Scriptures and the findings of geology accord. These come down to the Xisuthros of Greek tradition, our Noah. At his death colonies under the leadership of Titan (Nimrod), arrived in the plain of Sumer and essayed to build a tower that would scale the sky. On this spot at Babylon stood the temple of Anu. Then in these early Babylonian traditions follow the names of Gilgamesh, the Melcarth of Tyre and the Hercules of Greece, identified with the name of Nimrod of the Hebrews. The epic of the adventures of Nimrod, was preserved in the library at Erech and is identical with the twelve labors of Hercules. What significance lies under this common hero under the names of the greatest of the demi-gods of Egypt and Greece?

This overlapping of the geneology of antiquity shows that these heroes, Bel, Gilgamesh, Melcarth, Hercules, belonged to a common race. Belus (Nimrod), king of Chaldea serves to unite the Chaldeans with the Old Race of the Upper Nile, as does their building the temple of Anu,

another name of the original Cushite family. It
was for this reason that Greek and Armenian
geographers applied the name of Ethiopia to
Media, Persia, Susiana and Aria, or the entire
region between the Indus and Tigris in ancient
days. The records of the Hebrews connected the
Chaldeans, Ethiopians and Egyptians in ties of
kinship, and the findings of archeaological and
philological research prove those records true.
Rawlinson mentions a Cushite inscription found
in Susiana, in which there is a date going back
nearly to the year 3200 B. C. The language of
later Babylon was Semitic but that of the earlier
Chaldean monarchy was different, as can be
proved by the inscriptions upon the ruins. They
are distinctly Hamitic and like the Himyaritic of
Southern Arabia.

All the earliest traditions of Chaldea center
about Belus or Nimrod. We know that Nimrod
was the son of Cush. Babylon had two elements
in her population in the beginning. The northern
Accadians and the southern Sumerians were both
Cushites. The finds of recent explorations in the
Mesopotamian valley reveal that these ancient
inhabitants were black, with the cranial formation
of Ethiopians. On linguistic grounds a relationship with Turanians proves untenable. The Turanian is one of the oldest races of the world.
Some historians attempt to suggest that Noah
might have had other sons after the deluge. We
do not have to introduce other races to understand
the Turanian family. They were an important
branch of the Japhetic race just as Cush be-

came the name of an important branch of the Hamitic family. Once Turan and Cush occupied the greater part of Asia and Europe. The Turanians lived east of Lake Ural from remote antiquity. They possessed a peculiar civilization characterized by a gross Sabaenism. In them was complete want of moral development, though they had extraordinary advancement in some branches of knowledge. They were materialistic and incapable of having created the pure spiritual culture of the primitive Chaldeans. Turanians had absolute sovereignty over a great part of Asia and Europe for fifteen hundred years.

Moses of Chorene, the great Armenian historian, identifies Belus, king of Babylon, with Nimrod and makes Nimrod the son of Cush. Bochart and other authorities translate the passage of the Scriptures that deals with the beginning of Nineveh to read that it was also founded by Nimrod and that he was the god Ninus of early Assyria, which in its beginning was Cushite. Moses of Chorene connects Babylonia in the closest way with Ethiopia. From the Tigris eastward the names of the country and its formations in numerous cases were in honor of Belus and Cush. Some of these names have extended down to our times as Beluchistan and Hindu Cush. The precious document Toldoth Beni Noah, said that the primitive people of Babylonia were a subdivision of the Cushite race. There is no doubt that in later ages these Ethiopians became mixed with Turanians. The art, science and culture of the earlier unmixed Chaldeans was Cushite. The later religion became permeated with Turanian magic and the later Babylonian kingdom that was destroyed for its wickedness was an admixture of Semitic, Arian, and Ethiopian blood. The tendency of the modern book to make this commingling of the races extend back to earlier ages is unscientific, for all the kings whose monuments are found used the same language, professed the same religion and followed the same traditions, this proves continuity of race. 'It was universally attested by antiquity that from the Cushite element sprang the civilization of Chaldea.' The Scriptures say that Cush begat Nimrod and that he began to be mighty upon the earth. The beginning of this kingdom was Babel, Erech, Accad and Calneh, in the land of Shinar. Thus the Bible authenticates the Cushite claim. Rawlinson says that Nimrod set up a kingdom in lower Mesopotamia that attracted the attention of surrounding nations. The people that he led probably came from the sea. Their earliest settlements were upon the coast. Ur was the primitive capital. Nimrod was king of the city where the confusion of tongues took place. The people whom Nimrod found were probably Turanians or Semites. Babylonian traditions said that they were unlettered barbarians. Cushites pushed these people back and as the traditions of the fish-god reveal, taught them the arts of civilized life. Semitic inhabitants crowded back to Nineveh, later became predominant and appeared as the fierce Assyrians.

Rawlinson decided that the ruins of Chaldea

show Cushite origin. The names of Chaldea and Ethiopia are linked in a way to render any other interpretation impossible. The great city of the earlier period was Niffer a corruption of Nimrod. The language of the ruins is radically different from the Semetic tongue of the Assyrian empire. This is the report of all investigators who have studied the ruins. Long before the day of later Babylon, the land was full of all that would make a cultivated and flourishing nation. The strength of Nimrod's character and the greatness of his achievments are remarkably indicated by a variety of testimonies, which place him among the foremost characters of the ancient world. At least as early as the time of Moses, his name had passed into proverb. He was known as the mighty hunter before the lord. In his own nation he was deified and continued down to the latest times as the chief object of worship. In Arabian tradition Nimrod played a conspicuous part. Orion in the Arabian astronomy bears his title. His name lives in the tales of the people of Chaldea today. Wherever a mound is to be seen in Babylon or the adjoining countries, the local tradition attaches to it the name of Nimrod. The most striking ruins of the upper and lower Mesopotamian valley are thus made the mounments of his glory.

Indisputable proofs of the extreme antiquity of Chaldea have been unearthed. These evidences show that under the oldest cities lie the successive foundations of still older cities, seemingly stretching back into the antediluvian world. This substantiates the vast cycles of time included in the Babylonian chronology and the claims of the legend of the deluge upon the Babylonian tablets, which says that the survivors of the flood returned and rebuilt upon the old foundations of Babylon, which had gone down in the general destruction. ¡Rawlinson says that the race of Nimrod passed from east Africa by way of Arabia to the valley of the Euphrates before the beginning of history. Loftus speaks of this powerful stream of colonization from the south. The emigrants were called Accadians, the Accad of Genesis. Delineations found among the ruins of Nineveh, on the walls of the palaces, prove that their were two Ethiopian types, one the ancient Cushite and another a heavy southern face having the protuberant lips, the receeding forehead, broad thick nose and crisp hair of Africa. These were the primitive inhabitants of Susiana as well as Babylon. These were the lineaments of the inhabitants of the Upper Nile—the Old Race of Egypt.

Berosus, the Manetho of Babylon, who flourished at the time of Alexander's conquests, a priest of Bel, translated the records and astronomy of his nation into Greek. His works have unfortunately perished; but we have quotations of his in other authentic writings. His history of the deluge is almost identical with the one of the cunieform tablets. Berosus wrote a history of the Chaldeans in nine books. He gave the oldest traditions of the human race. We do not possess his works, only fragments remain in the writings of the Greek, Hebrew and Roman fathers.

We can no longer claim that tradition does not stand for actual happenings in the life of a race. Men once claimed that ancient Troy was a myth and that the Labyrinth of Minos was fiction; but archaeologists have unearthed the Troy of the Greek legends and the Labyrinth of Crete. Berosus mentioned Median and Arabian dynasties that ruled over Chaldea. The Medians were, Baldwin thinks, the Midianites of Arabia, for this was ages prior to the Medes of history. The Arabian dynasties were of the race of Southern Arabia for the language of the Chaldean inscriptions is the same as that of the South Arabian, called Himyaritic.

Berosus begins his story of Chaldean times with the primitive era, when a multitude of barbarous men of various tribes inhabited the Mesopotamian valley. These were very probably Turanian and Semites. The Japhethic people were not far from this first center of human life and we know that Abraham came from Ur of the Chaldeans. In the beginning Berosus said, that these men lived like animals without any order of government. Bel (Nimrod), god of the Chaldees and later Babylonians, saw the fruitfulness of the land. He sent to them from the sea, a fearful fish by the name of Onan. This was a ship which appeared to these barbarous people as a great fish. Its image half man and half fish is still preserved. It represents men who came to these untutored people by water. These primitive people of the Mesopotamian valley had not yet conquered the sea and this happening was

perpetuated from generation to generation as
they were first impressed. Then this vessel might
have had a fish shape. The early Cushite navigators used the figures of animals upon the prows
of their ships. The symbol of dolphins always
accompanied Bacchus, whom the ancients identified with Nimrod, the word meaning son of Cush.

The tradition continues: this animal came up at
morning out of the sea and passed the day with
men; but it took no nourishment and at sunset
went again into the sea; where it remained for
the night. This was because they were civilized
people who could not subsist upon such food as
these savages ate, but were fed in their own ship.
The fish taught men language, science, the har-
vesting of seeds and fruits and rules for the
boundries of lands. They gave to them the mode
of building temples and cities, arts, writing, and
all that pertains to the civilization of men. We
learn from the Babylonian inscriptions that Anu
the Babylonian god, was also the fish-god Oannes.
This Anu was king of the lower world. His worship was very ancient and the chief seat was at
Erech. At Nipper we find the name Tel-Anu.
This fish race by the same peaceful methods had
carried its civilization to Egypt of which Chaldea
was but a sister state. The Anu of Upper Egypt
were the only race at this early stage of the world
in possession of the arts of civilization. Turanians and Semites were barbaric nomads as late
as Persia and the conquests of Assyria. Turanians were still uncivilized when Christ was born.

This early tradition and the image of the fish-god, the sea-god of the Babylonians, worshipped on down through the ages, stands for a historic happening in the life of an undeveloped and untutored people. It was an age when every unexplained wonder was seen as a god. It was the totemic emblem that is seen among so many of the African races. This ship bringing civilized people to the untaught Turanians and Semites, who introduced the arts to these aborigines, proves that civilization did not originate in Chaldea, that it did not spring from the Turanian or Semitic races, or from Egypt, but came from elsewhere. It shows that Chaldea was not the original Cushite country but that civilization must have sprung from a parent root where it had developed during the long ages. In the Chaldean inscriptions the vernacular name of Ethiopia was Mirukh, and its maritime enterprise was very distinctly recognized. ' This civilization brought by Cushites to Chaldea must have developed in that first common cradle of mankind that the Greeks located upon the Upper Nile.

M. de Bolm tells us in *Early Cushite Navigation*, that the Cushite Ethiopians in primitive ages were a commercial people. It was due to their conquest of the sea that they so early covered three continents with colonies. With their ships they had in ancient days circumnavigated the globe, bequeathing maps, charts, and nautical instruments to their cousins and successors the Phoenicians, who called themselves Ethiopians. Cushite supremacy was everywhere marked by progress in the industries and science, with myths peculiar and original to the Cushite mind. These pushed back the original inhabitants of Chaldea everywhere except in the west, which afterwards became conquering Assyria. In the long course of ages these Cushites multiplied and built up the many cities of the Mesopotamian coast. One of these cities was named Kush. The Assyrians of historic times show how much their race was intermingled with Ethiopian blood for the sculptures represent them with wool hair waved.

The oldest cities of Chaldea were Ur, Eridu, Larsa, and Erech in the neighborhood of the Persian Gulf. These waters stretching out invited them to navigation and trade with distant states. Ur was built at the mouth of the Euphrates. It is now one hundred and fifty miles inland, the Persian Gulf having retired one foot in seventy years. Think to what remote antiquity this assigns Chaldea. The great temple of the moon-god was the oldest in the country. Ra-Zeus-Ammon was considered the sun god. An earlier worship was of the moon. It was of the Soudan. The moon god was considered father of the sun god. Moon worship took precedence over sun worship; but as the Cushite colonies grew stronger the worship of Ammon took precedence. Ammon-Ra was Cush. In the earliest ages the moon was considered king over the lesser rulers. Chaldea was filled with temples of vast size dedicated to Istar and Bel, the Isis and Osiris of Egypt. Ur rose to the leadership uniting the principalities of Chaldea. The hypothesis that Babylon was ruled by an Aryan dynasty was strictly contradicted by

Berosus and the records disentombed from the ruins. "Aryans," says Lenormant, "at this stage of the world had not yet crossed the great Sargartean desert."

Chaldea could not have been Semitic for there was difference in race between Assyria and Babylonia. The northern country in later times must have been overrun and conquered by the restless tribes of Semitic Arabians that in still later days formed the Saracenic conquest. By the time of the latter Babylonian empire, Assyria had become predominently Semitic. Diodorus Siculus spoke of Chaldea and Assyria as two separate and hostile nations distinct in every way in early times. Pliny draws a clear line between them. Classical traditions connect the primitive inhabitants of Assyria, Chaldea and Susiana, with Ethiopia. Æschylus and Herodotus regarded the Ethiopian king Memnon as the founder of Susa. At the same time he was claimed by the Ethiopians of the Upper Nile as their sovereign. Egypt claimed him as her ruling Pharaoh under the name of Amenhotep III, the Amenophis of the Greeks. His statute was known in Egypt as the Vocal Memnon. He perished at the Seige of Troy, after greatly distinguishing himself. Sometimes the expedition, that he led to the defense of the Trojan city is thought to have proceeded by way of Egypt from Ethiopia in Africa. There were palaces called Memnon at Susa and in Egypt. There were tribes called Memnon at Meroe. This common name thus unites the eastern and western

Ethiopians of Asia and Africa as but parts of a common empire.

The original name of Nippur was Belus, it was the capital of Chaldea during the most important part of its existance and perhaps the longest. As early as 4500 B. C. kings reigned there. Sargon of Agade flourished about 3800 B. C. He was the head of one of the Cushite-Arabian waves of conquest. He was one of the greatest in the long line of Babylonian monarchs. More than once he attacked Elam successfully. His empire extended from the Persian Gulf to the Mediterranean. He founded the city of Babylon. His kingdom was but a portion of the ancient realm of the Cushites, now broken into segments of which the Ægean, Egyptian, Ethiopian, Babylonian and Hindu nations were the parts of what in earlier ages had been a common empire. The legends about Sargon told of his winning the favor of Isthar (Isis) common to the worship of all these nations. The next great name in the line of monarchs is Hammurabi, who reigned about 2500 B. C. and was contemporary with Abraham. He expelled the Elamites from Babylonian soil and in reward was acknowledged king of all Babylonia. Gibbon calls him more than conqueror. He was a consummate statesman as well. He organized his kingdom upon so sure a foundation that his work endured for nearly two thousand years.

Hammurabi showed all the traits of Cushite genius. He cleaned out and cut out new canals and brought the system of irrigation to a high degree of efficiency. He built great embankments to protect the land from devastating floods. Throughout Babylonia he built and adorned the temples of the gods. He codified the laws and established courts of justice everywhere. He gave personal attention to the administration of the law. Babylonians of later days looked back upon the reign of Hammurabi as the golden age of their history. About 1750 B. C. Babylon was over-run by swarms of invaders called Kasshu or Cassites, who poured down from the mountains to the north of Babylon between Elam and Media. They subdued the whole land and established a dynasty lasting, according to the chronology, for 576 years. For a long time the rulers of Babylonia bear Cassite names and a number of Cassite divinities found a place in the Babylonian pantheon. The unchanging type of the inscriptions in form of writing bear out the belief now growing that these Cassites were but a late emigration of Cushites from the western branch of the race, scattered around the Ægean Sea, who were the people of Greece in the prehistoric ages. The correspondence between these Cassite kings and the Pharaohs of the Eighteenth Dynasty about 1400 B. C. and the fact that the royal houses were united by marriage again shows the Cushite relationship.

Let us examine ancient testimony to see if we can find the real origin of these Cassites. It was a race name of the original Chaldeans. Ezra V., 12, links the name Chaldean with the name Casdim. Daniel IX, 1, says that when the Babylonian army beseiged Jerusalem it was the army of the

Chaldee or Casdim. Taylor thought the Babylonians and the Casdim the same people. The races moved eastward from Kedem. Bryant in his *Ancient Mythology*, Vol. III, p. 226, fixes Kedem in the Caucasus. This more and more seems to be the center from which the three races emigrated, or near it. Let us look into the Caucasus and see if we can find the name Casdim. There today we find lingering remnants of the Iberians (ancient Cushites of Europe). Wilford in the *Asiatic Researches*, Vol. VI, p. 455, says that Ptolemy called the most ancient race of the Caucasus, Cassia or Chasas. They occupied this range from its eastern limits on the Euxine Sea to the confines of Persia. They are often mentioned in the sacred books of the Hindu and their descendants still inhabiting these regions are called Cassia to this day. One Cassite king of Babylon married an Assyrian princess. Their reign came to an end about 1207 B. C.

To what race did the Casdim belong? Sanchoniathon said that their great ancestor was Chasa or Chasya who lived before the flood and gave his name to the mountains that he seized upon. Some of the Greek legends centered about the Caucasus. This name Caucasus or Coh-Cas extended from India to the Mediterranean. The borders of Persia were inhabited by the Cassaei, there was a Mount Cassius on the border of Egypt and another in Syria. The titles of Cassius and Cassiopaeus are nearly synonymous with Jupiter, the god of Rome. The Casdim are a people mentioned in the Institutes of Menu of

India and their ancestor was Zeus-Cassius who lived before the flood. Jupiter of Rome was the Zeus of the Greeks and Zeus-Ammon or Amen-Ra of Egypt. One of the appellations of Zeus was Æthiops (Ethiopian),* the ancients also said that Zeus-Ammon was the Biblical Cush who ruled over the ancient Cushite Empire of Ethiopians, which in the earliest ages extended its colonies over three worlds. After he had seized the Caucasus, a considerable division of the people emigrated to Babylon, probably under Nimrod son of Cush. Thus we link the Cassites of the later emigrations with the earlier Chaldeans.

Let us look at the country directly north of Babylonia. Assyria until late ages was simply a province of Babylonia, and another proof that all these possessions were Cushite lay in the fact that all these northern towns had Accadian names. Accad was one of the primitive divisions under Nimrod. Many authorities translate Genesis X, 2, to read, "Out of that land, he (Nimrod) went forth into Assur or Assyria, and builded Nineveh." This is the proper translation of the passage and not that "Asher went forth and builded Ninevah," the connection is broken and destroyed by the latter mode of rendering. Asher a son of Shem being inserted among the descendants of Ham, and an event of his history narrated before his birth, first mentioned in verse 22. Mic. V, 6, calls Assyria, the land of Nimrod. Diod. Sic. II, 1, calls the founder of the kingdom Ninus.

---

*Eustathius, Schol. in Homerun.

In the unearthed remains we find the language of
the records of the early kingdom the old Hamitic
language of the Chaldeans. In later ages it became merely the language of the priests and scholars. The language of olden times changed to the
Arabic of encroaching Semitic peoples. That on
the ruins has the same origin as Hebrew; yet
only in the time of Ashurbanipal were translations made in vernacular. These things prove
that Assyria was colonized from Chaldea. The
oldest bricks are stamped with Babylonian
characters.

These inscriptions show that the northern
country was only a province of Babylonia from
which country she received her governors. Assyria had no chronology of her own until 1400 B. C.
and no certainly established date until 930 B. C.
Her line of rulers intermarried with the ruling
families of Babylon. We see the title Bel one
of the gods of the lower kingdom added to the
Assyrian line of kingly names. On the Assyrian
inscriptions we read "Bel-Lush" and very early
"Bel-Kepi." This name was in the Chaldean
titles. Some have thought Belus to have been
Jupiter, others that Belus was Nimrod, or Hercules. In both countries the external forms of
worship were alike. The special god Ashur was
unknown in the south. He must have been a
name of the Hamitic line or one of the Semitic
line of conquerors. No temple was ever built in
his honor. We find the worship of Anu and Vul
coincident with the founding of the empire. The
moon-god Sin stood at the head of the deities of

Assyria. He was connected with the beginnings
of life. As in Chaldea, this divinity outranked
the sun-god Shames. These earlier inhabitants
of Assyria had descended from the mountains
north of Elam from whence the Casdim came.
The chief Assyrian towns were built by them.
These people were very different from the later
Assyrian race.

The Assyrian monuments were full of the pride
and conceit of half savage conquerors. They
boasted of their deeds and belittled other na__ons.
They were nothing in original culture. The Assyrians at the time of their conquests were great
in invention of engins of war and in the organizing, equipping and training of armies. About
1300 B. C. we find Tig-lath-Adar signing himself
as the conqueror of Babylon. Another king was
Bel-Kudur, his line was unbroken until 1070 B. C.
He carried on destructive wars against Babylon.
1000 B. C. they had extended themselves into
Syria, this was in the time of David and Solomon.
The armies of Tiglath Pileser I, 1130 B. C. had
swept eastward and westward. He conquered
many nations just emerging from barbarism. We
find him restoring the temple of Anu out of the
spoils of conquest. His relations with Babylon
were at first friendly. Finally the southern
country was invaded. He met feeble resistance
but returning they were persued by Merodach
Iddin, the gods of Ashur were captured and carried to Babylon where they remained for four
hundred years. Up to the year 889 B. C. there
was a break in the records. 883 there was a re-

newal of vigor. 770 B. C. Pul made his appearance on the borders of Israel. Under Shalmaneser they reached their most flourishing point. Israel allying herself to Egypt refused to pay tribute. 720 B. C. the Assyrian king transported the inhabitants of Samaria to Mesopotamia, Assyria and Media.

Sargon the next king undertook the conquest of Egypt. These hosts were withdrawn from Egypt. Under his successor Media became independent, Babylon attempted to break away. Assyria was weakening and Nineveh fell under the combined armies of Media and Babylon. The ruins of Nineveh and three other distinct cities so near as to have been mistaken for one city, covered an oblong space 18 miles by 12 miles. This was ten times the area of London. Diodorus Siculus said that the suburbs of these places were so near that the whole region seemed one vast city. Xenophon said that the walls were 150 feet high and fifty feet thick so that three chariots could ride abreast on the top of the wall. The city was guarded by a moat which in one place was 200 feet broad and of great depth. Thirty miles from Nineveh was Nimrud (Nimrod). It covered an area of 1000 acres one half the extent of Nineveh. Xenophon said that these walls were one hundred feet high and twenty-five feet thick. The prostration and final weakness of Assyria sprang from the Scythic scourge, the monstrous brood from the north that swept like a disastrous flood over the southern civilizations. Attracted by the accumulated treasures and luxury of Assyria they sucked her very life's blood, that was already infested by luxury and license. It was left to the hardier Persians to deliver civilization.

The later religious beliefs of the Assyrians seemed to have but little influence upon their conduct. They broke their treaties with impunity. The spirituality of the old religion had flown, they had become materialists, even in their prayers. They sought favor of the gods by costly gifts. They sacrificed and spent seasons in times of calamity in religious fasting in which they made the beasts take part. They looked upon religon as politic and businesslike, and seemed to be but imitators of the southern race from whom the foundations of their earlier life had been laid. In science and literature they but copied and edited the contents of the Chaldean libraries. Had the Semitic race with which in later days they seemed so much intermingled been the race that gave civilization to the Mesopotamian lands, they would have been above imitation. Assyria had stone in abundance but down to the end of her dominion she used brick in slavish pattern after her neighbor at the south who did not have stone. The Babylonians were innately religious. Rich temples were devoted to the gods. In Assyria the temples were but mere annexes to the palaces and not like the earlier ones to Anu and Bel. Babylonia gave extreme attention to burial. Assyria had no tombs. The vast necropolis at Erech astonishes us with its innumerable graves. The potters of Babylon were largely employed in making clay coffins.

The Assyrians excelled as manufacturers; and foundationally had the blood of the old race. Conquest brought to them the skilled artisans of many nations. These were the producers of very much of her skilled wares. Ridpath (Vol. I, p. 199) names vases, jars, dishes and bottles of glass, bronzes, ornaments of ivory and pearl, engraved gems and broaches; rings and bells, musical instruments—cornets, flutes, harps—and implements of the house and field such were the products of Nineveh. Whatsoever the ancient soldier bore in beating down the enemy, in beseiging his town, in leading him captive from the battle, or in warding off his thrusts and blows, were produced in inexhaustible stores. In their architectural skill and mechanical genius we see the old Cushite race, it was not from the Arab in these early ages of Semitic strain to whom we can look for any development. The Saracen of a thousand years later was still a rude wanderer, saving as here in the Mesopotamian lands he had intermingled with the original inhabitants of Assyria; and when the Saracen made his sweeping conquests westward it was only to carry the precious seeds of the civilization of India, Babylonia and Egypt. Their leaders and teachers were the Cushite Arabians of the Hamitic race. India has not perished, she has the records proving these things to be true.

We must decide that Semitic infusion helped Assyria to be a race of military persuits. The blood of the Bedouin showed in their fierceness. The southern and all purely Cushite nations were ones of peaceful persuits. The men of the north were hook-nosed, larger framed, and delighted in blood and gore. Like the later Saracens they were perfect fighting machines. The ancient historian tells us that they transported and dispersed conquered nations with unimaginable sufferings. Frightful tortures were their deliberate policy. They exulted in transcribing the details of their fiendish deeds of cruelty. In the Chaldean we see the statute of the Ægean races and their genius. The southern race was shrewd, earnest. industrious, creative and humane. The Assyrian and Babylonian empires at their zenith represented all the difference of distinctive races. The rule of Assyria though extended, was very short compared to the length of the Cushite empire. Her strength was wasted by constant wars. She had waged most of them to crush her commercial rivals. After twenty years of subjection Egypt broke away. Twenty more and Babylon followed. Assyrian conquests were but an orgy of frightfulness, where they flayed alive, buried alive in living pyramids, others they impaled on stakes. They utterly destroyed rich cities, depopulated vast districts, in contrast to the Babylonians who spread the arts of civilization to prosperous and widely extended colonies.

CHAPTER XXII.

BABYLONIA THE LAND OF MARVELS.

Across the Mesopotamian plain flows two great rivers that rise in the Armenian mountains. These two great streams flowing from different angles, finally unite and enter the Persian Gulf. Here we find a rich alluvial delta like that of the Nile. North of this flat area rises the Chaldean plain, on the Tigris side being called Assyria. It was in the rich lowlands near the confluence of the rivers that the civilization of Western Asia first developed. The Mesopotamian plain is about 250 miles in length. The numerous mounds show how thickly this region was once populated. Babylon like Egypt was a country of scarcity of rain and depended upon the floods from the snowcapped mountains of Armenia for moisture. The flat low country was subject to overflow and the Babylonians had to dyke their country. Like Egypt these landmarks swept away and the knowledge of geometry developed in replacing the ancient dividing lines. Engineering developed from the building of the large and small canals that covered the country like a network, furnishing means of communication and irrigation.

The dams of the country were very ancient and the canals that covered the plains of Shinar must have required incredible skill and labor. They excavated natural lakes more deeply and turned into them the surplus waters of the Euphrates. The earth from the canals diked the rivers. The lakes were faced with stone. These stupendous dikes and canals protected the country from overflow and watered it in seasons of drought. In later days Nitrocris, princess of Egypt, assumed the direction of the great works at Babylon. Herodotus credits her with diverting the channels of the Euphrates to make a stone bridge connecting the two divisions of the city. If in no other way, we would recognize these people as Hamitic by their gigantic engineering achievements. Such works marked all their ancient sites. In India, in Arabia and in old Ethiopia, are to be found the ruins of similar indefatigable labors. We find lakes faced with heavy mortered stone, immense tanks as big as lakes, that stored water for irrigation. Under Turkish rule, the last vestages of these ancient works have gone to ruin.

5000 B. C. Mesopotamia was filled with little city republics like those of Greece and Italy. So great was the fertility of the soil that according to Herodotus, grain commonly returned two hundred fold and occasionally three hundred fold. Pliny said that wheat was cut twice from one sowing and afterwards was good keep for sheep. Quintius Curtius declared that the country between the Tigris and the Euphrates was so rich that the cattle were driven from these pastures lest they be destroyed by satiety. Berosus spoke of wheat, barley, sesame, ochrys, palms and many kinds of shelled fruits that grew wild, for here some of them originated. The soil needed only moderate labor to produce all that man required. It was natural that here should grow up one of the first populations of the ancient world. Everywhere we see the ancient remains of cities long gone to decay. In our day we have uncovered memorials that prove that the city of Niffer was the center of religious life for more than four thousand years. A period more than twice as long as Rome was the religious center of Catholic Christendom.

Delitzsch in describing Syria says, "As far as the eye can reach mounds may be seen of varying heights. They increase in size and number as we approach Susa. They are the remains of those ancient nations, the Hittites, the Assyrians, the Babylonians and the Elamites. Their palaces, temples, walls and gates, terraces and towers, lie buried beneath them." This had been a wide battle field of the armies of Egypt and western Asia, also it was the territory across which the trading caravans of these nations found their way to India or the Mediterranean. In the earliest ages the inhabitants of these regions were Ethiopians. Even in historical times the nations of Persia, Assyria, Mesopotamia, and Syria were largely permeated with this Cushite blood. This race was entirely responsible for the architectural wonders of these plains. The temples of Elam, Belbec and Babylon were reared by the same race that built the mighty structures of India and Egypt. At this age the Turanian race had produced no engineers and builders. The inscriptions of

Persepolis are of a race and age preceeding the nomadic Persians. The people of the sculptures of Nineveh are of a different lineage from the later Semitic conquerors of Nineveh. The sculptures of the Hittites and Philistines reveal the Ethiopian physiognomy.

The temples and palaces of Babylon were built upon enormous platforms high above the water soaked land. These structures were many acres in extent. They were cemented with bitumen in place of mortar made from lime. This cement has withstood the elements for ages and is superior to anything of the sort in modern masonry. The use of buttresses, drains, and of external ornamentation shows that architectural knowledge was already advanced. The temple with its huge masses of brick work, rising stage upon stage, each brilliantly painted and surmounted by a chamber, which was at once a shrine and an observatory; while the palace stood upon a heap of rubble, with open courts and imposing entrances; but never more than two or three stories high. These structures were made of sun-dried bricks. The outside was of burnt brick. These edifices have sunk down into great heaps mistaken for many centuries as hills. In the middle of the nineteenth century many were excavated. Magnificent statutes, ruins of great buildings and extensive writings, were revealed. These Sumerian libraries written upon clay tablets were composed of mythologies, religious knowledge, legal forms, astronomical, mathematical and geographical works, revealing a well developed civilization.

The material used in the body of the Babylonian structures was burnt brick of the finest and
most durable quality. The mortar was so lasting
that after the lapse of ages, the bricks can only
be separated by heavy blows. In early structures
of Babylonia we can trace the origin of the Doric
and Ionic pillars of Greece. Here Gibbon tells
us the columns branched out into fantastic forms.
These columns were rather an ornament than a
support. Like the walls overlaid with plaster and
painted with bright colors or overlaid with plates
of shining metal. The rain was carried off by elaborately constructed drains, some of which af-
ford us the earliest examples of the arch, and
which occasionally consisted of leaden pipes. In
Assyria sculpture was adopted instead of painting because they had not attained to the brilliancy
of the colors used in Babylon. The Greeks probably derived this art of painting sculpture from
the cultivated populations of the Euphrates. The
walls of their cities were of enormous thickness.
Herodotus said that the walls of Babylon were
fifty-six miles in circumference, which would include an area of two hundred square miles.

The conservative estimate of Ctesias would
make Babylon cover five times the area of London. These authorities said the walls were over
three hundred feet high with a width of eighty-
five feet. These writers were eye witnesses. Astonishing as is their report, we know that the
walls of Nineveh were one hundred and fifty feet
high at the time of Xenophon. Quintius Curtius
said that four horse chariots could pass each other

on them without danger. The city was entered
on each side by twenty-five gates of brass and
strengthened by two hundred and fifty towers.
Two of the gates were so massive that they were
opened and shut with a machine. From all the
gates proceeded streets, each 15 miles in length.
A river ran through the city from north to south.
On each side was a quay as broad as the walls
of the city. In these quays they had constructed
brass gates and steps leading down to the river.
A bridge of great beauty and ingeneous contriv-
ances was thrown across the river. On the western side of the city they had excavated an immense lake forty miles square. Herodotus said
it was thirty-five feet deep. Into this lake the
river was turned until the bridge was completed.
At the end of the bridge on each side was built
a palace and these had subterranean connections.

Babylon in those days might have been considered an enclosed district rather than a compact
city. In time of seige food could be produced
from within for the population. Perhaps the
most remarkable structure in Babylon was the
great temple of Belus. Its height was four hundred and eighty feet, being a few feet less than
the Great Pyramid of Egypt. Its summit over-
topped the city. From this height the whole
scene of the beautiful city lay spread below as a
picture. The shrine on the summit of the temple
had contained originally, Ridpath tells us, three
colossal statutes of Bel, of Beltis and of Isthar,
Here were two great censers and three golden
bowls. In front of Beltis were two lions of gold

and three silver serpents. These were accompanied by two huge bowls of silver. These splendid treasures were carried away at the time of the Persian conquest. When Herodotus visited the temple they were gone. In their place was a golden table and couch. A second and less pretentious shrine at the base of the temple was also despoiled by the Persians. Here had stood a colossal human figure wrought of solid gold, which was twelve cubits high.

Not as high but greater in ground dimensions was the royal palace. It was a quadrangular building with threefold ramparts of masonry. The outermost being nearly seven miles in extent. The inner wall measured more than two miles around. The basement of the palace was of almost incredible size. There were three bronze gates so heavy as to require machinery to open and close them. Within the enclosure were constructed the famous hanging gardens of Babylon one of the seven wonders of the ancient world. Nebuchadnezzar had constructed them for his Median wife Amyitis, who pined for the mountains of her native land. Babylon was flat. A rectangle was selected four hundred feet on one side. Around this space was built a series of open arches, and upon these serving as piers, other arches were erected. This vast structure was built to the height of seventy-five feet. Terraces rose until they over-topped the walls of the city. Earth was heaped to such depth that large trees could grow. Seeds were sown, flowers and shrubs were then set out and the largest trees transplanted from distant provinces and set up in all their beauty. A huge hydraulic machine was built on the banks of the Euphrates and by this means water was raised in pipes to the summit and distributed about the garden. From a distance the hanging gardens gave the appearance of woods overhanging mountains. From the highest terrace of his gardens the king had a perfect view of his magnificently constructed city.

The remains of the palace and gardens formed the vast mound called by the natives Kasr. Continued digging takes place in its inexhaustable quarries for brick of the finest and strongest quality. An endless succession of curious relics have been taken from this mound. Babylon in her treasury of antiquities became the rich prey of all the nations that were her conquerors. From the fallen towers and ruins of Babylon have been built all the cities of the vicinity, besides others which have gone to dust. Since the days of Alexander the Great, four capitals have been built out of the remains. The palaces of the Babylonians were splendidly decorated with the statutes of men and animals, with vessels of gold and silver and furnished with luxuries of all kinds. In the Assyrian temples everything was secular but the Chaldeans lavished their treasures upon the gods, showing the depth of their religious nature. The riches that this city possessed and her merchandise easily made her the emporium of the east and the true mistress of the ancient world. The Bible called Babylon the golden city, the glory of kingdoms and the beauty of the Chaldeans.

"Through her magnificent streets swept the
chariots of princes and monarchs. Out of her
gates of splendor, poured the bronzed cohorts of
well nigh invincible soldiers going forth to conquer. Into these same gates were driven the cap-
itves of a hundred vanquished provinces. In the
might of her power she saw her rivals one by
one expire and in her triumph she arrogated to
herself the rank and title of mistress of the world.
In the slow process of destiny her own time came
to suffer humiliation and downfall. No other
city reared by the genius and pride of man has
suffered a more complete extinction. Babylon is
literally in the dust. Only scattered mounds
which the rolling years have covered with grass
and shrubs, remain of the once mighty metropolis of the Babylonians. Birs Nimrud is the ruin
of the great temple of Nebo, that the blasts of
twenty-five centuries have not sufficed to level.
The great temple was the symbolization of Babylonian mythology. The seven platforms were
dedicated to the seven planets. To each a color
was assigned. The base was black. The second
platform dedicated to Jupiter was painted orange,
the third for Mars was red, the fourth a golden
square was for the sun, the fifth yellow, for Venus,
the sixth a blue platform for Mercury, and the
last assigned to the moon was silver." (*Ridpath's History of the World.*)

These colors were laid on in various ways,
some being burnt into the surface of the bricks,
some painted and the fourth and seventh squares
faced with thin layers of gold and silver and prob-

ably the shrine itself. This temple like that of the Medes in Ecbatana seen in successive bands of brilliant color, viewed from a distance, as the sun flashed its splendors upon the brilliant hues of the great pyramids or when the full orbed moon in milder radience diffused her light around the gigantic pile, the awe-struck worshiper may have well imagined that Nebo himself was inshrined on the summit. (*Ridpath's History of the World,* Vol. 1, pp. 263, 264.) In these temples the Babylonians offered at stated seasons human sacrifice. In the lowest strata of the excavated temples were found vessels of copper and bronze. Some of clay were lacquered in red and black in designs seemingly of Greek origin. This peculiar ware was co-eval with the products of Minoan culture which preceeded the historic Greek culture, in Hellas and was of itself Ethiopian.

To sum up, Rawlinson supposed these Chaldeans to have resembled the other Ethiopians. He concludes that the Cushites that occupied the country south of Egypt sent their colonies along the shores of Arabia, whence they crept into the Persian Gulf occupying Chaldea, Susiana and the Indus. Baldwin continuing his argument says, "The Bible points toward Africa for the central seat of the Ethiopians. It derives Nimrod from Cush not Cush from Nimrod. The monuments and traditions of Chaldea present some curious indications of East African origin. Much stress has been placed upon the theory that the Chaldeans were a mixed people but Berosus spoke of no influx of a foreign people. He identifies the

Chaldeans of the time of Nebuchadnezzar also with the primitive people of the country. The joint testimony of Berosus and the Scriptures should be sufficient. Babylonian tablets tell of an original race of black men called Admi, the Adites of the Cushite Arabian traditions. Scientists often make the statement that the original inhabitants of the earth were dark. The blond types that we see today may have developed by emigration to northern latitudes and the change was thus made from dark types to the fair-hued races of today. We will deal with the details of this argument later.

The earliest civilization of Babylonia was coeval with the earlier civilization of the Upper Nile. Ross says that Babylonian script goes back to 6000 B. C. Rawlinson mentions a Cushite inscription of 3200 B. C. Bochart points out Genises X, 7, as showing that Havelah son of Cush peopled the region where the Tigris and Euphrates unite. We know that the Hebrews while in captivity in Babylon secured the authentic geneologies of the first children of men. We would believe that the Babylonians could not have given them incorrect information as to their own origin. Diodorus Siculus said that the Chaldeans were a body of learned men resembling the priests of Egypt (both of the same race). Their whole time was spent in philosophic meditation. The learning of the Chaldeans was a family tradition. The Scriptures speak of them as the "Wise Men of the East." The son was taught by the father. Almanacs were to be found all over Babylon which was noted for its schools, libraries and temples, "The Cushite Ethiopians were the absolutely governing class in politics. They commanded the armies and held the offices of state. From them came the royal families of Babylon." (Diodorus Siculus, Bk II, Ch. 21.)

These Chaldeans were the same as the priestly race that ruled Egypt for many ages as priests and kings. As Chayas or Casdim they were the superior ruling caste of all Ethiopian colonies. Diodorus continues to speak of their great reputation in astronomy. They foretold the future and thought themselves able to ward off evil and procure benefits by their sacrifices and enchantments. They considered matter as eternal and that the arrangement and order of the world were the result of divine intelligence. Being of superior caste they inherited the stations of priests, governors and kings. Their positions of trust and dignity gave to the Babylonian kingdom the name of Chasyas or Chaldeans. Bryant in his *Ancient Mythology* (Vol. III, p. 226) quotes from Dionysus "The Chaldeans were the most ancient inhabitants of the country called by their name. They seemed to be the most early constituted and settled of any people on the earth. They seem to have been the only people who did not migrate at the general dispersion. They extended to Egypt westward and eastward to the Ganges. These were the Accadians of Chaldea, who looked to the southwest of the Caspian for the cradle of their race."

CHAPTER XIII.

THE CIVILIZATION OF BABYLONIA.

There was much disposition to underrate ancient civilization, until the recent finds of Egypt, which prove the height of the splendor of the ages that ancient tradition and records spoke of as the Golden Ages of antiquity. Rawlinson speaking in his *Ancient Monarchies,* concerning the Babylonians said, "Though not possessed of many natural advantages, the Chaldean people exhibited a fertility of invention, a genius of energy which places them high in the scale of nations and most especially those descended from Hamitic stock." Aristotle declares that the commencement is more than half the whole. Rawlinson continues, "The people who gave us our foundation in law, art and science are due more' than half the credit because they were the creators, we the promulgators. The human race lies under infinite obligation to the genius and industry of the early ages." That international egotism sweeping the continents, that would arrogate to our times the credit for the sum total of progress will only urge us to swifter retrogression. Nothing will so redeem us as study of the civilization of other races. Let us examine Babylonian culture minutely and compare it with the culture of today.

It is certain that we must credit Babylonians with possessing recorded knowledge of the creation and remembrance of epochs in the antediluvian world. The archaic account of Berosus bears the stamp of being genuine in origin. It runs a singular parallel with the Bible narrative. They both describe the beginning of the world as being one of chaos. The Bible makes but little more than the mere statement but the account of Berosus goes into the details. In the Babylonian story there was sad mixture of animal forms as well as of land and atmosphere until divine wisdem incarnated in God brought order out of confusion. There were monstrous animals and reptiles as the rocks of geology reveal. Nature from age and experience does not today so cross the germs of life. The primitive nations went to infinite pains in sculpture to reproduce these diabolical forms. A woman deity, as appears in Revelations, seemed to have presided at the beginning. All the unearthed sculptured idols of the primitive ages were feminine. Ancient art again supporting tradition. All Cushite colonies sculptured many animal forms.

There were revolting and seemingly impossible monstrosities in Greek and Babylonian cosmogony. They were but primitive conceptions of chaos and cannot be ignored because they are incomprehensible to us, from their vast distance in time and our evolution from such conditions. The real meaning of these pagan mysteries have at times focussed the mental ability of an age; but most of them still remain incomprehensible mysteries. They are traditions about conditions more accurately related by the, Bible. In no essential points do they differ. All men were distroyed because of wickedness. The, survivors of the flood had been warned of God. An ark of immense proportions was prepared. Archaeology has proved that the men of this age understood ship building. The Chaldean Noah entered the ark with his wife and children. Upon the recession of the waters he sent out three birds three times. He built an altar and offered sacrifice.

The life of the Semitic and Hamitic races must have been closely associated after the deluge. So close is the apparent relationship, that some authorities have looked upon Abraham as Hamitic. Abraham came from Ur of the Chaldees. But he descended by direct line from a Semitic father. His mother may have been Hamitic for Abraham was spoken of as a Chaldean. All down the line of the after years we find Hebrews taking wives out of the Ethiopian race. The Babylonian account of the deluge is older than the Biblical story. It does not take away from it but rather corroberates its truth. There is the same close relationship between the code of Hammurabi and the Mosaic law. Both were inspired by a common Creator. The Chaldean law was perhaps the Ethiopian remembrance of the best of the jurisprudence of the antediluvian world. Read the statutes of Hammurabi and you will be astounded at the likeness of these and the lesser laws of Israel. It was written long before the giving of the Mosaic law. The "Wisemen of the East," seeking the young child prove that they held the wires of revelation. The hope of the coming of a Messiah was written upon Babylonian tablets more than 2000 B. C.

The Babylonians were planet worshippers. This form was distinctly Hamitic. Abraham was called out of Chaldea because they had descended to the worship of idols. In their religious literature are penitential hymns that compare favorably with the Hebrew psalms. Though the seven planets and the sun were adored yet in early Chaldea the unity of God was distinctly taught. The cuniform tablets in the British museum address him as God-one. The famous Epic of Gilgamesh has been identified with the biblical Nimrod. The Seven Labors of Hercules were simply a Greek appropriation of the deeds of the Babylonian hero. The fragments of the tablets that tell the story of the creation and the deluge date back to 1900 B. C. and seem to be copies of still more ancient documents. With the later infusions from other races came the gross incantations and beliefs in evil spirits of later days. They sought to cope with them by magic. All the popular superstitions of the Middle Ages regarding demons, witchcraft and magic came from Babylon and to great extent were the cause of her downfall.

The study of the future through the stars became a popular false science. They sought to fix man's destiny through the good and evil influence of comets, planets and eclipses. These beliefs had great influence upon later Greece and Rome.

Those who seek to read their fate in the stars are following a Babylonian invention. Like the Etruscans they were very skillful in foretelling the future. By human sacrifice they sought to ward off evil and procure blessings for themselves. Africa is full of such superstitions. They divined from the flights of birds and were versed in the meaning of dreams and portents. Their philosophy passed down from father to son and constantly remained in the possession of one family. They believed that all that appears in heaven and earth is not the result of accident or fatal necessity but is the result of the wisdom of God. They believed that twelve superior stars ruled over the affairs of a man's life, and that he would be influenced by the peculiar attributes of the star of the month that gave him birth. (Diodorus Siculus Bk. II, ch. 21.)

The astronomy of the early Chaldeans was without the astrological features of later times. It was built upon scientific principles. Diodorus Siculus said that the Chaldeans could attribute comets to their natural causes and could fortell their reappearance. Seneca estimated that their theory of comets was as exact and intelligent as that of moderns. Ideler of Berlin, has shown that in their ancient calculations of the eclipse of the moon, quoted by Ptolemy, they differed from modern calculations only in minute degree. Observatories were set up in all the chief towns and royal astronomers sent regular reports to the king. In the British Museum are the fragments of a planisphere which marked the appearance

of the sky at the vernal equinox. The astronomical discoveries of the Chaldeans must have required long ages of patient observation. Alexander the Great, when he took possession of Babylon 331 B. C., found a series of astronomical observations taken by the Chaldeans stretching for
an unbroken period of 1903 years. These recorded observations dated from 2234 B. C. From this
foundation of indefatigable labors we have built
up the astronomical science of modern times.

The Chaldeans must have understood the manufacture of the telescope, for Layard reported
the discovery of a lens of power in the ruins of
Babylon. Nero the emperor of Rome had optical
glasses from the east. The most important work
of the Accadians, or the early Babylonians was
the invention and perfection of the calendar,
which with trifling changes we use today. At this
early day they had numbered and had also
named the stars. The equator was divided into
three hundred and sixty degrees. 2200 B. C. they
had named the twelve months of thirty days each
after the zodiacal signs. 2234 B. C. they had discovered the solar circuit. Their standard work
on astronomy was in seventy-two books and was
called the illumination of Bel and is now preserved in the British Museum. The duo-decimal
system was invented by the Babylonians. A tab-
let from the library at Larsa gives a table of
squares and cubes correctly calculated from one
to sixty. A series of geometrical figures used for
augural purposes implies a Babylonian Euclid.
They were the inventors of the dial for measur-

ing time. All the peoples of antiquity derived their systems of weights, measures and capacities from them. Those mathematical tables stand unchanged in our text books today, still used by our boasted civilization.

Myers says that aside from letters, the tables of weights, measures and capacity are the most indispensible agents in the life of a people. All the transactions of commercial life are dependent upon them. This race from its parent stock gave writing to the world. At a very early period the art was extensively practiced. In the early inscriptions there is no evidence of the wedge writing of the cuniform inscriptions. The wedge shape was caused by the later use of stylus to form the letters and the soft clay, which in drying produced the wedge shape. Semites borrowed this Sumerian system of writing. After Semitic conquest it continued the sacred ritual language of the Babylonian temples until the time of Alexander the Great. The modern man but little realizes how much the ancients contributed to our modes of thought, to our comforts and the accurate transaction of our business. At the dawn of history this ingenious people was in full possession of the principles of the wheel. When the Chaldeans first appear they were driving horses hitched to vehicles. Our method and the style of wheel are identical. There is so much in modern life that we are sure is our own invention, that has been appropriated out of that old life. Solomon truly said that there is no new thing under the sun.

Babylon was the seat of the costliest manufactures of the ancient world. Modern nations have developed more complicated machinery but the products that we weave are inferior. We are unable to produce linen as fine in texture as that wound around the mummies in the tombs of Egypt. The oldest Babylonian gems furnish us with pictures of richly embroidered dresses. She excelled all others in the manufacture of durably dyed and varigated goods. The carpets of Babylon were prized above those of every nation. Because of their greater elegance such products from the Orient are more costly than ours today. Their dyes were imperishable, the designs were artistic and beautiful, here also cotton goods were produced of the finest quality. Many of the carvings were so minute as to suggest the use of magnifying glasses, and modern ingenuity is taxed to know how their gem cutting was done. The minuteness of some of their engravings seem impossible. They were inventors of the art of inlaying metals. Modern artists learned from them the method of covering iron with bronze. Goldsmiths' work had attained a high perfection at a very early period. The elegance of their engravings excites the envy of the modern lapidary. The beauty of their furniture was worthy of imitation.

The ancient Babylonians were a legal-minded people. Law was highly developed. The mother occupied a prominent place in the community in early times. The Code of Hammurabi was in force 2250 B. C. It shows a high sense of justice.

It embodied the needs of a settled community whose chief occupations were agriculture and commerce. Gibbon tells us that the rights of persons and of property were clearly set forth and carefully guarded. Crimes were severely punished. Marriage and family were the subject of wise provisions. Inheritance was regulated and the interests of widow and orphans duly protected. Commerce was highly developed and Babylonian merchants had extensive connections with other lands. Judges were forbidden to accept bribes and prisons were to be found in every town. A son was fined who denied his father and banished if he disowned his mother. In contrast do not such wise provisions tower high beside tardy legislation of today? The expedition of the University of Pennsylvania unearthed documents at Thebes, which prove that Mesopotamian cities five thousand years ago had systems of municipal government similar in fundamental principles to those of modern cities. They had a postal system with a parcel post branch and a banking system with a reserve bank not unlike what we have today.

Babylonian bankers loaned money at high rate, the persons and families of the borrowers being the security. They were sold as slaves if the payment was not made. This was their method of settling the debtor, which question of the dishonest debtor we have not yet settled. Not violence but order was the rule. In those days public and private crooks were given but brief trial; if guilty they were summarily dumped into the

river. All deeds were drawn with that careful-
ness that denotes a wide-spread understanding of
the law. They were duly witnessed, sealed and
registered in the principal temple. Some of the
taxes were paid to support public brick-yards
and roads. No family was complete without
children. Bachelors were in ill repute. It was
common to adopt sons by law. Among the tablets
unearthed were religious texts, tax lists, real estate contracts. Houses were let on lease and the
deeds contained a careful inventory of their contents. These revelations set us wondering as to
the manifold forms and usages of modern life that
are not original as we have thought but that have
passed down to us from the hoary Babylonians.
Out of the ruined temples we have unearthed
images of divinities, terra cotta toys, weapons,
and instruments of stone and metals, ornaments
of gold, silver, copper, bronze and precious stones,
proving these people to have been far advanced
in the arts of civilization.

Agriculture occupied a prominent place. The
canals were of special importance and their man-
agement was superintended by the state. The
country was covered by gardens. This people
were skilled in pottery of unusual beauty and finish. Some of the dead were buried under huge
inverted dishes and in large earthenware jars.
They were skilled in terra cotta works. The images of King Gudea are quite astonishing when
we consider their antiquity. We may be sure
the best specimens have not come to us when we
remember the vandal destruction of the art of the

past. Some of their potteries were rude like those of Mexico and Peru. Others excelled the beauty of Greek vases. As other Cushite nations they sculptured the forms of animals. In Assyria no tombs appear, but the tombs of Chaldea are so plentiful that large spaces are literally filled with bones and relics of the dead. Sometimes the coffins were piled one upon another to the depth of from thirty to sixty feet, and for miles out into the desert the very soil under foot seems to be nothing but the accumulated dust of dead races.

We must conclude that the early Babylonians were skilled mechanics and engineers. They understood the use of the pulley, the lever, and the roller. Explorers found on the site of Babylon the remains of hydraulic machinery used for watering the hanging gardens. They were in possession of the microscope and telescope. Babylonian tablets contained zoological, botanical and geological writings in scientific classification. The capital had great libraries with the books grouped by subject and catalogued. The deftness and regularity with which the cuniform inscriptions were made are the amazement of modern scholars. The old Sumerian texts were accompanied by interlinear translations sometimes arranged in parallel lines. Great attention was paid to the ancient Sumerian speech by the Babylonian priestly scholars, as proved by the large number of texts of that kind that have been found. The tablets were hardened by a process which rendered them practically imperishable.

This race had taught writing and had established the institutions of city, home and state when other races were wandering barbarians. They gave the constellations of the heavens the names of the old kings of the ancient Cushite empire of Ethiopians and we in adopting them have not realized that the ancestors of the despised Ethiopians among us reached that height in ability to dare to name the stars. As the language of Babylonia changed there was a corresponding intermixture of blood with alien races. The habits and nature of the people changed. Amidst the luxuries and wealth that came from her conquests and commerce the people became effeminate and voluptuous. Curtiss said that at the last nothing could be more corrupt than their morals. Money dissolved every tie whether of kindred or esteem. They became immoderate in their use of wine. The women at the last threw away all sense of decency. On the grounds of this awful wickedness Babylon was threatened with destruction at the hands of the prophets. The prophecy was fulfilled. "Babylon is fallen, that great city, because she made all the nations to drink of the wine of the wrath of her fornication." The earlier Cushite life had been pure.

539 B. C. Babylon was invaded by the Persians. From behind the massive walls they were regarded with derision. Nabonadius in his profound contempt risked a battle in which his troops were defeated. The larger portion of the army retreated into the city but the king and the remainder sought to divide the forces of the enemy. In

Babylon there was little fear for they considered their city impregnable. For a season the forces of Cyrus beat against the city in vain. Leaving a portion of his army to engage the attention of the Babylonians, Cyrus departed from the city and going back up the course of the river he sought means to divert its channel. He cut canals for this purpose. He waited for the great pagan feast when the young prince and the court would give themselves up to a night of dissipation. A thousand nobles had been invited to the banquet at the palace. At a given signal, when the revelry was at its height, the sluices were opened by the Persians into their canals and the river began to fall. Land enough appeared for the Persians to make the passage along the edge of the channel. The river gates were seized and opened and the massacre began. Cyrus only dismantled the walls. 500 B. C. upon a revolt, Darius threw down the walls and expelled them from their homes. In the time of Strabo and Diodorus Siculus the place lay in ruins.

Recent investigations of Oxford University at Kish in Mesopotamia reveal that the Sumerians were a black people and the founders of the earliest civilization in the world. The value and variety of the unearthed art works have exceeded all expectation and reveal also that they were artizans possessing skill and knowledge unprecedented among other ancients. The report from the Field Museum says, "Jewels of exquisite ancient workmanship, finely engraved cylinder seals of inestimable historical value, glazed pottery of unique and rare design and artistic inlay work of silver and lapis lazuli are included in these discoveries according to D. C. Davies, director of the museum, and Professor S. Langdon, Assyriologist, who is heading the expedition. Most of the articles, all from 5000 to 7000 years old and of pre-Babylonian times, were found in a necropolis on the eastern side of the city and comprise personal property placed in the tombs and graves of the dead.

The various stages of craftmanship in cruder designs disclose that the Sumerians, a non-Semitic race, in addition to organizing the art of writing also developed metallurgy, glazing, glass making and various other arts. Excavations of the tombs and graves, which consist of brick lined chambers of uneven depth large enough to accommodate the body and the personal belongings is proceeding slowly owing to the fact that many objects once uncovered, crumble before they can be removed. The burial places and buildings are now completely covered with sand and soil and have the appearance of mounds linked together. Hairpins with ornamental heads of precious stones and worked metal were found in nearly all of the fifty or more graves already opened. Slender daggers of copper and silver, with handles of wood or bone inlaid with silver, were found in others. Silver medallions, engraved to represent the rising sun, silver fillets for elaborate coiffures, various sorts of delicately engraved cylindrical seals of silver, glass, copper and stone used in legal transactions, clay and metal pottery

and urns, battle axes of metal and stone and various kinds of precious stones have been removed.

"One unusual type of pottery was figured and possessed handles moulded to depict the bust of Nintud, the Sumerian mother goddess of child birth. Of the metal implements and ornaments uncovered, the copper because of its purity was in the best state of preservation, the other metals were corroded by the salts of the soil. Spindles and wheels, exemplifying the art of spinning wool were found in the tombs of several women. The whorls especially were artistically made of a porous white substance or shells and inlaid with lapis lazuli. Pins, finger rings, bracelets and other personal ornaments of copper and silver were also mounted with carnelian, haemtite, jasper, rock crystal and calcite. A gorgeous white pin setting that resembled a pearl, dissolved before the eyes of the excavators as the air came in contact with it. Despite the large variety of rare jewelry excavated, no gold was found in the tombs. The care and skill with which the silver was worked indicated it was probably the most precious metal of that day. The golden era of Kish in the later Babylonian period was, however, exemplified in the discovery of a solid gold earring, in the form of an opening pomegranite bud, an unparalleled **work** of art, in a clay coffiin of the fifth century **B. C.**

AMENEHAT I. (TWELFTH DYNASTY.)
Colossal head in red granite, from the ruins of the Great
Temple of Tanis.
Photographed by Mr. W. M. F. Petrie.

CHAPTER XV.

THE CIVILIZATION OF INDIA.

Asia is a continent in which republics were unusual in early ages. Here history reveals monarchies under despotic rulers, who were worshipped
as though the subjects were mere slaves. India
until late ages was under a very different form of
government. In early Buddhist times we find the
land full of aristocratic republics. This was the
same form of government to be found on other
Cushite sites. Here in a more isolated clime, remote from outside influences, the old Cushite
communal form of government has come on down
to our times. Much can be gained from a study
of this unique system. Out of it came the gentleness of the Hindu and it was the environment that
nourished his exalted mental attainments. Again
it is too lightly considered, when we remember
that this form of life produced artists and craftsmen who brought into existence lost arts and a
skill and originality that we do not today attain.
It is a common error to suppose that the tribes
that the Aryan invaders found were savages.
Ancient annals represented the Cushite Indi as
wise and skillful. Heeren said that these writings represented the early Hindu as a commercial
people, that their merchants could travel from one

of the Nile flowing through Barabra (Ethiopia) and the mountains of the Moon.

Even the name Hindu is Ethiopian. Ancient records of authority made Hind and Sind sons of Cush. Philostratus in Vit. Apollon (Lib. II), says, "The Indi are the wisest of mankind. The Ethiopians are a colony of them, and they inherit the wisdom of their fathers." The separation of India from the parent Cushite stock was in ages long before the rise of the so-called Aryans in India. The older Greeks always associated the sacred waves of the Indian Sea with the wonderful Ethiopians. Ephorus stated that they occupied all the southern coasts of Asia and Africa. As in Chaldea they brought to the aboriginal tribes of India the knowledge of metals to take the place of stone implements, they brought the knowledge of the arts. Their funeral remains all over India reveal the stone circles and upright massive menhirs of North Africa. They understood in those far distant ages how to make hard earthenware, iron weapons and ornaments of gold. Today in a state of degenerated art, Sind is the only province where the potters craft is artistic. Before Megathenes, a Greek ambassador to the court of the non-Aryan Chandra Gupta, about 300 B. C., the Greeks mentioned as Indi only the Cushites of the areas between the Hindu Kush and Persia.

The name India means black, and Condor thinks that it was employed only to designate the home of the Asiatic Ethiopians. Let us look for a brief space at the land. India has often been described as almost a continent of itself, surrounded as it is by high mountain ranges to the north with the spurs stretching out to east and west, leaving only two natural passages down into the peninsula. India has a rich and varied climate and landscape. First come the Himalayas with their colder atmosphere, then the vast, fertile, densely populated plains of northern India watered by the Indus, the great Ganges and the Bramaputra. These have the greatest volume of any rivers of the world. South of the great northern plain is the elevated plateau of Decan. The Ganges has meant so much to the life and development of the country that it is a sacred river to the Hindu. Almost all the traffic of the country passes up and down this river. Southern India has a tropical climate. The Indian plains are sultry but Decan and the slopes of the Himalayas enjoy a temperate climate. There are two annual seasons the rainy and the dry.

Modern books deal with forest destruction in India and the wearing out of the land. These are the result of conquest and the crowding back of tribes upon the more waste areas. The great Indian rivers cause terrible disasters through floods that sweep off cattle, grain, stores and houses. The mighty currents undermine and carry away soil to build up monstrous deltas. Still with all these disasters India has an age old system of agriculture and we see everywhere the evidences of a people long skilled in agriculture. Northern India produces the plants of the temperate zone in profusion. Southern India abounds in tropical verdue. Two harvests are sometimes reaped in one year. Rice grows in the irrigated districts. Many think that cotton was first developed in India and that many other important plants found there their origin. We find indigo, jute, tobacco, sugar cane, cocoa, the date and other palms. Among the tropical fruits are the orange, lime, citron, melon, pineapple, fig and other fruits. The dense growth of tropical woods affords some of the world's most important plants. Here we find resins, gums, perfumes and varnishes with hundreds of other articles of commerce or luxury.

These wonderful and useful plants and fruits of India are not the result of accident, but are the fruit of the genius of some continuously agricultural race. These products were the foundation of the age old art and commerce of the Indies, that in the days of Columbus made the route to India the world sought quest of western nations. Nearly every article that produces commerce abounds in India. All the shrubs and herbs needed for the healing of the nations may be found there and are used as native medicines. Rice and millet are the staple foods, though sweet potatoes, onions, barley and garlic are much used. The vast forests are densely populated with wild animals and birds. The leopard, wolf, tiger, hyena, fox and jackal abound, the lion is extinct. Snakes and reptiles cause innumerable deaths. The tiger is in every part of the country. One tiger in the course of three years killed one hundred and eight persons and another caused thirteen villages to be abandoned. There is a government price on the tiger's head. The tamer animals are deer, sheep, goats, antelope, oxen, camels, mules, horses and many birds. With this rich flora and fauna a distinctive ancient life developed and flowered as gorgeously in religion and art.

A glance at India today reveals a great difference from the old condition of opulence. The country has grown overpopulated. Many districts are so overcrowded that the natives can hardly secure land to cultivate. Life in the British Isles is very conjested, the population being about 213 to a square mile, but in India we find 271 to the square mile. In England the people support themselves by working in the industries. India has very few large towns. Millions are struggling to live and support themselves on half an acre. If the rains fall short by only a few inches, there is terrible scaricity of food and thousands die. This condition is due to the fact also that the old industrial system of the Hindu has been destroyed. Once they manufactured in their homes and thus kept themselves from want. During the centuries of misrule after the various conquests of India, the land became full of robbers and armed bands. Since introduction of railroads by the English, the natives are slowly moving from the conjested districts to the few remaining spare lands. In ancient days each rural family was rooted to the spot of its ancestry.

The first glimpses that we catch of the Hindu in historical times we find a people of varied ethnology. The popular theory emphasizes an Aryan invasion that took place in late ages, compared to the primitive times when the deeds of the Indian epics were enacted. As late as the authoritative records of history, the most powerful kingdoms of India were ruled over by non-Aryan princes. These were the Indi of the ancient records. This ruling race had produced the culture that passed down, and just as across all the wide belt of the equator the civilization of the ancient Cushite was appropriated—here it was not destroyed. So intermixed are all the classes of the Hindu today that all Brahmin, and Soudra have identically the same formation of skull, the old formation of Ethiopia. This later Brahmic type which has only ruled India in the Christian Era is Turanian in the same sense that the races of western Europe may be so called. These Turanians entering India were inferior in culture to the Indi. Today after continued conquest, we find great peoples using literary languages among the Dravidians who represent the primitive Cushite stock. Such are the Tamlis, Telugu, Malayalam and Kanarese. Authorities dispute the claim that the black Rajputs were the same race as the invading Turanians. The ancient books read without prejudice reveal a deadly contest between Brahmins and the Kshattriyas, the original royal stock.

The literature reveals that this hostility did not come to an end until the Brahmins gave up the hope of holding the sovereignty and took over the custody of the ancient books and the priesthood. We read in *Buddhist India,* p. 44, that it is a common error to suppose that the tribes with whom the so-called Aryans came in contact were savages. Some were, but there were also settled communities with a highly developed social organization, wealthy enough to excite the cupidity of invaders. These people were too much addicted to peace to be able to offer prolonged resistance, but they were strong enough to impose many of their ideas and institutions upon their conquerors. On page 59 we read, "It is now generally admitted that there are no pure Aryans in India, in spite of the theoretical restricions on intermarriage. Aryan, Kolarin and Dravidian could not at the time of the rise of Buddah be recognized. Long before the theory of caste had been brought into working order a fusion sufficient at least to obliterate completely the old landmarks had been accomplished." In the ancient books of India there is, no mention of caste. Long before the time of Alexander all the Hindu were a dark race.

Baldwin declares that Indo-Aryans were but a small proportion of the whole population of India. All over the country are masses, whose dialects reveal that they did not belong to the Indo-European group. Cushites entering India in primitive ages perhaps found aboriginal Malays. They did not exterminate them but conciliated, civilized and to some extent absorbed them. This was the Ethiopian custom over their wide domains. In the central provinces an aboriginal Malay race forms a large proportion of the population, showing that the Cushites may have refused to intermix. The struggle represented as taking place between these Cushites and their conquerors might have been but a later emigration of their race as the Cassite invaders of Chaldea. We would think this from the identity of skull formation of all the racial divisions of India. The hill people of the Himalayas have always been fair, as we find Cushite people on all the continents where they were not exposed to the torrid rays of the sun. The Casdim or Cassites of ancient days occupied the highlands of southwestern Asia from Caucasus to the highlands of India. Does it not seem more reasonable that this learned race as proved by the Chaldeans and Elamites sent the type into India that made her ruling class.

(5000 years ago we have shown there was no branch of the Aryan race that could have produced the Rig-Veda. 5000 years ago no Japhethic nation possessed blacksmiths, chariots, and the civilization that the Rig-Veda reveals. It seems to be the story of the passage to the southwest of Hindu colonists from the mountains of Hindu-Kush (Cush) down into the plains of India. Note the name of the region from which they came. In the beginning these invaders took Dravadian wives because most probably they were primarily of the same stock. 3000 to 4500 B. C. the father is represented with the ancient Cushite traits in all their glory. He was priest of the family. He conducted human sacrifice, for which the horse sacrifice was substituted in later ages. There was no burning of widows and woman enjoyed a high position. The Rig-Veda represents these people at this far distant age as blacksmiths, barbers, coppersmiths, goldsmiths, carpenters and husbandmen. They fought from chariots as did all Cushite nations. They settled down as husbandmen to till the fields. Unlike the modern Hindu they ate beef. They adored gods identical with those of Egypt, Chaldea and Ethiopia. Who were these people who 4500 B. C. possessed towns and built ships? Semites and Turanians had no such arts.

When the Hebrews left Egypt they did not understand the art of welding iron. Persians in late ages used Egyptians as their carpenters. The historic Greek and Roman at this early age had not emerged from caves and use of rude stone tools. Let us glance at the Goths as they appeared on the plains of western Europe as late as the Christian Era and see if we find the race traits that the Rig-Veda reveals. They possessed no knowledge of metals. They scorned images and temples, therefore they had no priests. The name of not a single Gothic deity has come down to us. They showed not the faintest glimmer of the mentality and austerity of life of the Buddhist. They were coarse and gluttonous. They loved strong drink and would lay for days in drunken stupor in the ashes of their hearths. They appropriated the gods of the long headed race of western Europe, Odin and Thor. They knew nothing of agriculture being a nomadic race fitted for conquest. They had no communal interests as the people of India, they were extreme individualists. They battered down the grand structures of antiquity, they did not create them and smashed the art treasures of ages. Even in the Middle Ages they had developed none of the traits of the gentle Hindu and regarded not the rights of others unless compelled to do so by the sword.

Beside this picture let us line the Hindu priest. His is a type that early was devoted to ceremony. His whole life was mapped out for stages of discipline. When he had reared a family and gained a practical knowledge of the world, he retired into the forest as a recluse, using nature's wild foods. Here he practiced religious duties with increased devotion. Next he entered upon an ascetic and rigorous self-denial, wandering as a religious mendicant, wholly withdrawn from joy or pain, wholly absorbed in final absorption into the deity. He ate nothing but what was given him unasked, remained not more than one day in a village. Throughout his life he took no wine, curbed desire, shut out tumults of war, his duty was to pray and not to fight, to study and practice self restraint. The Brahmin represents a race in India that holds supremacy not by force of arms but by vigor of hereditary culture and temperence. Dynasties have fallen, religions have spread themselves over the land and disappeared, but since the dawn of history the Brahmin has calmly ruled.

As late as the Græco-Bactrian and Scythian inroads 327 B. C. to 544 A. D. we find the fairest districts of northern India still in possession of Cushites. In almost every part of Oudh and the northwestern provinces are to be found ruins ascribed to this race, which reigned at different periods from the fifth to the eleventh centuries A. D. The early invaders found as the Vedas describe, these people in possession of wealth, having cattle, cities and forts. The literature represents them as making alliances with the native Cushite princes, this would have been impossible if they had not been of the same race. The Nubians (Cushites) of old Ethiopia will not intermarry with Arabs or Egyptians. Some superficial interpretations of the Vedas attempt to make out the Dravidian Cushites as disturbers of sacrifices, lawless, without gods, and without rites. This would not describe Cushites anywhere in the world. For at no stage of their development do they seem to be without sacrifice, law and religion, which rites they gave to the ancient world. That section of the Vedas describes Cushites finding the aborigines of the country without these rites, which they naturally at first opposed.

To those who read the Rig-Veda intelligently and without the confusing glasses of prejudice, these mutilated and interpolated writings are but a description of the familiar traits and customs of Cushite Ethiopians. The Brahmins were probably a much later and intermixed branch of the inhabitants of Hindu-Kush. That they were intermixed we can tell by their cruelty. Full blooded Cushites are very gentle. The fact that the Brahmins altered the Sanskrit writings to such great extent is proof itself that they were not the original authors of these works. They took over and appropriated much from Buddhism that would appeal to the masses when they found it otherwise impossible for them to sit in the saddle of the priesthood. An ancient treatise tells us of the early Cushite element, that they adorned their dead with gifts, with raiment, and ornaments, immagining thereby that they shall attain the world to come. Their ornaments were bronze, copper and gold. One non-Aryan chief described this race as of fearful swiftness, unyielding in battle, in color like a dark blue cloud. This old type is represented today by the compact masses at the south. These Dravidians constitute forty-six millions of southern Indians today. They represent the unmixed Cushite type. All the rest of the blood of India is heavily mixed with this strain.

These Dravidians that the untruthful book seeks to represent today as despised outcasts when they are still a very important division of the Hindu population, entered India in primitive times by the northwest passage. They were a part of that advancing wave of the Old Race that swept eastward and westward, peopling primitive Arabia, Egypt and Chaldea. The rich merchants of the ancient Indian commerce had been Dravidians. One of their greatest kingdoms was Pandya so noted in the Sanskrit writings. The Nandas in Behar of whom the great Chandra Gupta sprang and his greater grandson Asoka, were non-Aryan. These were of the supposed-to-be degraded Sudra. The Takshak and Naga nations who figure so largely in Sanskrit traditions are words purely African. Koch or Kush (Cush) form the masses of Bengal and Behar. By virtue of their descent from the old dominant race they retain their name of Kshattriya and call themselves Rajbansis a term exactly corresponding to Rajput. The rajas of Kuch Behar claim a divine descent. The name Rajput means of royal descent. It was the title of the old conquering class of the ancient Cushites. There was alliance between them and the Brahmins. We find distinguished bodies of the Kshattriyan so-called caste received into the Brahmin caste and for the same reason sections of aboriginal races manufactured into Brahmins.

In the Hindu Puranas the Dravidian kingdom of Pandya was given two dynasties. The first had seventy-three kings, the second forty-three kings. The last king of the second dynasty was overthrown 1324 A. D. by the Mohammedans. No other Dravidian kingdom can boast so continuous a succession as the kings of Madura. The chronicles enumerate fifty Chara kings and fifty-six Chola kings as well as many minor dynasties. Dr. Deiche and Isaac Taylor thought the Hindu alphabet derived from the south Arabian and adopted a thousand years later by the Brahmins. The early history of the Dravidians is yet to be deciphered from mouldering palm leaves and more trustworthy inscriptions on copper and stone. Like the Minoan script of Crete and the Merotic of Ethiopia this is a third of the Ethiopic stem that has not been interpreted. In the territory of the Dravidians, we find extensive ruins of ancient temples, fortifications, tanks, bridges and vast remains.

The Dravidians in ethnic type are Ethiopian and are the race of India from which her civilization originated. Megathenes said that the naitves of India and Ethiopia were not much different in complexion or feature. Dravidians are short like the race of the Mediterranean called Iberians and the Chaldeans. Their complexions are black or very dark. Their hair is plentiful and crispy. Their heads are elongated with the nose very broad. They occupy the oldest geological formation of India. They are descendants of that race of black men with short woolly hair that were the primitive inhabitants of ancient Media, Susiana and Persia, mentioned repeatedly in the Iranian legends, and whose faces look out at us from the sculptures of Babylon and Nineveh Dravidian is spoken by forty-six millions of India, not including the numerous uncultivated hill tribes and retired communities. A form of speech similar to it is spoken in Beluchistan, which originally was Cushite. In all the political changes that come to India, the communal type of life to which these natives cling never changes.

In ancient times India was ruled by Rajas, who were assisted by a council of elders. Sometimes the Raja was influenced by a queen mother or dowager. In Cushite races lineage was traced through the mother. The succession of the Rajah was traced in the same way. This was changed upon the ascendency of the Brahmins. Turanians trace lineage from the father's side. Some authors have sought to prove that the metronymic system or inheritance through the female line is evidence of promiscuity in the beginning of human life. In savage life men and women pair in mating, also among anthropoid apes proving that this instinct is as old as the human species. The spirit of the Cushite was to honor and exalt woman, therefore lineage was thus traced. Nephews when born of sisters were treated as sons and inherited the property to the exclusion of sons. Devalle described the queen of Ilaza as a black Ethiopian. He said she ruled like a woman of judgment. Marco Polo described the inhabitants of India as black and adorned with massive gold bracelets and strings of rare and precious gems. They had temples and priests. Vasco de Gama while circumnavigating the globe found the inhabitants black.

CHAPTER XIV.

ANCIENT INDIA THE LAND OF MYSTERY.

India has always been a land of mystery. The facts of her beginning and the origin of her culture have been the subject of much contradiction. Some would pronounce her a land of late development and that her rock hewn temples and hoary monuments were built after the beginning of the Christian era. Rawlinson says of the early founders of Indian civilization, "Recent linguistic discoveries show that a Cushite race did in the earliest times extend itself along the southern shores of the continents from Abyssinia to India. The whole peninsula of India, the sea coast of Beluchistan and Kerman by the inscriptions belonged to this race." Wilford who had an extended and thorough knowledge of Hindu mythology points out that the Sanskrit writings, the sacred literature of India, describe the extended domains of the ancient Cushite empire. In these books are relations about early Egyptian history. It mentioned one of the emigrations going out from the Upper Nile as having peopled India. The Puranas divided the world into seven dwipas or divisions. Sancha Dwipa was Africa in general. Cusha Dwipa was the land of Cush, India and the Mediterranean. These books speak place to another with perfect security to themselves and their merchandise.

Alexander the Great found the natives of India not living under a monarchial system, but in republics. From very ancient times there had been indirect trade between India and the Mediterranean but it was with the Ægean civilization that had preceeded the historic Greek and of which Greece had no record. Alexander found that Nysa had a senate of three hundred members. Many of these republics were very powerful and warlike, opposing Alexander as he had scarcely been resisted anywhere else. His victories were purchased at vast price of blood. Walls and ramparts encircled their cities. Their encampments were protected by triple lines of military wagons and cars. They had boats and vessels. One of the temple reliefs represents the fore part of a vessel filled with strangers. In Multan, in Malle and Oxydracae, nearer the Ganges, there were still more powerful nations. (Ibid. V, 23-24.) At Sangola thousands perished. Many tribes deserted their cities preferring exile to subjugation. The reports of the mighty armies of the native Parsii, the modern Bengal, and Oude, so terrified the hitherto unconquered Macedonians that they retreated. (*Historical Researches in the Nations of Antiquity,* Heeren, Vol. I, p. 319.) How different is this report by a careful student of the records of the past, to what we read in the hastily written volumes of today.

Buddhist India, by Rhys-Davids gives a clear and interesting picture of the communal system of India. The villages consist of houses all built together, separated by narrow lanes. Immediately adjoining is the sacred grove or primeval forest, left standing when the first clearing was made. Beyond is the wide expanse of cultivated fields. There are grazing grounds for cattle and jungle where every villager has the equal right of wood and waste. The cattle belonged severally to the householders of the village. After crops they roam the fields under the charge of herdsmen hired collectively and a man skilled in cattle care. The fields are all cultivated at the same time. Irrigation channels are laid out by the community. The supply of water is regulated by rule under the supervision of head men. There is a common fence. The great fields are divided into plots corresponding to the heads of the families in each village. Each family takes the produce of its share.'' Compare our system of monster bonds to make community improvements, that after multitudinous shavings bring us back meager results, with this communal system of co-operation which brought almost perfect results with little expenditure.

In India it is impossible for a shareholder to mortgage his part of the village field without the consent of the village council. No individual had the right of bequest. All such matters were settled by the general sense of the community as to what was right and proper. The superintendence of the estate fell to the elder son. Women had personal property and daughters could inherit from their mothers. They had no need of a

separate share of the land for they were supported from the produce falling to husbands or brothers.   The villagers united of their own accord to
build motes, halls and rest houses.   They followed
the same plan in building reservoirs, in road
mending and park building.   There were no land-
lords and no paupers.   There was little if any
crime.   The people dwelt with open doors.   These
people occupied a social grade quite above our
village folk.   They held it degradation to hire.
These traits are quite contrary to the nature of
the races called Indo-European that peopled western Europe.   They were quite contrary to Turanian or Semitic nature as it developed in Asia, but
was the nature of Ethiopians and from this foundation of communal life that they layed in southern Europe, in early Chaldea and elsewhere,
evolved the foundation and ideals from which the
democracies of our times were developed.

It was by this simple system, as revealed in
the communal districts of India—which cannot
function perfectly, because of the spirit of exploitation and foreign rule—this system of co-
operation, of the Cushite race that built the wonderful temples, palaces and giant engineering
works of the past that today bewilder the be-
holder.   The basis of the wonderful achievments
of Babylonia, Egypt and Ethiopia was this communal system.   It is for the results they gained
that we should weigh this system, seemingly impossible to us, for its value.   It was by their combined strength that they gained and held world
sovereignty for so many thousands of years.

There are things in Cushite forms that would relieve some of the insufferable miseries of today that are a reproach to our civilization. The placing of every man upon an actual basis of equality seems a thing impossible to our natures, though it is written in our civil confessions of faith. Metcalf says, "These little village communities are little republics, having everything they want within themselves and almost independent of any foreign relations. They seem to last when nothing else lasts. Dynasty after dynasty tumbles in India, revolution succeeds revolution, the Mogul, Sikh, and English, all have been master but the village communities remain the same."

Megathenes, the Greek ambassador to the court of a non-Aryan king about 300 B. C., gives us another picture of Indian Cushite life. He observed with admiration the absence of slavery in India, the chastity of the women and the courage of the men. In valor they excelled all other Asiatics. They required no locks to their doors, above all no Indian was ever known to tell a lie. They were sober and industrious, good farmers and skillful artisans. They scarcely ever had recourse to a law suit and lived peaceably under their native chiefs. The kingly government was portrayed almost as described in Manu, with its hereditary caste of councilors and soldiers. Husbandmen were exempt from war and public service. These were worthy descendants of the "Blameless Ethiopians," of old traditions. Though we are told that the Greeks and Hindu are kindred the Hellenes were very ignorant of

India prior to the expedition of Alexander. The prehistoric Greek and the Hindu were both branches of the Old Race. The native tribes which Megathenes found esteemed their constitution as an inheritance from Dionysus, an ancient Cushite king. The names Nysa, Malli, Nanda, and many other names of cities and nations are purely African words, alive today in the Soudan.

Missionaries to India have given further pictures of the working of the communal system in the home. When a man and wife have reared a family, the sons bring their wives to the paternal home to live together and raise families in the common home of their father. The supreme authority rests with this parent. The whole income goes into a common treasury. There is no individual property. So loyal is the Hindu to paternal authority that no question is ever raised by anyone as to obedience to his commands. (We may scoff at such a system as impossible to individualism and freedom but where is there any family of any civilization that has succeeded by any other plan. Families that learn to pull together soon rise to position or wealth. The tendency of our civilization is toward a dangerous freedom that weakens and enslaves us.) In India the weak, the sick and the feebleminded have the same claim on the family resources as the others. His claim is universally recognized by the race. No poorhouses are needed. The Hindu considers this as his most cherished and ancient institution. He should be proud of it, for it indeed proves his humanity. They have a sublime conception of reverence for parental authority and obligation to the ties of blood.

Jones tells us, that Buddhism has produced in India, a higher type of womanhood than Brahminism; yet the women of no other land wield a greater power than the much abused women of India. We are made to feel by superficial observers of Hindu life, that the women of this race are undervalued. This is misrepresentation. No woman on earth today reveals a greater attachment for her husband. She allowed herself to be burned upon the funeral pyre as a sublime exhibition of wifely devotion. So the African wife for ages desired to pass on into the unknown with the mate. In the narrow home sphere, in religion and the training of children, her influence is supreme. The conversion of the husband to another faith will not be permanent if the wife persists in the ancestral faith. Millions of money is expended in the manufacture of female ornaments. The Hindu expresses his love in this way to his bride. There are four hundred thousand goldsmiths constantly employed. The wealth of the family in the Middle Ages was largely measured by the amount of jewels possessed by the women of the family. Hindu clothing is beautiful and suited to the climate. The one-cloth of the Hindu women bright with colors and deftly wound around her body is the most exquisitely beautiful garment in the world.

Did the Indian race create anything in architecture? The ancient ruins and remarkable

structural remains were built in ages remote from
ours. A period long before any Aryan, Scythian
or Mohammedan invasion. They are the work of
the native races that inhabited India. The Brahmins only reached power and overthrew Buddhism in the year 700 A. D. They took over the
ancient records and they themselves say that the
ancient ruins were constructed 7000 years ago.
This was coeval with the pyramids. They were
both built by the same race. Everything in these
grottoes is of Indian character, they belong to the
time when India was under no foreign yoke. In
Ellora, Hindu mythology is shown in perfect development. In the rock in the excavations of
Elephante, we find a stone so hard that ordinary
steel cannot work it. The same hand that carved
the rock of Egypt worked here. The temple
grotto, at Salsette, has inscriptions but the alphabet no one has been able to decipher. This
would all prove that these forms of architecture
had their origin from the primitive Cushite race
of India.

All the scenes of the mythology on the walls of
these ancient temples are southern and do not
represent any phase of the life of Aryans or Turanians. Heeren, in *Asiatic Nations, The Indians*
(Vol. III, p. 43), tells us that in the carvings may
be seen armies on elephants, never on horses,
which would disprove the 1000 A. D. theory of
their building. Their plan is simple yet grand.
Ponderous roofs rest on seemingly slender and
inadequate supports. There are halls with roofs
of solid rock supported on massive piers, which

are richly carved with pictures and friezes. Painted reliefs and numerous colossal animals enliven
the temples. The inscriptions are in Sanskrit.
If this be true, then 'Sanskrit must have been the
language of the primitive race. Langles says, "If
these structures were reared nine hundred years
ago, then Ethiopia alone could have furnished
the architects, for at that late date, the world
had lost the art of carving in granite." The plains
around the Indian temples were once highly cultivated but now are inpenetrable jungle and the
lair of wild beasts. The topes of India prove the
Hindu to have been acquainted with both the
pointed and circular arch, which were unknown to
both the Egyptians and Greeks.

Heeren describes Mavalipurian, a royal city,
hewn out of the living rock. A large part of this
city had been engulfed by the sea. Immense
blocks of stone in Cyclopaean style show that
these ruins must have been very ancient. They
were built by the same race that at that age in
other parts of the world, in Phoenicia, in Arabia,
in Nubia, and in Egypt, left similar massive ruins.
These Indian works were built so long ago that
the very recollection of their origin is lost. The
pagodas are pyramidal temples of Cyclopaean
construction. The Brahmins must be right in
their estimate of the age of these ruins. Heeren
thinks that nine hundred years ago, there were
no powerful princes that could have erected such
stupendous monuments. Bardesanes reported,
that at the beginning of the Christian Era almost
two thousand years ago, Indian messengers said

that in a large grotto under a lofty hill is an image of Siva, half man and half woman twelve ells high. At that day Elephante was completely deserted, unused and as mysterious as now. Mohammedans destroyed all of the ancient monuments of India and Heeren thinks we may be sure that they borrowed from Indian architectural ideals. The Hindu far surpassed Egypt and Greece in the richness of their ornamentation.

Maurice, that eminent authority on Indian antiquities, says, "One would suppose that such astonishing works would have been called the eight wonder of the world and would have a fixed place in any country as an era never to be forgotten."

The presence of the image of Siva would give us the impression that these temples might have come from beyond the deluge, for Siva worship and its abominable rites were a part of the idolatrous religion for which God destroyed the antediluvian world. The Tartar nations north of India are addicted to the worship of this god and may justly be credited with bringing it into India; for two streams of emigration have swept into the peninsula, one from the northeast and the other from the northwest. The rite polyandry, a wife having a number of husbands, exists among these Tartars and we find this custom in India even among Brahmins. The early Cushite worship was pure and included no part of Siva worship that has prostituted the morals of a once pure race. Siva worship must have been introduced by the Brahmins as it is one of the chief deities of Brahminism. Nowhere in these ancient ruins is there a temple dedicated to **Brahma or Vishnu** showing that Turanians had nothing to do with the erection of the structures. The rock temples of India were built at the same age as the building of the Great Sphinx.

From 100 B. C. to 700 A. D. Indian civilization suffered from the inroads of Tartars or Scythians. For five hundred years the native dynasties waged war against them. The Greeks called these invaders Huns. They were shepherds or herdsmen who roamed across the plains of central Asia. It was from this element that the caste of Brahmins may have sprung or from earlier invasions, for about 700 A. D. the Brahmins began to gain the upper hand in India. The old religion of Buddhism was falling to decay from age. Brahma's apostles having caught the central gist of the life of Buddha began to invent varying philosophies upon the central thought of Buddha's—self denial and restraint. A mass of impossible miracles and divine incantations were fostered upon the people. Siva worship was adopted in the national religion. With the introduction of cremation came the burning of the widow on the funeral pyre. Human sacrifice was incorporated. Krishna which means black was taken out of the old cult and incorporated in Brahminism, anything to insure the strengthening of the claim of the Brahmin to the priesthood. Some sought to teach the equality of caste, others sought to establish a religion of pleasure.

The Scythic invasions were followed by the Mohammedan conquest. In which the idols of India were broken and her treasures carried away. Mohammed died 632 A. D. One hundred years after his death his followers had invaded Asia as far as Hindu Kush. It took three hundred years more for them to be strong enough to grasp at India. The first invaders were struck with wonder at the despairing valor of the Hindus. One Rajput garrison preferred extermination to submission. They raised a huge funeral pyre upon which the women and children first threw themselves. The men having bathed, took a solemn farewell of each other, and throwing open the gates, rushed upon the weapons of the beseigers and perished as a man. The difficulty of the Mohammedan entrance into India lay in the daring of the Hindu tribes, for they did not enter easily as is commonly supposed. Not only the Sind Rajputs but the kingdoms of the lower Ganges from Bahar downward of non-Aryan extraction represented by the Chers, Chola and Pandya dynasties made the conquest of India a very tedious progress. The Hindu power in southern India was not fully broken until 1565 A. D. At no time was Islam triumphant throughout all India. Hindu dynasties always ruled over a large area. The Mogul empire was fast falling into the hands of the Hindu when the English power fastened itself upon this afflicted people.

The three ancient kingdoms of Chers, Chola and Pandya were of Dravidians. They were Tamil speaking races. No European kingdom can boast a continuous succession such as that of Pandya or Madura, traced back by the piety of genealogists for more than two thousand years. In the sections of India that were conquered it was because these were essentially a creative and not a naturally ferocious people. The Mohammedans stripped the temples of gold and the idols of precious stones. The Tartar invasion of 1316 was indescribable in its atrocities. From 1350 to 1550 A. D. the Dekan was a theatre of war between the Hindu and the Mohammedans. Then began the intermingling of Arabian and Indian blood, both of which were foundationally Cushite. From this union of genius has risen the richest architecture in the world. The Taj Mahal, the Indian Mohammedan temple is perhaps the most beautiful edifice in the universe. It is described as though it was conceived by Titans and finished by jewelers. Its grandeur of conception and wonderful delicacy of workmanship enthralls all. The visitor exclaims, ''The half has never been told.'' The Taj is the highest expression of art human affection has ever attained.

Akbar the Great, was the founder of the Mogul dynasty. Mogul is the Arabic word for Mongol. This empire lasted for one hundred and fifty years His grandfather had married a Rajput princess. His favorite wife was of the old race. The tomb of Akbar the Great almost equals the Taj. In this great mausoleum, the famous Kohinor diamond was exhibited for years in the open air. Would this have been possible in our civilization? The Shah of Persia in 1739 sacked the palace of the Moguls and carried this diamond and other fabuious wealth back to Persia. These vast treasures seemed to convey a curse. This famous diamond passed into the hand of Queen Victoria. The imperial grandeur of the Moguls arose from the sacking of Hindu cities of the accumulated wealth of the ages. Their display has probably never been surpassed. The temple of the Sikhs is only fifty three feet square but it is largely covered with gold plate, it is a beautiful object to behold. The Mohammedans though they left wonderful archetectural beauty did not seriously change the undercurrents of the life of the people. The Hindu charge the Mohammedans with compelling them to the necessity of secluding their women, who before their invasion were free and independent. The licentiousness of the Arab caused them to withdraw their women into the home.

Modern literature places great emphasis upon the caste system of India. Some books represent the seeming four castes as subdividing into as many as 3000 castes. These cannot intermarry and most cannot eat together. Each caste is supposed to keep to the same occupation. Though we read this, in reality, the castes often change employment and lower ones rise in the social scale. Vaisyas were once tillers of the soil, now they are great merchants and bankers of India. The system of castes helped to bring the crafts up to perfection. The famous manufacturers of medieval India, its muslins, silk, cloth of gold, inlaid weapons, and exquisite work in precious stones, were brought to perfection under the system of casts or trade guilds. Such guilds may still be found in full force in India today. These in their organization prevent undue competition among the members and each upholds the interest of its own body in any dispute arising among craftsmen. Their trade disputes are settled and a stamped agreement fixes the rate for the future. The trade guild charges a fee and acts as an insurance society. (*History of the Nations, India-Persia,* p. 78.)

We may pass over to the west coast of Africa and we will find these same trade guilds and clans that eat only with their caste and only certain kinds of food. In India some are vegetarians, others eat beef. All of this grew out of that African custom where a tribe is forbidden to eat the animal that is its totem. Caste difference in India has no existance because of color. Caste keeps Aryans in Hindustan outside the pale as well as other aliens. Europeans delight in calling themselves of the same race as the Persians, but Jones tells us that the Parsee, driven from Persia twelve hundred years ago into India, declined the other day to receive into their fold, the English bride of one of their number. Caste delights in calling all foreigners unclean wretches and teaches that contact with other races brings ceremonial polution and sin. Some of the native rulers have set the time of audience with Englishmen at impossible hours, that the visit might not take place. They look upon the Hindu who has crossed the ocean into foreign lands and who has associated with us, as engulfed in polution. In early Cushite days there were no child marriages, prohibition of widow marriages and rite of suttee. These abominations have been added in later ages by the Brahmins.

The Hindu of today lives in ages that have long gone by. The present to him is an age of corruption with ones more deeply degraded to ensue. He looks with contempt upon our modern scientific investigations and modern haste. He feels that they do not add to real progress or to our happiness. His life is introspective, dealing with the mystic. He renounces outer attractions to seek communion with God. In early ages he had evolved a subtle system of philosophy. He has developed a sixth sense, which we of modern civilization cannot comprehend. 350 B. C. or 2350 years ago he had attained the same degree of civilization that is his today. Jones declares, "the people of India are the most religious upon the face of the earth. The Chinese and Japanese beside them are worldly and prosaic." The Hindu are deeply spiritual. They are not materialistic like the people of western nations. In India religion enters every detail of life as it did in Egypt and old Ethiopia. In remote ages, when our ancestors were in the depth of savagery, the Hindu were endulging in metaphysical disquisitions, which even today are admired by western sages. Many Hindu writings express aspirations and yearnings so beautiful as to excite our highest admiration.

CHAPTER XVI.

HINDU RELIGION AND LITERATURE.

India with its deeply religious people has given two great religions to the world. Buddhism and Brahminism are typical of the intermingled races from which they have come. Buddhism arose from the more ancient civilization. The older temples of India are to Buddha. His worship was anterior to that of Brahma. In the Ramayana they are spoken of as opponents. Buddhism was older than Buddha-Gautema, who was only one of the incarnations of the old faith. In India, China, Thibet and Nepal six mortal predecessors of Buddha are recognized. The Jains celebrated one of his forerunners. Because of this the various sects differed and disputed about his coming. The dates of the incarnations of Buddha ranged from 2450 B. C. to 453 B. C. Buddhism was the evolution of many centuries. It sprang from some earlier form of Cushite faith. Buddhists when they pray call upon ''Ad.'' The early Cushites were Adites. This religion preached equality and held the primitive inhabitants. The Cushites of western Europe possessed the worship of Buddha in primitive ages. There had been religious pilgrimages between them and the people of India in those old days. Woden father of the gods of northern Europe was the Indian

Buddha. (See *Ancient Races of Western Europe,* Chapter XX.)

Buddha Gautema a prince of a Sakya clan, was an Indian sage of the fifth century before Christ. He was a prince filled with compassion for the human race and works of charity. He left the courts of royalty and lived in hermitage striving to read the mysterious riddle of life. He became the incarnation of Buddha. His teaching was that there is no escape from pain, that to attain perfection our appetites and emotions must be kept in subjection. He practiced extreme renunciation, giving up his princely rights, wife and infant son. He sought to forget self in a life of service for others. The principles of his faith were abstinence from lying, stealing, adultery, drunkenness, indulgence in extravagant entertainment feasting and theatrical performances. He idealized and made beautiful by his life and teachings the primal virtues—purity, charity, patience, courage, introspection and understanding. His ethics warned his disciples against coarse language and indulgence in vain and frivolous talk. This faith was accepted by the later Scythian hoards, though they made changes in it. Thus it became a great bond of union between the races of India and the fiercer Mongolian peoples.

Gautema did not leave his doctrines in writing. He taught and talked to the people. His words were carefully treasured and reduced to writing after his death. There is an almost identical likeness between his teachings and those of the Saviour but Gautema preceeded Him by five hundred years. Buddha carried his message not to caste but to the common men. He brought a spiritual deliverence to the people not through imaginary deities but by conduct. The Buddhist books we now possess are the work of several cannons and were completed two full centuries before the birth of Christ. Buddhism was a protest against caste distinctions. It permeates and softens even to-day the Brahminism that thrust it out of India. Buddha forbade the worship of images. The religion was pure in its beginning, but has become confounded with the worship of the sage. Though now banished from India by the persecutions of the Brahmins, Buddhism prevails in Ceylon, Burmah, Siam, Thibet, Mongolia, Java and Japan. Buddhism became established in China 65 A. D. The Graeco-Bactrians accepted it with the Scythian dynasty that succeeded them. It was carried to Thibet, Afghanistan and to the Caspian.

247 B. C. Asoka of the non-Aryan race, the grandson of Chandra Gupta, supported many Buddhist priests, 64,000 in number. He founded many religious houses. He did for Buddhism what Constantine did for Christianity. He corrected the heresies of evil men who had taken upon themselves the yellow robe of Buddha, without the life. Britannica says that Buddhism has won greater triumphs in its exile than it could have achieved in the land of its birth. It has created a religion and literature for more than one-third of the human race, and has profoundly affected the beliefs of the rest. Five hundred million men still follow the teachings of Buddha.

His shrines and monasteries stretch in a continuous line from the Caspian to the Pacific and still extend from the confines of the Russian empire to the equitorial archipelago. The most reliable of the books of Buddha are written in Pali, a dialect direct from the Old Race. It is not surprising that teachings so high and earnest should have met with eager acceptance by a people as intensely religious as the Hindu. 400 A. D. Buddhism was still flourishing over a large area in India. In the ninth and tenth centuries a great persecution arose and Buddhists were utterly exterminated. For two centuries Brahmins had been gaining the upper hand.

Brahminism and Buddhism had lived side by side from 250 B. C. till about 900 A. D. Modern Hinduism is but the product of both. 400 A. D. temples of the two faiths could be found side by side. Fah Hian, traveling in India saw many Brahmins in their idol temples. He found Buddhist monks maintained at public expense. He carried back revised copies of the Buddhist scriptures to his brethren in China. He saw Buddhist hospitals where the crippled, destitute, and diseased were attended by physicians and supplied with medicines and food until relieved. There was a huge monastary of Buddhists at Nalanda, the ruins of which are still to be seen. It was a vast university where a thousand Buddhist monks and novices were lodged and supplied with every necessity. Towers and domes rose and pavilions were to be seen amidst a paradise of trees, gardens and fountains. There were six large ranges of buildings, four stories high, as well as a hundred lecture rooms. Food, bed, and vestments were furnished free. They were thus enabled to devote their whole lives to the acquisition of learning. They studied the sacred books of all religions and all sciences especially arithmetic and medicine. The people of India became gentle, honest and just. There was no capital punishment.

Many miraculous stories grew up around the life and death of Buddha. Great festivals were held in which the monarch stripped off his jewels and royal raiment and handed them to bystanders in imitation of the great renunciation of Buddha. In the architecture of India, the Pagoda is the symbol of Buddhism. It is one massive solid structure of an elongated bell shape. The highest part is usually covered with precious metal. The Schway Dagon is 370 feet high on an artificial mound of 170 feet. Its top is mostly of solid gold incrusted with precious stones. It is surrounded with numberless shrines or temples every one of which holds an image of the Great Buddha. The shrines are built of marble, richly carved teak, or glass mosaics, every one trying to excel the other in delicate charm. In each are sweet little bells which upon the winds blowing, ring gentle peals of sacred music to the great founder of the faith. In Mandelay, Burmah is an immense brazen statute of Buddha. The devout among his believers gild the image with leaf gold. At least a dozen men and women can be seen at any time thus expressing their devotion. Here

Brahma holds no sway. Here the women, modest and self-respecting possess equality with men.

Brahminism claims to be founded upon the Vedas, the sacred books of India, taken over by the Brahmins. They were not the creators of the writings, though today they are the custodians, interpretors and priests. They only attained this place after a bloody struggle with the native races. Upon the suppression of Buddhism a line of apostles of Brahminism appeared, with a philosophy built upon the peculiar mystic, ascetic, teachings of Buddha. A mass of Hindu legends sprang up around them. Some were born of virgins, others overcame lions, others raised the dead. When hands and feet were cut off they sprouted again; while the earth opened up and swallowed their slanderers. In Brahminism, Brahma was the first person of the trinity. He was the creator. Vishnu was the preserver and the abominable Siva, the destroyer. Brahma who was at first the most exalted sunk into the background and today Vishnu and Siva form the two worshipped deities of India. Though Siva was revered in a philosophical way by the Brahmins, he is worshipped with the most degrading rites by the masses of India. In the image of Siva of the Grotto of Elephante obsenity is displayed that surpasses anything that depravity can imagine.

Buddha and Siva were two hostile sects, Heeren tells us emphatically that in the Pallic emblems and the female counterpart, there are no evidences of grossness. In one place Vishnu is represented as a servant of Buddha. The Brahmins attempted to incorporate the pure worship of Buddha into their religion by making him an incarnation of Vishnu. As time went on Brahmins added to and corrupted the Vedas to confirm their excessive pretentions. Brahminism is full of elements foreign to the Aryas. It worships gods that they did not bring into India and the traditions are borrowed from the darker race. Brahminism as a power came in by political changes about 700 A. D. Dr. Stevenson declares that wherever Brahmins found a god whom it was politic to reverence they made him one of their own. Later Brahmins tried to conciliate and absorb everything. Their religion was not pure or attractive enough to supplant Buddhism fairly, so they destroyed, revised and interpolated the historical books of India, suppressing its real religious history. "Thus we find two strains running through the Vedas, one pure and devotional, in the other," Barnett says, "are bursts of filthy obsenity, a mass of vulgar superstitions and magic rites enwrapping almost every function of life."

High in the Himalayas in an eastern direction from Bramaputra of Thibet the original seat of the Brahmins was found in 1807. There were seven hundred cities. Here the predominant sect is Siva, showing that this abominable god had a Mogol origin. This is the birthplace of a people who came down into the India plains to bring their faith, which in the seven hundredth year of the Christian Era gained the upper hand. The cruel nature of Brahmic law reveals their Tartar origin. By torture they forced Brahminism upon the Indian Cushites. They punished theft by the cutting off of hands and feet. One who defamed the Brahmins or the caste spirit they sought to force upon the people had his tongue torn out, red hot irons thrust into his mouth, or the lips cut off. (*Antiquities of India,* Barnett, p. 116, 122.) Under their law the husband could whip or kill his wife and confiscate her property. The polyandry of the Malay tribes of Thibet was among them where brothers had a common wife. The burning of the widow on the funeral pyre persisted down to modern times. Time has treated the Brahmin roughly. He had a better start than any other Hindu, he appropriated learning ready made, but he made but little of the great chance. He has been too proud and self centered. The Brahmin has the proud conviction of superiority depicted in every muscle of his face. His is not the nature that could have created the wonderful literature of India. Pride is manifested in every movement of his body. Though he is in possession of the richest literature and the deepest philosophy of the ages, he adds nothing to the solution of India's bitter problems today. We must look to Ghandi and the masses for that. Brahmins added fictions to the great Indian epic poem Maha Bharata to satisfy their hatred of the Buddhists. Some modern books claim that Buddha belonged to the Aryas but history proves the Brahmins to have been the hostile sect that drove Buddhism from India. Buddha could not have been Turanian. Heeren says, "This god is easily known by his

woolly hair and long ears as he sits cross-legged.''
So we see him in the great temple dedicated to
him at Kinnery. Brahims in the altered literature represented the heads of Buddhist monasteries as monsters and the charioteer, whom the
priests envied were represented as lowborn
carters and wagoneers.

Barnett speaking of the Aryas or Brahmins in
their beginning says of them that, whatever was
their inception, their race was very quarrelsome.
They brought no women with them to India but
took Dravidian wives. They established themselves in the midlands and here amidst Aryas
mixed with Cushite blood the Vedas developed
their classic culture. Sanskrit was the language
in which it was written because it was the tongue
of the predominent race. In the Vedas we find
but a very rudimentary knowledge of astronomy.
Their enlightenment on medicine is very obscure
and mixed with sorcery. History and geography,
says Barnett, were left solely to the immagination.
Vedic society was patriarchial or masculine, the
Cushite life matriarchial. In the Vedas were
tales of endless blood-feuds, capital punishment,
roasting alive, drowning, trampling by elephants,
devouring by dogs, tearing in pieces, impalement
and other horrors that sound more like the Assyrian cruelties of a later age or Hunnish atrocities,
rather than the deeds and customs of the noble
Indo-European race in its beginning. The Rig-
Veda written not later than 1000 B. C. represents
a civilization similar to the Iliad. Both represent
a society moulded by foreign invasion, a race of

stalwart strangers, strong in culture and armour, of the late bronze and early iron ages, descending upon a darker, weaker people, subjecting them and mixing blood and culture.

Leaving the enigma of the origin and meaning of the Rig-Veda, we come to the two allegorical poems, the Ramayana and the Maha Bharta, which eclipse anything in Sanskrit. The Ramayana is very ancient. It represents a culture and ideals very different from the early Vedas. It is an allegory in which good triumphs over evil. It begins with the description of a city founded by Manu (Menes), first sovereign of mankind. The streets are full of merchants, elephants, horses and chariots, beautiful temples and palaces decorated with precious stones, incense and flowers. No covetous person was there, no liar, deceiver, or evil disposition. This poem is uncontaminated with foreign alloy. It is a picture of Hindu life prior to 1000 B. C. It is also a picture of Cushite civilization at that age. It is the story of the deeds of primitive heroes. The poem contains 2400 verses and is divided into seven books. It was written about 500 B. C. Another Hindu book is the Code of Manu, dating 1000 B. C. It regulated the moral and social life. The Maha Bharata is 240,000 lines, the longest epic poem ever written, being eight times as long as the Iliad and Oddessy put together. The sacred books of Buddha contain five times as much matter as the Old and New Testaments combined.

The Rig-Veda is composed of songs of praise, prayers and commandments. They sprang from

an immaginative and creative, as well as serious
and thoughtful people. Much of the grossness
found in these writings cannot be attributed to
the creators but to the interpolations of the Brahmins. The Puranas, the Fifth Veda, consists of
prehistoric legends. With the voluminous additions of the Brahmins, they have become a kind
of encyclopedia of general knowledge. They are
based upon older books of less extended scope.
None of them are older than 1000 B. C. The
Jains, wealthy southern Dravidians, an offshoot
from Buddhism, accuse the Brahmins of destroying the real historical books of India, wherever
they gained ascendency. They assert that the
Puranas were formerly historical books and that
some of the divine heroes were merely kings of
Oude. As Buddhism declined Jainism grew in
southern India. Heeren tells us that the mythology of the Indian Bacchus (Dionysus), son of
Cush, seems to have been transformed by the
Brahmins into Brahma. Siva one of the great
gods of the religion does not appear in the Veda
as a god but is simply an invention of the Brahmins. Buddha-Gautema denied the claims of the
Brahmins that they were the divinely appointed
teachers of sacred knowledge.

The literature of India is vast beyond all comprehension. The library of one of its kings was
so huge that it required a hundred Brahmins to
carry it from place to place. Sanskrit is supposed to bear the closest resemblance to the primitive language. Its writings have furnished a
storehouse for the rest of the world. The Vedas,

as the Homeric poems, and the folk lore of western Europe, were probably sung and recited for hundreds of years before they were committed to writing. Sanskrit has not been a living langauge since 200 B. C. The rising supremacy of the Brahmins must have hastened its decay. Had it been their language it would have come over into the Christian Era. It is a carefully constructed tongue and very symmetrical. Great masses of the literature are in meter. Indian jurisprudence is a standing proof of the ancient moral and intellectual refinement of the people. It has striking similarity to German and Jewish law. All of these nations were in close contact with ancient Cushite law. The poetry of India reveals the high moral status of the female sex. A deep feeling of tenderness and regard for woman is invariably represented.

The epic narrative of the Hindu poems, bears great resemblance to the Homeric stories, yet in subject and prevailing tone, they are more gigantic. They are full of tenderness and female charm, like the mass element of India that was once Buddhist. The poems describe their character and relations with women as pure and noble. The great poems are prevaded by a most subtle philosophy and their history of metaphysics extends back into the mythical ages and cannot be attributed to the creation of the Brahmitical mind, which dominated and appropriated far down to our era. The first system of philosophy is founded upon nature, the second upon the psychic self, the third upon the revelations of the Vedas. Of the different systems of philosophy, the Vedanta was founded by the author of the Maha Bharata, which is from the Cushite element. The Sanchya philosophy gave the highest place to nature and seems athestic. It reveals absorption of thought in the deity as necessary to the gaining of miraculous power. The Yoga system of philosophy teaches complete union of thought and faculty with God. It leads to hermitage. Buddha was the author of the Nyaya system of philosophy. It was logical, dialectic or the metaphyiscs of logical science. He taught that this vain world was but an illusion and that our personality must be absorbed in the god-head.

In grammatical structure the language of India is absolutely similar to Greek and Latin in the minutest particulars, only Sanskrit is far richer and more varied. The sacred books of Buddha were written in Palli, the language of native India. If we examine the language of Persia, we find no relation between it and Sanskrit, yet we are led to believe by linguists that Sanskrit with its roots common to the nations of western Europe, passed across Asia with succeeding emigrations of Aryans. "It is impossible to acknowledge the indebtedness of western literature to the literary thought of India. We have borrowed from every department, but nowhere have we found richer treasures than in its romances and fairy tales. Stories written in far away India have been the favorites of the story tellers of the world. Many of the fairy tales like Cinderella were written to delight some Hindu child. India is rich in literary as well as material treasures and we are far richer for having borrowed from them.''* Grammar seems to have had a special fascination for the Hindu. The oldest extant grammar dates from 300 B. C. In mathematics and astronomy they have greatly distinguished themselves.

*Standard Dictionary of Facts, p. 278.

CHAPTER XVIII.

ANCIENT MEDIA AND PERSIA WERE CUSHITE.

In the mythology of the Greeks we find the most probable origin of the Medes and the records of the Hindu give us the source of the Persians. Yet this may or may not have meant that they were of the same race. The Persians so famous under Cyrus were anciently called Elamites. The Code of Manu of India said that the Persians were originally one of the divisions of their race. The Iranian legends said that the whole region of ancient Persia to India was inhabited by a race of black men with short wooly hair. They were undoubtedly closely akin to the Cossaei of Strabo XI, 5-6. From them all Elam was called Cissia (Her. III, 91; V. 49) they had come from Elwend where the ark rested./ The father of Cyrus was a king of Anzan. Southern Suisiana was called Anzan in the cuniform inscriptions. The ancient Zend writings said that anciently the Medes, Persians and Bactrians were the same, having one common language, the Zend, and one religion. Cyrus belonged to this old division. Later Persians were utterly ignorant of the history of their country before Alexander. The incoming northern Scythians had the same effect of obliterating the real historical remembrances just as happened in Greece.

The traditions of the Greeks said that the Medes were descended from Medus son of Jason and Media. His brother Armenus was the ancestor of the Armenians. The legends of Lydia said that the founders of Babylon and Nineveh were Lydian princes. Colonies from these centers had been planted in the remotest parts of the world. Such an origin the Lydians claimed for the Etruscans and the primitive states of western Europe. The interior of Media and Armenia were full of memorials of Jason, the Greek hero of the Old Race, and Media the enchantress, daughter of the king of Colchis. The Magi certainly must have been descended from her, for they filled the ancient world in the days of Babylonian supremecy with their enchantments. The belief in charms and omens spread to India, Egypt and the western world. Their legends told of the first home of their race as having been in a land of perpetual spring, of sunshine and peace. Geology teaches us that this once was the climate of Europe and western Asia. Then winter came with bitter frosts. Their people emigrated to a land more delightful than the first, where there was neither poverty, violence or deceit. This was the golden epoch and the most glorious state of the human race.

Media is today the northern portion of the Persian empire. The ancient area is in dispute. This region is in a direct southeastern direction from ancient Colchis and Armenia, in the line of the Accadian race that peopled Assyria and Elam. Media had not the plentiful water supply of old Mesopotamia or India and because of this deficiency her civilization was tardy. The capital Ecbatana is more favorably situated, surrounded by verdure and mountain streams. Because of the freshness of the air it became the summer residence of the king of Persia. Diodorus Siculus said that the ancient city had an area of fifty square miles. Herodotus (Bk. I, 98) tells us the walls were 178 furlongs. Thucydides said they were nearly eight leagues long. The inhabitants, however, did not depend upon their walls but rather looked to valor. But for its lack of rainfall, Media had a delightful climate. In these regions appears the mirage, that wonder of travelers and the puzzle of science. Mountains appear where there are none, villages arise in the waste, and springs in the desert. In the distance appear the domes and minarets of phantom cities.

In the river valleys and the parts of Media protected from the chilly winds of the north, almost every fruit grows to perfection. These regions seem the native home of apples, pears and peaches. Here also the vine flourishes. The olive, apricot and the almond can be found growing wild. Western Media has more rainfall and we may find all the vegetables and cereals that are to be found on other Cushite sites, pumpkins, melons, cucumbers, wheat, barley, millet, sesame, corn and rice. There were flourishing cotton and tobacco fields. Media was rich in' minerals and stone. Her quarries were the equal of those of

Assyria and more widely distributed. There was
a famous yellow marble that could be cut in thin
strips and used for glass. The fauna was represented by the lion, tiger, leopard and bear. The
most important domestic animal was the camel
of both the Arabian and Bactrian breeds. The
celebrated Nisaean horses were praised by the
ancients. The Macedonian greyhound was strong
and swift. The great bird of the upper air was
the eagle. The lakes being salt were without fish.
There were many reptiles and plague pests of
locusts.

The old religion of the Medes and Persians can
be found in the Zend Avesta, which is written in
a language older than the Median. Among the
later inhabitants, outside of political papers and
messages, there remains little evidence of any
native literature or the expression of idealism in
art. The Zend Avesta is in eight books. It is
from the old foundational race of ancient Bac-
trinia, the earlier name of Media and Persia.
The utterances of these religious books reveal the
deep reverence and the awe of nature that shows
in all forms of Cushite faith. The Zend Avesta
represents their praises and supplications to the
invisible spirit world. The gods of the ancient
Bactrians were Indra (Cushite) the storm god,
Agni, fire, and Soma, god of intoxication. These
religious books portray the unceasing conflict between good and evil. Intermixed with this faith
as the ages rolled on were the rites of Siva, from
the tribes of the north that began to pour as a
flood over the Iranian plains. In this way Siva

worship was added to the Hindu pantheon by the Brahmins. In their sacrifices the horse was generally offered. These northern races did not as the old race believe in the resurrection of the body. They taught that the body could not be buried or burned lest it pollute the earth or air.

Let us scrutinize the Zend Avesta closely and the religion it represented, for the false conspiracy of literature claims it to have found its source and its best features from the Japhethic Turanians of the north. The original Avesta contained twenty-one books. Most of it has been lost. There are numerous indications that show that these books once existed. Pausanius (V. 27, 3), said that the Magi read from a book. Hermippus affirmed in the third century that Zoroaster, the founder of the religion, was the author of twenty books. The Arabian historian testified that they had been written on hides, 1200 in number. West Africans told Frobenius that their ancient annals had been written on cow-hides. Masudi wrote, "Zartusht gave to the Persians the book called Avesta. It contained twenty-one parts, each containing 200 leaves. This book in the writing which Zarthusht invented and which the Magi called the writing of religion was written on 1200 cow-hides, bound together by golden bands. Its language was the old Persian, which no one now understands." The Parsee testify that the Avesta was burned by Alexander, that it was written on leather in golden ink and preserved in the archives of Persepolis. Alexander did permit Per. sepolis to be burned (Diodorus, XVII, 72). After his death, the Zoroastrian priests met and gathered the scattered fragments which had escaped the ravages of war, which were but a small portion of the original. More of the Avesta disappeared with the wave of religious persecution after the Mohammedan invasion. Later it was translated into its present form.

Everything concerning Persian history, and literature is contradictory. In the ancient testimony Zoroaster was called a Persian. By others a king of the Bactrians, also an Arian. We can reconcile all of these statements when we remember that Bactria, Aria and Persia were anciently Cushite. Zoroaster is represented as having had intercourse with the deity. Dio Chrysostem declared that neither Homer or Hesoid sang so worthily of Zeus and his chariots and horses. There is the same conflict about his birth. Hermipphus placed him 5000 years before the Trojan war. Xanthus made his 6000 years before Xerxes. Aristotle gave him similar antiquity. All ancient testimony spoke of him as a historical character. He must have belonged to the earliest ages of the Cushite empire. His name is nowhere on the cuniform inscriptions though Darius and his successors were firm adherents of his doctrines. The later books of the Avesta made him a supernatural being but the earlier refer to him as a personage of remote antiquity (Yasma, 57, 8). In these hymns he is a mere man trusting in his God. He had had to face all forms of outward opposition as the lukewarmness and unbelief of his adherents and the inward misgivings of his own heart as to the truth and final victory of his cause.

The Avesta names a seemingly mythical country, which we cannot identify with Bactrina. He taught under the patronage of Vishtaspa, who was not the later Hystaspes of the Greeks. There were ties of kinship between them. One striking peculiarity of the Avesta is that the evil spirits are called daeva. The people of India, the Italians, the Celts and Lets gave the name deva to their good spirits, the spirits of light. In India evil spirits were the asuras, while in Iran ahura meant god. No solution has yet been found to explain the peculiar difference. In the Rig-Veda there is rivalry between Varuna and Indra. Varuna the old king of the gods was asura and Indra was the type of Deva. The distinction in the Iranian countries represents the struggle between two hostile and different sects. The contest most probably between an old and an incoming race. In the Shah-Nama, Zoroaster was said to have been murdered at the altar by Turanians. He is usually spoken of as a reformer of the old Iranian faith. The meaning of the names deva and asura may have been perverted in the Avesta from the original text of Zoroaster, just as the Brahmins changed the books of India. It was this opposition that Zoroaster reveals in the hymns. The Magi altered but claimed to be the representatives of the great teacher. It was these interpolations that Darius sought to purify.

Examining this religion, Ormund resembles no Japhethic type, but in the mutilated books is like an oriental king surrounded by Magi. In the world are two opposing forces, the creatures of good and evil. They wage war with man's soul as the stake. No religion of the world shows more clearly that the goods deeds we perform strengthen the powers for right and evil deeds render service for Satan. Wicked deeds cannot be undone but can be counterbalanced by good works. Of remission of sins Zoroaster knew nothing. He speaks of dreams, visions and conversations with God. He has firm conviction of the final triumph of good over evil and the final reward of the just and upright. He believed that the fullness of time was near, when the faithful would gain power over their enemies. The good would be assigned to the hoped for reward and Satan confined in the abyss in which from henceforth he shall lie powerless. He speaks of the one undivided kingdom of God in heaven and upon earth. To this pure faith were added other divinities and prohibitions. 3000 years after Zoroaster a new leader would be born of his seed. The dead were to come to life and a new incorruptable world to begin. This was an early forerunner of our Saviour, who promised a new heaven and a new earth.

Whether the Magi were a division of the old race directly, descended from the Medea of the Greek myths or were a ruling class of the Scythic invasions that early began to shift into the northern country we do not know, but we might judge from the innovations so different from the rites of the old race of Persia that they were from the new race. These priests seemed to deal wholly in magic, to which the Scythic tribes were addicted. They claimed the gift of divination and prophecy. Exposure of dead bodies was an innovation of the Magi, for in Persia proper as late as the time of Herodotus they refused to expose and buried their dead (Her. I, 140). The actual annals of the Medes begin about 950 B. C., when Assyria devastated a portion of her territory. Whole colonies of Medes were carried to Assyria and their places filled by Assyrians or Samaritans. Cyaxares leading a horde of untrained soldiers, sought vengence on the Assyrians for the death of his father. In his onslaught against the decaying power of Assyria he was routed. Training his soldiers, he returned and drove the Assyrians within their ramparts. He received the intelligence that the Scythians were overrunning Media. He retreated and for twenty-six years struggled against these rude, fierce enemies.

Uniting with the Babylonians, after three onslaughts Nineveh was taken. The Medes and Babylonians seemed able easily to make an amicable division of the empire. Media taking the north countries and Babylon the south. Cyaxares turned his attention to Lydia. War continued six years until an eclipse of the sun caused these superstitious nations to sign a truce. After the fall of Nineveh, the three great kingdoms of Asia were Babylonia, Media and Lydia. The princes and princesses of these three kingdoms intermarried because of the common Cushite blood. Aryenis, the sister of Croesus, was married to Astyges, the crown prince of Media. Amyitis, the sister of Astyges, was wedded to Nebuchadnezzar, the heir to the throne of Babylonia. Herodotus reported that the founder of the Lydian Herakleid dynasty was the son of Ninus and the grandson of Belus (Nimrod). Assyria we must not forget, except for six or seven centuries was but a province of Babylonia. At the death of Cyaxares, Media passed to Astyages and 556 B. C. to his grandson Cyrus, king of the Persians. Her. I, 95, calls Cyrus, the son of Cambyses, a Persian prince and the daughter of king Astyages. Because of a dream he was delivered to a herdsman to be put to death.

Xenophon agrees in making him the grandson of Astyages. Other accounts say that he was given the hardy Persian training until twelve. Then he was placed with his grandfather at the luxurious Median court. Ktesias connected Cyrus with the old race. He called him an Amardian. At the fall of Babylon when he entered the capital, the priests and scribes welcomed him as though he had been a native king. Cyrus was a zealous worshipper of the Babylonian deities. They were restored to their places in great state. These were the same gods as those of the Sumerian race to which he belonged. He was one of the last of the Cushite kings trying to restore the old widespread empire. Cyrus gave his son the title "King of the World." At the death of Cyrus, acceptable to the old race, the Sumerians threw off the yoke (Her. I, 95).

The name Cyrus in the nominative is Kurush (Kush). The capital and chief residence of Darius was at Susa the city which had been capital of ancient Elam. The tomb at Murghab that reads, "I am Cyrus the Achaemenian," cannot be Cyrus the Great. It is of a period subsequent to Darius. The figure on the tomb is Cushite.

The young Cyrus sent from the hardy virtues of Persian training to the luxuries of the Median court, looked with contempt upon the perverisons there from the old life. Persia tolerated not the gross and unspiritual practices of the Magi. When his grandfather's kingdom was invaded by the Assyrians he accompanied him in the campaign. Cyrus pled to return to his father's court but was refused. On the night of a feast he made his escape. Astyages persued him and invaded Persia. Cyrus and his father with their war chariots awaited the onslaught. Cambyses was killed and the Persian army put to route Cyrus with remarkable heroism reorganized the army but the Medes succeeded in driving the Persians, though they made valorous resistance, to the very summit of their hills. There the beseeching cries of their women and the challenge to their valor and patriotism caused Persia to turn with ferocity and thrust back the foe. Astyages fell back to the vicinity of the Persian capital and there in the watches of the night Cyrus surprised them. The victory was on the side of the Persians. Astyages was overtaken and captured. The Medes welcomed Cyrus as a deliverer from the rising domination of incoming usurping Turanian

Scyths. Zoroasterism was reestablished and Magism for the time overthrown.

Cyrus subdued Cappadocia, marched against Croesus and defeated him. He took Sardis. Having reduced almost all Asia, he turned and repassed the, Euphrates and attacked Assyria. Josephus (*Antiquity*, Bk II, Ch. 2) speaks of how the prophets of Israel had foretold the coming of Cyrus. After the times of Cyrus, we find Darius and his nobles seeking to put a check upon the wild strains of northern barbarism. Darius was of the old race as we shall proceed to prove. Under the fierceness and cruelty of the intermingled Median people noble families of both Media and Persia of the old race had been banished, but Darius and his notables overthrew the tyrants and restored the exiled. He republished the Avesta, the sacred books of the old Bactrian race, which had become polluted with Turanian magic. The language of the books was different from that of Media today. The language and the religion were undoubtedly that of ancient Susiana and Elam as well as of Bactrina. Darius sought to change the book back to the old faith of his fathers. Darmesteter supposes Magism not to have gained power until 600 B. C. Zoroasterism was a thousand years older. In contrast to the Cushite race, the Magi had no respect for human corpses, but abandoned them to beasts of prey, there were no sacrifices of bloodshed, no images of the gods, no temples. Their rites were resisted by true Persians and Medes. Finally the new forms fought their way and prevailed.

Ancient testimony revealed that the doctrines of Zoroaster met determined resistance among the mixed Arians with the fierce struggle ending in religious wars. Lenormant calls his most persistent enemies the Indo-Aryan priests called Brahmins. It seems rather queer does it not to attribute the creation of Zoroasterianism to that race of opposite concepts, that pours maledictions upon the head of Zoroaster in the Rig-Veda. (*Ancient History of the East*, Vol. II, p. 37, 38.) By Strabo's time the name of Magi was applied indiscrimininately to all priests of Persia. Darius tells us positively on the engraved rock of Behistan, that the Magi usurpation had destroyed the temples of his gods and the sacred hymns of the primitive Zoroasterian faith. He says: "I restored the ancient book in all the countries and the people followd it." Thus in the inscriptions he allies himself with the old race, that was fundamentally Cushite. The inscription at Behistan also allies Zoroaster with the old race. In the restoration we see the burying again of the dead, the Cushite gods Indra, Mithra and Krishma, ancient kings, reappear. The deva had been turned from gods tu devils.

Persian art was like that of Susiana and Babylon because all were Cushites. The palaces were reared upon lofty platforms. The columns and sculptured figures of animals were like Nineveh and Babylon. The subjects of the sculptures were the figures of the old Cushite mythology. The art of the Sumerian was written strongly on the walls. Persian architecture can best be studied in the remains of the palace near Persepolis burned by Alexander. The buildings on the different terraces are not connected with each other. Of the five largest, one was dedicated to Darius, another to Xerxes, another is known as Chel Minar or the Hall of a Hundred Columns. To attribute the construction to the later Persian race would be erroneous. Heeren says that mystery surrounds the construction of the ruins of Persepolis. The pillars belong to no known order of architecture. The inscriptions are an enigma. Fabulous animals are on guard at the entrance. Allegorical figures decorate the walls. It is the art of remote antiquity. It is doubtful Heeren thinks that the historical Persians used Persepolis as a capital. No contemporary author mentions it by name. The stones of its buildings are laid without mortar. They were fastened with iron clamps that were stolen or destroyed by rust at an age when Japhethic people did not understand working in iron or the construction of temples.

Heeren thinks Persepolis might have come from the ancient Median race because the later inhabitants were incapable of erecting palaces. Cambyses imported Egyptian builders to rear the buildings of Susa. At Persepolis are no traces of Egyptian art. At Ecbatna we find forms and inscriptions like those at Chel Menar. There are the double columns of the collossal Cushite proportions. Winged monsters guard the portals having the bodies of lions, the feet of horses and human heads. These were mythological Cushite forms. The pillars were unrelated to Greece or Egypt. The figures have the dress of ancient Medes. The reliefs on the walls show the people to have been commercial. Various nations are depicted, one wrapped in furs, another naked except for an apron, numbers wearing loose flowing robes, others wearing close fitting clothes like the Minoans. These came bearing the products of the widely scattered colonies of the old empire. Some presented spices, dress ornaments, implements, fruits and animals. (*Ancient Commerce,* Heeren, Vol. I, p. 167.) The inscriptions in these ruins are of unknown language, showing their antiquity. Bactrians had preceeded the Medes at Ecbatana. Heeren says that Chehl Menar did not arise by enchantment but sprang from the same source.

Persian kings by repeated invasions into Scythic countries saved civilization. They evolved a more centralized government, yet in no way essentially different from ancient Cushite rule. The power of each province was divided between the satrap and the commander-in-chief. So in Greece and Carthage two heads had been a check upon each other, whether they were consuls or kings. In each province their was the king's ear, a secretary who kept him informed as to the fulfillment of his commands and the loyalty of his subjects. There was the king's eye, troopers who appeared at intervals to arrest those who proved disloyal. This system was very effective but back behind it we cannot fail to see the break up of the old trade and commerce that had covered the Orient.

Heeren points to the anarchy and confusion produced by the rule of Assyria and the destruction
wrought by the headlong conquests of Persia,
which destroyed and ruined the royal cities of the
Euphrates and the Indus. The commerce of Asia
of which the Scythians had once been the trusted
carriers had disappeared. The rule of Persia
compared to the old empire was very short. She
was supreme two hundred years.

Persian literature has perished. References
in ancient books reveal that once there was much
of it. The later race was not commercial. The
language in which the Avesta now exists is Pah-
lavi a mixture of old Persian and Semitic speech,
the tongue of a conqueror grafted on the language
of the old race. The oldest book is very archaic
and written in meter. Some of the books are of
Sasanian origin. The oldest portion must have
come from Zoroaster himself. Some of the Yashts
are of Iranian gods and heroes that had their
origin in the Orient. Another treats of the blessings of agriculture, in poetical form. The interpretation of this literature is a difficult problem.
Old Persian is impossible to have been Semitic
and is unlike Sanskrit. A multitude of contra-
dictions occur in Persian history. The ancient
records must have been falsified as the religion
of Zoroaster was altered. Heeren says, that contemporary historians and Persian chronicles give
completely different accounts. When the Medes
and Persians attacked Lydia they appeared as
fierce barbarians because the old civilization was
changing, when the old monarchy became again

predominant the genius of the Cushite blood sprang forth. They checked the onrush of the Scythians, who were a real menace to the culture of the world.

In mediaeval times Persia became the mistress of the civilization of Islam. Bagdad was an intellectual center, a paradise of poetry and the literary light of the east. After the marvels described in the *Arabian Nights* she sank rapidly to decay. The spirit of worship toward the monarch was as abject as in Egypt. The harem of the monarch was guarded by eunuchs, a type quite common among ancients. The couch of the king had golden feet. In the mixed race drunkenness was as prominent a feature as the proverbial truthfulness which had been the virtue of the Indi. Criminals were put to death for slight offenses in peculiarly cruel ways as among the Brahmins. Distinctions of caste came to prevail as in India. It was the method by which Turanians could show their hatred to the more civilized, darker race. In the mixed race polygamy grew apace and education was neglected. As of old the queen mother exercised a preponderant influence over the king, court and empire. Greek legends said that the expeditions of Cyrus and Alexander were but the surging backward and forward of divisions of the old race of Greece and that the Persian invasion was retaliatory upon Europe for the fall of Troy, when Europe first resisted the growing power of the east.

In ages as late as 652 A. D. we note the late flowering of the ancient Persian genius. The sculptures of this time show remarkable skill and vigor. Sir William Hunter, late Director General of Statistics of India, tells us that the decorations were a bewildering mass of vines and foliage combined with birds and animals. For richness and delicacy this sculpture is unsurpassed by any age or clime. When S'ad leading the hosts of Islam, captured the magnificent capital of the Persians, among the treasures seized was a great carpet of white brocade 450 feet long and 90 feet broad with a border worked in precious stones to represent a garden of flowers, the leaves formed of emeralds, the blossoms of rubies, sapphires and pearls. Centuries of ravage and decay have left few remains of these splendors. (*History of the Nations,* Lodge, India, p. 322.) The native Persians of today are sadly degenerated from constant mixture with foreign races. The bulk of the population are merchants and agriculturalists. From these come the wonderful tapestries and shawls hardly equalled by any other descendants of the old race today. The finest of the natives still cling despite persecution to the old faith of Iran.

FINAL WORD.

The story of India, Persia, Arabia, Chaldea, Egypt and Ethiopia has been astonishing, but more amazing and fascinating is the recital describing the life and deeds of the Cushite nations of western Europe. The beautiful, world renowned mythology of the Greeks throws upon the screen of literature the mystic figures of the Cushites who played a mighty drama in western Europe and the circle of magic cities around the Mediterranean in ages long preceeding the life of the Grecian period of history.

The prints of Cushite footsteps are found all over the three regions, as proved by the facts of accepted sciences today. We learn that the strange surge of races backward and forward across the plains of western Europe at the dawn of recorded history was but the reaction of earlier age old conflicts between Cush and Turan, the most western of the sons of Japheth.

The story solves the baffling problem of who were the Celts and the origin of the so-called Aryan race of modern times. Reliable authorities confess that Aryans do not know their own origin. Careful mining into the authentic testimony of the ancients and a study of the relics and remains of western Europe proves that the greatest names of the old traditions, the heroic figures of the Greek mythology and the subjects of classic culture were the sons of Cush, the founder of the ancient Cushite empire of Ethiopians. Hercules Bacchus, Apollo, Hermes and other heroes were his descendants.

The world just now is witnessing a revival of interest in the myths of ancient races. Reason has always told man that myth was but confused pictures of literal truth. The scholarship of entire ages has wrestled with the enigma of the meaning of the beautiful legends of the Greeks. The most beautiful and intensely interesting of these now have scientific proofs that they but pictured the figures and told the heroic deeds of ancient Cushites and their cousins, the descendants of the African brothers of Cush, the Zeus of the Greeks, the Jupiter of Rome and the Amen-Ra of Egypt.

So fascinating and vital has the world considered these classic stories that they are still the commanding literature of Aryan college life everywhere; for strange as it may seem the most powerful branches of the so-called Aryan race, as can be indisputably proven, are as well as the African Ethiopians, descendants of Cushite Ethiopian blood. Another volumn of this work (Book II) gives more authentic information upon this subject than any other book extant, in it has been interwoven the undeniable proofs of the Cushite origin of western Europe, linked with the intense drama that was the foundation of the Greek legends.

AFTERWORD
TO
WONDERFUL ETHIOPEANS OF THE ANCIENT CUSHITE EMPIRE
by
Asa G. Hilliard III

An individual who loses his or her memory is disabled. So it is with a people. African and African diasporan people have, in large measure, been deprived of the most important memories or history. Those who have enslaved and colonised Africans have understood fully the powerful role that history plays in the life of a people. Enslavers and colonizers have spared no effort to keep the truths of African history hidden.

During all ages of the enslavement and colonization of African and African diasporan people, there have been those among us who have never lost consciousness. Brilliant and courageous historians and writers have kept our story alive. They have done so, often without the benefit of an audience from their people in general or even from those scholars of African descent who have been trained in the traditions of our conquerors.

In writing **Wonderful Ethiopians of the Ancient Cushite Empire**, Drusilla Dunjee Houston stands out as an historian of rare comprehensive vision—one of the few to gain a real sense of Africans in world history. For example, Joel Rogers' main interest was in race mixing. He did a monumental job of recording data on the African ancestry of many notable world figures. Earlier writers such as Edward Wilmont Blyden were aware of African development on the continent, especially in the Nile Valley. Later writers, such as **William Leo Hansberry**, saw the influence of Africa on locations outside Africa. In Hansberry's case, the influence shown was on European classical civilizations. But it was Houston who, for her time, seemed least weighted down by the racist and colonial mind set, which kept even the most respected African and European historians confined in a false perspective of Africa and the world. For example:

> In the 1830s, the German philosopher Hegel, in his lectures on history at Berlin had put it in rather more philsophical terms when he had spoken of Africa as 'no historical part of the world; it has no movement of development to exhibit... (Du Bois, 1970, p. xi)

Drusilla Dunjee Houston avoided a major conceptual problem by her choice of a title for her book. It was a master stroke for her to focus on the Cushite Empire with reference to the fact that they were "Ethiopians." To have done it the other way around, i.e., to have focused on Ethiopia alone, would have been a mistake of major proportions. For it was the **work** of Blacks or "Ethiops" in nation building that is of prime interest. As far as we can tell, the name Kush or Kvsh (Massey, 1974) is the indigenous name of an ancient African kingdom and civilization. As Houston shows, this indigenous African civilization spreads, not only through the African continent but through the broader world as well. This spread included Arabia, Greece, Persia, and India. Remnants of the name Kush as well as the culture and the people of Kush can be found in these and other places, e.g., Hindu Kush in India and the Black Dravidian population there.

Houston's focus is upon African **peoplehood** rather than upon Black individuals. So often African Americans appear to become intrigued by a kind of "Ripley's Believe-It-Or-Not" treatment of the history of African people. The achievements of individuals are highlighted. What is usually missing in African history presentations is the basic story of a people. The scope, depth, and continuity of the African experience must be understood if any real appreciation of African identity and creativity is to be gained.

Houston has been criticized for some scholarly laxity:

> . . .she was not always careful in her evaluation of historical sources, sometimes choosing lively adjectives to compensate for a much needed critique of the author's work. The failure to include proper citations, a bibliography, and an index makes it difficult for the reader to verify her sources without extensive, careful sifting. In all fairness to Houston, she may have intended to include an index and bibliography in the last of her projected three volume work but only the first volume was ever published.   (Spady, 1978, p. 105)

Yet, in spite of these limitations, the general outline of Houston's arguments hold. In fact, so do the details. The fault lies not in errors of fact but in a failure to leave a clear trail for easy verification.

It is most interesting to see that Houston's general thesis is gaining strong support as contemporary scholars pursue the same questions and do their work with the benefit of finer tools and broader more up-to-date background.

During the past two decades, a growing number of excellent African and African diasporan researchers have added greatly to our body of knowledge of the story of Africa in the world. Almost without exception, they verify the general lines of Houston's thesis.

1.   The earliest world civilization was developed in the Nile Valley by native Africans who were Black people.

2.   Africa's early civilization was the parent civilization of later civilizations in the East, the Middle East, and in Europe.

Cheikh Anta Diop (1974), Senegal's intellectual giant and undisputed leader among Egyptologists, has shown the antiquity of Egypt, its Black origins, and its cultural unity with Africa. Chancellor Williams (1974) of Howard University in Washington, D.C. has linked the history of Cush and Egypt and explained how these high civilizations were destroyed. John Jackson (1970) has shown the evolution of African civilization and shares much with Diop in his treatment of the subject. More recently LeGrande Clegg (1978) and Ivan Van Sertima (1976) have offered strong evidence for the presence of Africans in America long before the birth of Christ. Clegg has also documented the presence of Africoids in Europe as Europe's first homo sapiens. Runoko Rashidi (1983) is one of the leading African American researchers to study the spread of Africans and African civilization in all parts of Asia. While each of these historians and a whole series of others not mentioned have followed their on research priorities, collectively they offer a sound basis for supporting the comprehensive view of Houston.

Recently, Bernal (1984) has written to show that Greece, in its early days, was an African colony of Egypt drawing its cultural forms from Egypt. According to Bernal, this was the view of the ancient European historians. It was changed in recent times as a result of racism. Bernal's work is more important for its documentation of the politics of scholarship than for any new insight about African contributions to world civilization, since Africa's connection to Greece, while important to Greece, was only a small part of a larger sweep of events.

Houston had no army of doctoral students and graduate assistants to help with her work. She had no word processors and no access to computer searches of the literature. She was not located centrally among a core group of African American researchers or an interdisciplinary team of researchers. Yet she was able to extract a theme from raw data and to extend its application to appropriate limits.

Today, the body of evidence in support of Houston's main argument is growing at a phenomenal rate. For example, we now have the results of important anlayses of archaeological finds from Nubian sites south of Egypt, sites now covered by Lake Nasser behind the Aswan High Dam on the Nile (Williams, 1974). It shows the Nubia nation of Ta Seti was older than Egypt. We see a growing body of linguistic date (Diop, 1974). It is fascinating to see the gradual, if reluctant, shift in mainstream thought among establishment Egyptologists and other African history scholars in the face of overwhelming amounts of new data about old African cultures (Mokhtar, 1981). Where Houston's work was met with a wall of silence, assuming that historians knew of it at all, the more recent work of Diop and others has bludgeoned the historical establishment to the point where they have begun to rationalize their former Eurocentric positions.

The archeological finds on early hominoids are stunning. In sum, the greatest number of these sites, and the oldest ones as well, are found in East Africa in the Great Lakes region. While the presence of five million year old humanlike beings (more than four million years older than hominoid bones at any other sites in the world) does not prove the antiquity of civilized human behavior, it would seem to minimize any element of surprise when we find from other evidence an African origin for the earliest civilization.

Many historians have been trained during the days since Drusilla Dunjee Houston and other such historians have written. What seems remarkable to me is how few African American historians have picked up on these themes. A review of the titles in the issues of the **Journal of Negro History** since its beginning in 1916 will show an appalling lack of attention to areas of vital concern to African and African American people. World history cannot be written correctly if African history is treated incorrectly.

If any other group of people on the face of the earth had a history as that of Africa to which they could appeal, we would be hearing about it constantly. But be that as it may, the real tragedy is that so many Africans and African diasporans are attempting to understand their own place in the world without the benefit of an accurate history. That is unnecessary today. As one reads such accounts as the **Wonderful Ethiopians of the Ancient Cushite Empire** by Houston, it can be seen that it has been unnecessary for some time to function without the missing pages in African history.

The wonderful Ethiopians of Cush have stretched out their hands to God over the centuries. They do so here once more, in the work of Drusilla Dunjee Houston.

SELECTED REFERENCES AND BIBLIOGRAPHY

Bernal, Martin. **Black Athena to White Goddess: The Denial of the Afroasiatic Roots of Greece: 1780-1980,** Unpub Ms 1984

Blyden, E. Wilmot. **Christianity Islam and the Negro Race.** Edinborough; University of Edinborough Press, 1967 (first published 1887)

Clegg, LeGrand (1978). "Ancient Racism: A Lesson From the Past" in John Williams (ed) **Y'Bird,** pp. 28-39

Diop, Cheikh A. (1974). **The African Origin of Civilization: Myth or Reality.** New York: Lawrence Hill

Du Bois, W.E.B. (1970). **The Negro.** New York: Oxford University Press

_____ (1972). **The World and Africa: An Inquiry Into the Part Which Africa Has Played in World History.** New York: International Publishers

Gladwin, H.W. (1947). **Men Out of Asia.** New York: McGraw Hill

Hegel, Georg Wilhelm Friedrich (1965). **The Philosophy of History,** translated by J. Subree, New York, p. 99.

Jackson, John (1970). **Introduction to African Civilization.** New York: University Books

Massey, G. (1974). **A Book of the Beginnings.** Secacus, New Jersey: University Books, (first published 1881)

Mokhtar, G. [ed. (1981)]. **General History of Africa II: Ancient Civilization of Africa.** Berkeley: University of California Press

Parker, George Wells (1917). "The African Origin of Grecian Civilization." **Journal of Negro History**

Rashidi, Runoko (1983). **Kushite Case Studies.** Unpub. MS.

Spady, James G. (1978). "Tri-Muse: The Historiography of Joel A. Rogers, Drusilla Dunjee Houston, and William Leo Hansberry" in John A. Williams (ed) **Y'Bird,** pp. 98-116

Van Sertima, Ivan (1976). **They Came Before Columbus.** New York: Random House

Williams, Chancellor (1974). **The Destruction of Black Civilization.** Chicago: Third World Press

DRUSILLA D. HOUSTON: A UMUM COMMENTARY, A SEARCH AND PERSONAL NOTES

Dedicated to Thomas W. Harvey, Lewis Michaux,
F.H. Hammurabi and Ralph Ellison.

Drusilla Dunjee Houston is one of the least known of early Black writers of the ancient past. This is due largely to the scarcity of printed data available on Blacks in places like Oklahoma, Idaho and Nebraska. A great deal of "national" Black historical works are, in reality, a cursive history of Blacks in large urban centers. Even in works by specialists in Black Oklahoma history, Drusilla Houston is given little attention. Only a few decades ago her columns on political, social and educational issues affecting Blacks in Oklahoma were widely published, read and discussed. Significantly, for this study, she is the only known Black woman to write a multi-volume history of Blacks in antiquity.

This is the way we began the chapter "Tri-Muse: The Historiography of Joel A. Rogers, Drusilla Dunjee Houston and William Leo Hansberry", which appeared in the volume on Black pre-history (Ybird: 1978) edited by John A. Williams, in one of the many publishing ventures by that remarkable man of arts and letters—Ishmael Reed. How ironic! Two of the most outstanding novelists in America must be credited with publishing the above mentioned chapter, the first and only scholarly assessment of Houston's work to appear in fifty years. What a sad commentary on "Black" Studies!!!

Drusilla Dunjee Houston's pioneering efforts are like those of Drs. Irene Diggs and Merze Tate. All three of these Black women's scholarly works must be given serious attention. Tate's **The Disarmament Illusion—The Movement for a Limitation of Arms to 1907** (1942) and **The United States and Armaments** (1948), influenced Henry Kissinger and McGeorge Bundy, as well as many other armament specialists all over the world. Diggs' published and unpublished writings on W.E.B. Du Bois are first class. It is hoped that she will publish the correspondence between herself and Dr. Du Bois as well as a full biography of that scholar. Clearly, Diggs can provide insight missing from the current body of scholarship on Du Bois.

Houston was born in Harpers Ferry, West Virginia, lived in Minneapolis, Minnesota and later settled in Oklahoma. Merze Tate was born and educated in central Michigan and Irene Diggs was born and educated in Minnesota.

This brings us back to our opening statement regarding the inattention given to Blacks in the Midwest and Western United States. Part of Houston's absence from Black studies is that she is from the Southwest and not a stereotypical "angry" or "deprived" Black women.

How did we learn of her? First of all being in Philadelphia and surrounded by a rich culture and oral history, the names and deeds of our progenitors were ever present. One of the great oral historians of our era was Thomas W. Harvey, president of the Universal Improvement Association and a close associate of Marcus Garvey. Among the many experiences he shared with us in a typical Saturday session was this dynamic Black author of **Wonderful Ethiopians of the Ancient Cushite Empire**. He had met her and read the book and her columns years before. Efforts to find the book at public and university libraries were unsuccessful. Not able to find it there we checked a local Columbia Avenue bookstore—Sheikh Muhammad's—where Cecil B. Moore, (erstwhile leader of Black Philadelphia during the 1960's, builder of the largest branch of the NAACP during his tenure as president and clearly one of the best criminal lawyers in the U.S.A.), Malcolm X and Joel A. Rogers all visited. My first Rogers book, **100 Amazing Facts About The Negro,** was obtained there. This bookstore was only twelve blocks from the International Headquarters of the U.N.I.A.

Still searching for those Wonderful Ethiopians, we went to Lewis Michaux's National Memorial African Bookstore, where Patrice Lummumba, Malcolm X, W.E.B. Du Bois, Kwame Nkrumah and Nnamdi Azikiwe searched for rare books. This "Proper House Of Propaganda" was at that time located near the corner of 125th and 7th Avenue in Harlem. Michaux knew of her work, had once sold copies, but no longer had any for sale. Actually, Michaux's bookstore was a street university. He was a professor in the very best sense of the word. Witty, sardonic, prophetic, preacherman, he kept our history alive for nearly five decades. Having begun as a street gambler and pool shark in Philadelphia, he transferred the same skill and knowledge to developing a remarkable bookstore that had a mass appeal. A bookstore that provided mass self-knowledge to so many who were attracted to this institution.

It is important to state these things so that one does not get the impression that Houston was totally forgotten. In later years, Joe Goncalves published a part of her book in **The Journal of Black Poetry** as **Soulbook** had done with excerpts from Cheikh Anta Diop's **Anteriorite' des Civilisations Negres: Mythe ou Verite' Historique.** Scholars who claim to be discovering these things must begin to give credit to the Sheikh Muhammad's, the Lewis Michaux's and of course the F.H. Hammurabi's.

On the desk in front of us is a copy of **Where is Black Man Headed in the Post War World??** by F. H. Hammurabi, who did for the Chicago Black community what Thomas W. Harvey and Lewis Michaux did in Philadelphia and New York, respectively, they kept the fire burning for the current generation. On page seventy-three of Hammurabi's book Houston is mentioned under "Open House For All Who Seek The Truth", along with Harry Dean's **Pedro Gorino,** Willis King's **African Outline** and J. A. Rogers' **Sex and Race.** On page ninety-one, Houston's work is advertised as available at $3.00. That was in 1942-43. In 1985 that same book is valued at $45.00. Buying Black books is a double investment and should therefore be seen as a heritage and property investment. Libraries must aggressively collect small press publications.

In addition to citing Drusilla Houston in **Where is Black Man Headed in Post War World??,** Hammurabi kept her name alive in his **The Chicago Round Up 1779-1951: A Vest Pocket Encyclopedia** (1951). **Wonderful Ethiopians Of The Ancient Cushite Empire** was offered for purchase through a mail order, twenty-five years after it was published. Additionally, he features Houston in several of his **Quizzers and Calendar's.** In correspondence and discussions with Hammurabi he shared much information about Drusilla, including the assertion that she was well known in musical and journalistic circles in Chicago. It is known that she wrote for Claude Barnett's Chicago-based Associated Negro Press (A.N.P.) as did Irene Diggs during her stay in Havana, Cuba. If it were not for Barnett's A.N.P. would Houston's and Digg's views have been accessible to a mass audience?

In reconstructing the careers of scholars like Drusilla D. Houston and F. H. Hammurabi one encounters several problems. Perhaps they can be summarized as one problem. Their historical publications did not conform to "traditional standards", i.e. were not indexed and could not be researched by chronological, alphabetical or other usual means. Although Hammurabi earned a Juris Doctorate at Northwestern University's School of Law in 1927, and did post graduate work in political economy at the London School of Economics and the University of Vienna in Austria, his historical writings are still subjected to criticism for not conforming to "traditional standards". Hammurabi and Houston must be given more serious attention by Afro-American scholars and Africanists. Hammurabi is the single individual who kept Houston's work before the public for nearly five decades.

Eight years after publishing volume I of the **Wonderful Ethiopians**, Houston states:

> I stopped my Associated Negro Press articles to do research work on the second book of the series **Wonderful Ethiopians**. I will be able in a book, **Origin Of The Aryans**, to prove that I have risen above merely thinking as a Negro to tackle world problems.

It is useful to point out, this book was due to be published during the Ethiopian-Italian War and at a time when the spirit of "pure white-Aryans" was much popularized in the media. What role did Houston's work play in cementing racial affinity between Ethiopians and Blacks in the United States?

As a working journalist, Houston wrote about a wide range of topics from "America Needs Another Alexander Hamilton to Deliver Her," to "Parents Of Today Held To Blame For Youth Waywardness" and "Writer Urges Back To The Farm Movement." The latter was written prior to Elijah Muhammad's ascendancy to the leadership of the Nation of Islam.

In early 1932 she advises:

> Select crops for a five acre tract that are intensive. Foreign people live on small tracts and reap from them more than our farmers on 160 acres. Plant things that other people are not raising.

This is during the same period that Zora Neale Hurston and Langston Hughes are quarreling over a play—**Mule Bone**. Perhaps they should have left the "Mason Plantation", thrown out the mule bone and selected rotating crops and a five acre tract to raise dreams on.

A collection of columns by Drusilla Houston should be published. Journalists looking for a thesis might examine Houston's many topical pieces that are scattered throughout the Black newspapers of the 1920's, 30's and 40's. Her musical career should be explored. Was she trained at the Northwestern Conservatory of Music? Where did she perform?

Drusilla Houston was remembered by Ralph Ellison as a kind aggressive lady. He told me about Drusilla and her brother Roscoe Dunjee, editor of the **Black Dispatch** newspaper of Oklahoma. Ellison recalls her serving ice cream at the corner soda fountain store. John Hope Franklin remembers her columns and the Tulsa, Oklahoma riot of which she writes so brilliantly and moving:

> No better thing could have happened for the Negro race than the brutal race riot at Tulsa.
> The white man got a chance to look at the naked heart of its masses. In headlining the
> The white man got a chance to look at the naked herat of its masses. In headlines the
> Negro's sins, he has grown callous to the corruptions growing in the white race. The
> sufferers of Tulsa are but our martyrs, that shall bring to us a quicker and brighter dawn. I
> am not much impressed with the terror and cowardice showing up in some of the advice
> we are getting from some of our leadership.

She was an even handed critic of both Blacks and whites, leaders and followers. On
the other hand she won the respect of Black and white critics with the publication of
Wonderful Ethiopians. Mary White Ovington, a white NAACP leader, describes the
book's impact:

> One feels in laying down this book how foolish have been the old time statements that
> the white race was centuries ahead of the African. It is just the other way. The Negro has
> had the greater civilization. In Africa he is now decadent. The white race is younger, more
> vigorous. The two together, ought in America to produce a noble culture and a powerful
> just state.

Joel A. Rogers, the pioneer twentieth century Black global historian places Houston
within the context of other writers on the Negro.

> White writers like Count de Volney, Weisberger, Prof. Chamberlain and Lady Lugar have
> long pointed out the important part the Negro played in ancient history. And now an
> increasing number of Negro writers are following in their wake, the latest of these being
> Mrs. Drusilla Dunjee Houston, whose interesting articles on Negro history will be recalled
> by the readers of the colored newspapers of a year or two ago.

William Pickens, author of **Bursting Bonds**, (his most representative work), former
NAACP field secretary and director of branches, was an associate of Houston's and a
strong supporter of all her volumes: **Origin Of Civilization, The Origin of Aryans,
Astounding Last African Empire** and **Wonderful Ethiopians Of The Ancient
Cushite Empire.**

Why not locate those unpublished manuscripts, give them a critical reading and
determine if they should be published during the 1980's; edit a collection of her columns,
establish a Drusilla Dunjee Houston Scholarship at Langston University in Oklahoma?
For it was Ms. Denyvette Fields of the M.B. Tolson Heritage Center and Jimmy Stewart of
Oklahoma who were most helpful to me in locating relatives and friends whose memory
of Drusilla Dunjee Houston helped to resuscitate this women's role in restoring the
African to his rightful place.

Her "discovery" and remembrance is due to the tradition bearers who kept her words
and deeds alive—Harvey, Michaux, Hammurabi, among others. May her tribe increase.

INDEX

Where author uses variant spellings, all forms have been included. Forenames have been supplied as far as possible.

INDEX

A Select List of Black Classic Press Titles

The Osiris Papers
Reflections on the Life and Writings of
Dr. Frances Cress Welsing
Raymond Winbush • Denise Wright

The Osiris Papers: Reflections on the Life and Writings of Dr. Frances Cress Welsing is intended to be the first of many treatises written to examine the life, theories, and contributions of Dr. Frances Cress Welsing. Some of these writings will be hagiographic. Some will be critical, but all will expand our understanding of one of the greatest African thinkers of the past 100 years.
ISBN 978-1-57478-162-5. 2020. 315 pp. Paper $24.95.

Race First:
The Ideological & Organizational Struggles
of Marcus Garvey and the
Universal Negro Improvement Association
Tony Martin

This book has the important element that is missing in most of the books and articles on Garvey—a political analysis of what the Garvey Movement was about.... John Henrik Clarke, The Black Scholar.
ISBN 978-1-57478-177-9. 1976*, 2020. 421 pp. Paper $24.95.

Journey of the Songhai People
Calvin Robinson • Redman Battle • Edward Robinson

The Journey of the Songhai People attempts to piece together the tapestry of world culture that was deliberately unraveled by the Europeans. As a result of their destroying the black threads of world culture, it has caused all people, including African Americans, to disrespect and loathe us.
ISBN 978-1-57478-175-5.1987*, 2020. 417 pp. illus. Paper $29.95.

Pillars in Ethiopian History
Joseph E. Harris

In the first of two groundbreaking volumes, the father of African Studies, William Leo Hansberry, examines the myth and legend surrounding some of the African continent's most dynamic countries. *Pillars in Ethiopian History* (Volume I) consists of four of Hansberry's lectures on the theme of Ethiopian history—the Queen of Sheba legend, the origin and development of Ethiopian Christianity, medieval international relations, and the Prester John legend. The essays included in *Pillars in Ethiopian History* are taken from Hansberry's private papers amassed while he taught at Howard University from 1922-1959. During these thirty-seven years, Hansberry laid the foundation for the systematic study of African history, culture, and politics.
ISBN 978-1-57478-155-7 1974*, 2019. 156 pp. Paper. $18.95.

Africa & Africans
As Seen by Classical Writers
Joseph E. Harris

In *African and Africans As Seen by Classical Writers*, the second of two groundbreaking volumes, the father of African Studies, William Leo Hansberry, examines classical references to the African continent and its people. The writings of Homer, Pliny, Ovid, Virgil, Herodotus, and others are discussed and analyzed in a lively and highly readable manner. The essays included in *Africa and Africans As Seen by Classical Writers* are taken from Hansberry's private papers amassed while he taught at Howard University from 1922-1959. During these thirty-seven years, Hansberry laid the foundation for the systematic study of African history, culture, and politics.
ISBN 978-1-57478-154-0. 1977*, 2019. 163 pp. Paper $18.95.

My Global Journeys
in Search of the African Presence
Runoko Rashidi

This book documents Rashidi's inspired *Global Journeys in Search of the African Presence*. This unique travelogue records his country-by-country travels in Africa, Asia, Australia, Europe, Russia, the Pacific and Caribbean Islands, and Central and South America. It also recounts his day-by-day encounters with people, historical markers, art, and cultural practices that both separate and unite Blacks around the world.
ISBN 978-1-57478-121-2, 2017. 370 pp. Paper $39.95.

Christianity Islam and the Negro Race
Edward W. Blyden

A native of St. Thomas, West Indies, Edward Wilmot Blyden (1832-1912) lived most of his life on the African continent. He was an accomplished educator, linguist, writer and world traveler, who strongly defended the unique character of Africa and its people. Christianity, Islam and the Negro Race is an essential collection of his writings on race, culture, and the African Personality. The Black Classis Press edition is a complete reproduction of the 1888 revised and corrected edition. It remains an important source for examining an early African-centered perspective on race, religion, and the socioeconomic development of Africa.
ISBN 978-0-933121-41-6. 1888*, 1994. 432 pp. Paper $18.95.

The Name "Negro": Its Origin and Evil Use
Richard B. Moore

This study focuses on the exploitive nature of the word "Negro." Tracing its origins to the African slave trade, Moore shows how the label "Negro" was used to separate African descendants and to confirm their supposed inferiority.
ISBN 978-0-933121-35-5. 1960*, 1992. 108 pp. Paper $10.95.

A Tropical Dependency
Flora Shaw Lugard

When Lady Lugard sat down to write A Tropical Dependency, it was not her intention to inspire generations of Africans to regain the independence of their countries. Lugard writes of slavery as though it was a God-given right of Europeans to own Africans as slaves. Ironically, her text on Africa's place in history reaffirms the belief that "If Africa did it once, Africa can do it again!" Introduction by John Henrik Clarke.
ISBN 978-0-933121-92-8 1906*, 1997. 508 pp. Paper. $24.95

To order, visit: www.blackclassicbooks.com
Or call 410 242-6954

*Indicates first year published.